BOURBON DEMOCRACY IN ALABAMA

1874-1890

Bourbon Democracy in Alabama 1874-1890

ALLEN JOHNSTON GOING

UNIVERSITY OF ALABAMA PRESS

University, Alabama
1951

Preface

I n 1 8 8 0 Alexander K. McClure on a trip through the South wrote, "Alabama is rich in natural resources, rich in products and richer in Bourbonism than is best for her people." The term *Bourbon* had originated during the Reconstruction period and was used by the Radicals to label their Democratic opponents as anti-progressive and ultra-conservative. Although some Alabama Democrats readily accepted the designation, the majority of the party resented its implications. The term, nevertheless, has been generally adopted to describe the period in Southern history following the overthrow of Radical Reconstruction, and for some states at least has come to imply exactly the opposite of its literal meaning. For the sake of clarity, the terms *Bourbon* and *Bourbonism* have been utilized in this work only when they could be applied literally to some of the Alabama Democrats.

The purpose of this study is to analyze and describe the state government of Alabama during this Bourbon period as it operated under the Democratic and Conservative party. Comprehensive studies such as Walter L. Fleming's *Civil War and Reconstruction in Alabama* and John B. Clark's *Populism in Alabama* cover respectively the period before 1874 and after 1890. It is hoped that the present work will fill in the intervening gap and will shed light on the question of just how conservative

v

(or Bourbon) Alabama Democrats really were. It should also contribute to an understanding of the background of Populism and of some twentieth century problems faced by Alabama Democrats.

In a study of this nature it has been impossible to treat in detail the numerous topics considered. Consequently some of the generalizations may not stand the test of time. I have attempted, however, to present the facts impartially as the material available seemed to warrant. Perhaps this general treatment may stimulate further interest in the period and lead to more detailed studies that will counteract the faults of this one. Most of the material was found in the Alabama State Department of Archives and History at Montgomery, the University of Alabama Library, the Birmingham Public Library, and the Library of Congress. A grant from the University of Alabama Research Fund assisted in defraying expenses connected with the research and the preparation of the manuscript. I wish to express my appreciation to Professor Fletcher Melvin Green of the University of North Carolina for inspiring and guiding this study and to the following individuals for valuable assistance in research and criticism: Dean Anne Gary Pannell of Goucher College, Dean Albert Burton Moore of the University of Alabama, Professor Howard Kennedy Beale of the University of Wisconsin, Miss Jesse Ham of the Birmingham Library, and Miss Frances Hails of the Alabama Archives. My thanks for assistance in the preparation of maps go to my mother, Louise Thornbury Going, and Mr. Jack H. Furman.

A. J. G.

June, 1950

Table of Contents

Maps and Charts

CHAPTER ONE

Introduction
Party Politics During
Radical Reconstruction

THE CIVIL WAR left political parties in Alabama, as in other Southern states, confused and disorganized. The ante-bellum parties had lost their identities because of the controversy over state rights and secession. After 1865 the Democrats could re-unite with their national party, but ex-Whig, Know-nothing, and Union men had to form new allegiances. The Alabama Democrats succeeded in attracting a great many of this latter group in 1866 by reorganizing as the Democratic and Conservative party.

It is difficult to ascertain the strength of the Republican party in Alabama before the Radicals won control over Congress. The small farmers, who were more numerous in north Alabama, had long resented the political domination of Black Belt leaders, and many of them had sympathized with the Union. Undoubtedly some of this group leaned toward Republicanism after 1865. Before 1868, however, the state government rested in the hands of moderates, most of whom had opposed secession and had given little or no support to the Confederacy. These leaders belonged to the Democratic and Conservative party and supported the mild reconstruction program of President Andrew Johnson.

The controversy over the ratification of the Fourteenth Amendment to the federal constitution brought political differ-

1

ences into focus, and a group of "unconditional union men" in north Alabama supported the amendment and other demands of the Radical-dominated Congress.[1] As Congress began to win the ascendancy over the President, the Alabama Republican party increased its strength and activities under the leadership of such men as Milton Jefferson Saffold, Nicholas Davis, Adam Felder, Davis C. Humphreys, Charles Christopher Sheets, and other radical Unionists.[2] The Passage of the Reconstruction Acts by Congress in 1867 found the Alabama Republicans ready to take over the state government, basing their strength on Negro votes backed up by federal troops.

For some time after Congress forced Radical Reconstruction on Alabama in 1868 opposition seemed futile. Because of disturbed conditions following the war and the disfranchisement of many whites, few experienced political leaders were active in the state. But those opposed to Radicalism both in principle and in practice soon coalesced in a definite opposition movement. Undoubtedly chief credit for organizing the Democratic movement against the Radicals should go to General James Holt Clanton, a former Whig and hitherto unknown as a leader in political circles. Clanton had distinguished himself as a brigadier general of cavalry and had been appointed chairman of the State Democratic Executive Committee in 1866. The Democrats could offer little opposition to the election of Radical delegates to the constitutional convention which met in November, 1867; but when the new constitution came up for ratification in February, 1868, so many whites were persuaded to stay away from the polls that the document failed of ratification by 13,550 votes. The Democrats made no nominations for state offices. In June of the same year, however, Congress arbitrarily declared the constitution adopted and the Radical nominees duly elected to their offices.[3]

In the wake of such peremptory action, followed by the election of General Ulysses S. Grant to the presidency in November, 1868, a number of prominent political leaders felt that their own welfare and the future of Alabama depended on support of the

---

[1] Cincinnati *Commercial* quoted in New York *Times*, January 23, 1867.
[2] Walter L. Fleming, *Civil War and Reconstruction in Alabama*, pp. 398, 402-405.
[3] *Ibid.*, pp. 536-541, 550-552.

Radical cause. Consequently such Democrats as Lewis Eliphalet Parsons, Alexander McKinstry, Judge Samuel Farrow Rice, and Alexander White left their party to join the Republicans.[4] These men were undoubtedly motivated to some extent by personal political ambition, but they rationalized their move as the only sensible course of action in the face of existing circumstances. They believed that Alabama could best recover from the political and economic disasters of the War by co-operating with the Radicals, and that the advantages of strong national support should outweigh the disadvantages of associating with a party that locally included some untrustworthy political adventurers and based its power on questionable methods of controlling the Negro vote.

These defections caused resentment in Democratic ranks and also precipitated a controversy over future party strategy. Some felt that the proper attitude should be acquiescence in Radical Reconstruction as a *fait accompli*. Advocates of this policy recommended accepting, if not openly approving, the Fourteenth and Fifteenth Amendments; they would then proceed to beat the Radicals at their own game of winning and controlling the Negro vote.[5] Other Democrats advocated the establishment of an independent white man's party devoted to some of the Reconstruction policies but without the onus of Negro and "carpetbag" domination. One supporter of such a policy was General Jones M. Withers, editor of the Mobile *Tribune*.[6] Still others, such as Ryland Randolph, editor of the Tuscaloosa *Monitor*, and John Forsyth, of the Mobile *Register*, advocated waging an all-out attack against the Radical program in an attempt to unite the white people against Negro and alien rule.[7]

With the approach of the 1870 state election, Chairman Clanton feared the effects of this internal rift and postponed as long

---

[4] Alabama Testimony in Ku Klux Report, February 19, 1872, *Senate Reports*, 42 Cong., 2 Sess., no. 22, VIII, 502; Mobile *Register* (weekly), January 30, 1869.

[5] Selma *Times and Messenger* quoted in Mobile *Register*, April 5, 1870; Montgomery *Advertiser* and Wilcox *Vindicator* quoted in Mobile *Register*, April 31, 1870.

[6] Mobile *Register*, January 19, 22, February 5, 15, 1870; Montgomery *Advertiser*, January 17, 1870.

[7] Mobile *Register* (weekly), February 2, 1869; Mobile *Register*, April 5, 1870; Montgomery *Alabama State Journal* [hereinafter cited as Montgomery *Journal*] (weekly), May 6, 13, 1870.

as possible the summoning of a convention. He took no part in the controversy but stated, "The least said . . . the soonest mended."[8] The appeasement forces, however, put their ideas across in the convention; the Democratic platform and the candidate for governor, Robert Burns Lindsay, failed to condemn the fundamental points of the Reconstruction program. Lindsay himself had publicly recommended passive acceptance of Radical Reconstruction, and the platform emphasized the flagrant inefficiency and misconduct of the Radicals without condemning their program per se.[9]

The split within the Radical party between Governor William Hugh Smith and the "carpet-bag" element played into the hands of the Democrats, who hoped that their candidate from north Alabama would win many votes from whites who had become disgusted with the Radicals.[10] It was rumored that Senator George E. Spencer, "carpet-bagger" and bitter rival of Governor Smith, secretly supported Lindsay in some north Alabama counties. The Senator probably hoped that a Democratic legislature would defeat, as it ultimately did, the re-election of his colleague and enemy, Willard Warner, whose senatorial term expired in 1871.[11]

The Democrats made no effort to campaign in the Black Belt counties and avoided any moves that might bring forth retaliatory action from the national government. The absence of a presidential election in 1870 promised less interference from Federal soldiers and authorities. The strategy succeeded; Lindsay was elected by a close vote of 77,721 to 76,292, with practically all of his support coming from the northern and southeastern counties.[12]

The newly elected House of Representatives consisted of thirty-five Radicals (including fourteen Negroes) and sixty-five Democrats; the Senate, consisting of thirty-two Radicals (in-

[8] James H. Clanton to Robert McKee, March 27, 1870, McKee Papers.
[9] John Witherspoon DuBose and James K. Greer, *Alabama's Tragic Decade*, pp. 292-295. See Lindsay's testimony in Ku Klux Report, *loc. cit.*, VIII, 205.
[10] William Hugh Smith, *Letter . . . In Defense of his Administration.*
[11] DuBose and Greer, *op. cit.*, p. 342.
[12] *Journal . . . of the House of Representatives of the State of Alabama* [hereinafter cited as *House Journal*] (1870-71), p. 30.

cluding one Negro) and one Democrat, was carried over with
no changes because its members had refused to classify for two
and four year terms as specified by the Constitution of 1868.[13]
A virtual legislative deadlock resulted from this situation, and
the troublesome financial and railroad problems became more
confused than ever. As far as many Democrats were concerned,
Governor Lindsay left much to be desired. He was severely
criticized for his seizure, in the name of the state, of the Alabama and Chattanooga Railroad and for continuing the state-aid
policy to certain other lines. Opinions concerning the governor
varied, but even his supporters had to admit that Lindsay blund-
ered as an executive and that his two-year administration
brought little improvement in the sad condition of the state
government.[14]

With the next state election approaching, the Democratic
party found itself once again divided in its fight against Radicalism. The controversy over Governor Lindsay's conduct split
the party, and, as in the 1870 election, there arose dissension
over how far the party should go in accepting basic principles
of Reconstruction. During the months preceding the 1872 election, the term *New Departure* came to describe the tendency
toward co-operation particularly with the Liberal Republican
group in the North. Opponents of such a "Departure" came to
be called Bourbons, and some adopted the designation as de-
scriptive of their stable and conservative ideas.[15] The Democratic newspapers argued bitterly over the question of strategy.
The Montgomery *Advertiser's* Departurist tactics led another
Black Belt paper to wonder why there was no "sound Democratic paper" in Montgomery.[16] Opposed to the *Advertiser's* con-
ciliatory policy stood the Mobile *Register* and the Montgomery
Mail, papers which continued to insist on a program of "self-

[13] Arthur Williams, "Participation of Negroes in the Government of
Alabama" (unpublished M.A. thesis, Atlanta University, 1946), pp. 27, 42.
See the maps illustrating the political composition of the various legislative
sessions in the Appendix.

[14] Montgomery *Journal,* February 2, March 30, 1872. See below,
pp. 63-64, 67-68.

[15] Mobile *Register* (weekly), July 15, 22, October 21, 1871.

[16] Hayneville *Examiner* quoted in Montgomery *Journal,* January 11,
1872.

assertion of the whites" and no compromise with Radicalism or the Negro.[17]

The state Democratic convention in June, 1872, had to face the difficult problems of nominations and organization of the campaign without the aid of their foremost leader, General Clanton, who had been killed September 27, 1871, in Knoxville, Tennessee, by David M. Nelson following a personal quarrel.[18] All incumbents except Governor Lindsay were renominated for office. Because of Lindsay's record during the past two years, the party preferred to stake its chances on a more conservative leader from the southern part of the state. After protracted balloting on a number of candidates, the convention chose Thomas Hord Herndon of Mobile, an outspoken secessionist in 1861.[19] The northern counties complained bitterly over their lack of representation on the party ticket.[20] After the national Democratic convention in July, 1872, had ratified the Greeley-Brown, Liberal Republican ticket, state Democratic leaders gave it their unqualified support and hoped that it would swing many votes in north Alabama. Liberal Republicans in Alabama, including such leaders as Frederick George Bromberg, Samuel Rice, and Willard Warner, and a Republican newspaper in Huntsville supported the Democratic nominees for state offices.[21] Consequently discussion of state issues was held to a minimum so that attention could be focused on the national campaign against Grant and the Radicals. This action of prominent Republicans strengthened the arguments of the New Departurist faction in the Democratic party.

The regular Republican organization attempted to capitalize on Lindsay's unpopularity and the Democratic choice of what it considered "extreme and ultra" candidates. Early in the year its principal newspaper organ set out to win support from con-

[17] Mobile *Register* (weekly), April 8, 1871; Montgomery *Mail*, March 1, 1871; Montgomery *Journal*, September 23, 1871.

[18] William Garrett, *Reminiscences of Public Men in Alabama*, pp. 634-645.

[19] DuBose and Greer, *op. cit.*, pp. 341-345; Montgomery *Journal*, June 20-23, 1872.

[20] Huntsville *Advocate*, June 25, 1872; Mobile *Register* (weekly), July 6, 13, 1872.

[21] Mobile *Register* (weekly), August 10, October 26, and *passim* July-August, 1872; Huntsville *Advocate*, October 12, 1872.

servatives, especially old-line Whigs and Douglas Democrats.[22] Although a group of office holders and Negro leaders resented the leadership exercised by Senator Spencer, Alexander White, and others, the latter group controlled the state convention. The ticket nominated consisted exclusively of native Alabamians and was headed by David Peter Lewis of Huntsville, a former Douglas Democrat and law partner of Leroy Pope Walker, prominent Democrat and former member of the Confederate cabinet.[23] During the campaign Republicans took advantage of Democratic dissension and failures during the Lindsay administration, and pictured their own party as one of moderation. The opposition to Lindsay, the unpopularity of Greeley, and clever campaigning by the Radicals, all combined to defeat the Democratic ticket, with a vote of 89,878 for Lewis and 81,371 for Herndon.[24]

Elections for members of the legislature proved to be extremely close, and because of numerous contested elections, both parties claimed a working majority. For two months rival legislatures met in Montgomery until the attorney general of the United States proposed a compromise that was accepted by both sides. Through the use of arbitrary tactics by Lieutenant Governor Alexander McKinstry, Spencer was re-elected United States senator.[25] In the reorganized legislature the Republicans had a majority of two in the House, while the Democrats had a majority of one in the Senate after a Republican senator died in 1873.[26]

With the legislature so evenly divided between the parties, it became practically impossible to pass legislation on any subject whatsoever. While the state government approached bankruptcy, schools languished, and agriculture suffered from the country-wide depression, the legislature could reach no agreement on solving or alleviating the distress, although it remained

[22] Montgomery *Journal*, January 5, 7, May 28, June 22, 1872.

[23] *Ibid.*, January 11, February 6, April 2, 1872; Mobile *Register* (weekly), August 24, 1872; Williams, *op. cit.*, pp. 47-48.

[24] Montgomery *Journal*, June 25, August 16, 1872; *House Journal* (1873), p. 289.

[25] Report of Spencer Investigating Committee, *Journal of the Senate of Alabama* [hereinafter cited as *Senate Journal*] (1875-76), pp. 31-73; *Which Was the Lawful Legislature of Alabama?* (pamphlet, 1875).

[26] Mobile *Register* (weekly), March 1, 8, 1873. See maps in the Appendix, pp. 216-217.

in session until near the end of April, 1873. A great deal of its time was consumed in the fruitless discussion of civil rights bills intended to guarantee social equality for Negroes; the chief result was the aggrevation of existing racial fears and bitterness. When people complained about paying tax money to a legislature that did no work, the Mobile *Register* replied: "Be quiet, good people . . . . While the Republican members are engaged in this work they are not passing bad laws, and no laws must be better than bad ones under existing circumstances".[27]

Thus by 1873 the Democratic and Conservative party had been unsuccessful in its attempt to oust completely the Radical regime in Alabama. It had failed to maintain a united front largely because of disagreement over strategy. Although it had won control of the governorship and one house of the legislature in 1870, it failed to make secure its victory because of internal party strife. The Republican party was also suffering from serious internal troubles, which in the next few years would bring about its complete collapse.

[27] Mobile *Register* (weekly), February 22, 1873.

CHAPTER TWO

The Overthrow
of Radical Reconstruction

ELECTION OF 1874

D URING 1873 and 1874, a dark period for the state as a whole, the Democratic and Conservative party exerted every effort to take advantage of the Radicals' discomfiture and to formulate a unified plan for the "battle of redemption" at the next election. For the first time practically all leaders and factions agreed that the struggle with Radicalism should be an all-out fight on the issue of white supremacy. In all previous state elections the worst stumbling block for the Conservatives had been the rivalry between small farmers, particularly in the hill country, and large farmers or planters in the Black Belt. In spite of the fact that the small farmer group disliked Negro suffrage and Northern politicians, the Radicals had won considerable support from them because of the liberal features of the constitution and the promises to encourage and subsidize the economic development of north Alabama. By 1873, however, the small farmers were becoming increasingly suspicious of Radical promises and Radical leadership and were showing a tendency to drift toward the Democrats, provided that party would denounce any intention of courting the Negro vote in order to maintain Black Belt supremacy. Favorable reports came in from Democratic leaders

9

in the northern counties. "Everywhere now throughout the county," said one, "the political condition of affairs indicates a return to the old landmarks of our party and you do not now see and read so often the sneering allusions to bourbonism, etc."[1]

The Democratic leaders in south Alabama were forced ostensibly to give up any idea of courting the Negro vote. A former governor wrote: "Local advantages might result from a mongrel ticket, but there is more strength in an open out-and-out White Man's Ticket. We can carry some prudent and sensible negroes— but as a party we have tendered them the olive branch which they have spurned with derision. Any further effort on our part will be simply throwing pearls before swine."[2] A newspaper commented that it seemed hopeless to court the Negro vote because the Negroes invariably voted Radical in spite of all the advice given them.[3]

Other factors played into the hands of the Democrats. They could capitalize on the economic destitution resulting from the depression of 1873, and could accuse the Radicals of maintaining an extravagant and corrupt government in the face of depressed economic conditions. The national political situation also favored the local Democratic cause. Radical Republicanism was rapidly losing favor in the North thanks to the exposures of graft and corruption in the Grant administration and to attacks by Liberal Republicans. At the same time the Democrats of the South in both word and deed were proving that their party was not strictly Bourbon in its outlook and that the state governments and the Union would be safe in their hands. In 1874 Alabamians, as well as other Southerners, felt that there would be little likelihood of Federal interference in state elections because of President Grant's increasing distrust of the Radicals and because no presidential election would be at stake.

The most hopeful sign for Alabama Democrats, however, lay in the rapid breakdown of the Radical party in the state. Even after the victory in 1872, internal conflicts raged within the party ranks. Resentment began to grow against the party leader-

[1] Rufus King Boyd to Robert McKee, April 29, 1874, McKee Papers.
[2] John Anthony Winston to Charles Lewis Scott, April 20, 1870, in Mobile *Register* (weekly), June 6, 1874.
[3] Mobile *Register* (weekly), October 19, 1872.

ship of Spencer, White, Ex-governor Parsons, and Congressman Charles Hays, who generally counseled a conservative approach to such matters as force bills, civil rights, and mixed schools. As a Republican writer some years later saw it, political success had made the party careless, and a number of factions tended to engage in violent quarrels.[4] The Montgomery *Journal* had a brief quarrel with Alabama Republicans in Congress when the paper failed to receive the public printing contract.[5] Another serious controversy centered around Federal Judge Richard Busteed, who had been accused of supporting Democratic Governor Lindsay in the struggle over the Alabama and Chattanooga Railroad. At the instigation of Parsons, impeachment proceedings were begun, and Busteed resigned October 9, 1874.[6]

The primary cause of dissension in Republican ranks, however, was the increasing cleavage between some of the white leaders and the Negroes. By and large, the prominent leaders in the Lewis administration and those in Congress tended toward a moderate, white-dominated party, while some whites such as Adam Felder and Paul Strobach continued to seek and to win Negro support. The debates over both national and state civil rights bills focused the spotlight on this cleavage. As an illustration, Alexander White was accused of bringing about the defeat of the civil rights bill in the Alabama legislature, but the Republican organ held that the Negroes themselves were responsible.[7] One Democrat in recommending an immediate vote on an extreme civil rights bill said, "This will compel Parsons & White either to take the bill pure et simple which will kill them in the Northern counties or vote against it which will throttle them in the nigger counties."[8] One student of the subject has concluded that the bills were defeated because the scalawag faction of the "demoralized Republican Party" conspired with the Democrats.[9]

[4] Montgomery *Journal*, October 12, 1875.
[5] *Ibid.*, February 1, 1874.
[6] Selma *Southern Argus*, March 27, 1874; Mobile *Register*, January 14, February 27, 1875; New York *World* quoted in Mobile *Register* (weekly), October 17, 1874. Busteed broke with the party and left the state.
[7] Montgomery *Journal*, August 14, 1873.
[8] Rufus K. Boyd to Robert McKee, February 18, 1873, McKee Papers.
[9] Williams, *op. cit.*, p. 50.

As the time for the 1874 state Republican convention approached, intra-party disputes increased in bitterness. Two meetings exclusively for Negroes assembled in Montgomery in January and June respectively; in both the discussions concerned social equality and mixed schools.[10] The Negro faction opposed the renomination of Governor Lewis and favored Adam Felder for the gubernatorial nomination.[11] The Negro newspaper in Montgomery, a few days before the convention, viciously attacked Parsons, White, Sheets, and other white leaders and stated that Lewis had displayed an "utter lack of backbone."[12] In spite of such strong feelings, the party did not split openly; the white leaders who were accused of gerrymandering districts, maintained a firm control over the convention. Lewis received the nomination, and the platform declared, "The Republican party does not desire mixed schools or mixed accommodations for the colored people; but we ask for them that in all of these the advantages shall be equal."[13] The quarreling factions had, however, severely weakened the party. "The Republican party entered upon the campaign in 1874," said the party organ a year later, "divided against itself, its leaders embittered against each other, and the rank and file . . . torn and distracted."[14]

The Democratic campaign began officially when the state executive committee issued resolutions calling for the "fraternal co-operation of all white men in the state." The county conventions followed the lead of Barbour in adopting resolutions that emphasized the idea of a white man's campaign.[15] The major difficulty faced by the party was the selection of a gubernatorial candidate who would not alienate north Alabama votes because of a secessionist or extreme pro-Confederate rec-

[10] Fleming, *op. cit.*, pp. 772-773; Mobile *Register* (weekly), July 4, 1874; Montgomery *Journal*, August 23, 1874.
[11] Selma *Southern Argus*, March 27, 1874; Mobile *Register* (weekly), July 18, 1874.
[12] Montgomery *Republican* quoted in Mobile *Register* (weekly), August 1, 1874.
[13] Montgomery *Journal*, August 21-25, 1875; Mobile *Register* (weekly), August 1, 1874.
[14] Montgomery *Journal*, October 9, 1875.
[15] Mobile *Register* (weekly), March 21, 1874; John Witherspoon DuBose, "Forty Years of Alabama, 1861-1901" (unpublished manuscript), pp. 984-986.

ord. At the same time he must not have adhered to any Reconstruction ideas which south Alabama Democrats might construe as leaning toward Republicanism. George Smith Houston of Limestone County seemed to meet the demands. Prominent in Democratic circles before the war, opposed to secession, and more or less neutral during the war, he had avoided active politics during the turbulent Reconstruction years. By devoting himself to his law practice and railroad interests, Houston had become by the early 1870's one of the wealthiest men in the state.[16]

After some hesitation Houston gave in to the persuasions of Democratic leaders and consented to make the race.[17] Hoping to avoid unnecessary public debate, the party leaders arranged matters so well that the Democratic convention, which met in Montgomery, July 29, 1874, nominated Houston unanimously. To break a deadlock over the position of lieutenant-governor, the convention chose Robert Fulwood Ligon, who was supposed to attract the votes of Whig-Bell men.[18] Not all Democrats approved the selection of Houston, and some of the Black Belt Bourbons opposed him because of his known opposition to repudiating any of Alabama's large Reconstruction debt. Houston's name had been prominently mentioned early in 1874, and his opponents went so far as to organize a meeting in Selma previous to the Democratic convention. Robert McKee, editor of the Selma *Southern Argus,* led this unsuccessful fight and received considerable encouragement from many quarters of the state.[19] After the nomination the Mobile *Register* could not work up much enthusiasm over another north Alabama candidate. Republican opposition labeled Houston a front man, stating that his party would actually be dominated by "secession-

[16] Thomas McAdory Owen, *History of Alabama and Dictionary of Alabama Biography,* III, 848; Alpheus Baker to Robert McKee, May 11, 1874, McKee Papers.

[17] Alpheus Baker to George S. Houston, January 27, 1874; Robert Hugh Ervin to Houston, Janaury 19, 1874, Houston Papers.

[18] Montgomery *Advertiser,* July 30, 1874; Montgomery *Journal,* July 29-31, 1874.

[19] C. C. Langdon to McKee, May 16, 30, July 20, 1874; Burwell Boykin Lewis to McKee, May 14, June 3, 1874; Rufus K. Boyd to McKee, April 29, May 17, 1874, McKee Papers; Selma *Southern Argus,* June 12, 1874.

K.K.-White League Democrats," whose principal aim was repudiation.[20]

The Democratic platform was agreed upon well in advance of the convention.[21] Chief emphasis was placed on the race issue, and the first half of the document in no uncertain terms denounced the civil rights bills. The last two planks emphasized the necessity for a more economical government and pledged the Democrats to make good every dollar "justly owed by the state."[22] A large and colorful public ratification meeting, held around the famous fountain in Montgomery, followed the convention and launched the campaign. Houston made a stirring oration against a background of Japanese lanterns, skyrockets, and transparencies depicting such scenes as a school house with white and Negro children side by side and a scalawag attempting to ride both a white and a black horse at the same time.[23]

Walter Lawrence Bragg, of Montgomery, served as chairman of the State Democratic Executive Committee, and employed every means at his disposal to draw out a record vote and to whip up support for the Democratic, white man's cause. Newspaper editorials and pamphlets were widely circulated, and speakers penetrated deep into the rural areas; John Tyler Morgan and Hilary A. Herbert both traveled and spoke extensively in the hill country, Morgan often employing the Bible as his text. Since Bragg did not trust the Federal mails in the distribution of literature, he worked closely with the railroad, telegraph, and express companies.[24]

The Democratic strategy minimized such vital questions as the handling of Reconstruction bonds and the plight of the school system. Instead, the campaigners focused attention primarily on the necessity of white unity against Negro rule and secondarily on the failures and corruptions of the incumbent Radical regime. A moderate statement of the case declared:

[20] Mobile *Register* (weekly), August 8, 1874; Montgomery *Journal*, February 3, June 16, October 23, 1874.

[21] Montgomery *Journal*, July 29, 1874.

[22] Mobile *Register* (weekly), August 1, 1874.

[23] Montgomery *Advertiser*, July 31, 1874; Montgomery *Journal*, July 31, 1874.

[24] J. W. DuBose, *op. cit.*, pp. 1009-1011; Hilary A. Herbert, "How We Redeemed Alabama," *Century Magazine*, LXXXV (1913), p. 860; Selma *Southern Argus*, September 11, 1874.

"We are in favor of giving the Negro every right which the Constitution guarantees to him, but we are not in favor of placing him with all his ignorance and prejudices, over the white man as a ruler. He is incompetent and unfitted by nature for such a position."[25] The discussion of the civil rights bill and social equality drew forth stronger statements. "The poor man must either see his little boys and girls on the benches with miscellaneous black raggedness in person and morals, or allow them to grow up in absolute ignorance," stated one paper; another issue of the same paper declared: "The bill means miscegenation."[26] While some Democrats fomented antipathy for the blacks in the white counties, others toned down the race issue in black counties and did not hesitate to court the Negro vote whenever they saw an opportunity.[27] The Selma *Argus*, in the heart of the Black Belt and chief supporter of the Patrons of Husbandry, did not emphasize the race issue or Radical corruption. Instead, it urged farmers and planters to vote for Democrats because their party displayed a more sincere devotion to the interests of agriculturists; the struggle should be the "People's Fight" against the vested interests supporting Radicalism.[28]

The Radicals necessarily conducted an almost entirely defensive campaign. They bitterly assailed the Democrats for unnecessarily stirring up racial discord and pointed back to 1868 and 1872 when the party had courted Negro votes. "We reject the issue of race against race," stated the Republican Executive Committee, "as fraught with incalculable evils to our whole people, which sows the seeds of ruin to all our material interests and which will, if persisted in by the party [Democratic], speedily plunge us again into war with the government of the United States."[29] A north Alabama Republican paper accused the "false

[25] Tuscumbia *Alabamian and Times* quoted in Mobile *Register* (weekly), July 11, 1874.
[26] Mobile *Register* (weekly), May 30, June 6, 1874.
[27] Affairs in Alabama, February 23, 1875, *House Reports*, 43 Cong., 2 Sess., no. 262, pp. 144, 299, 309. See also the account of the Montgomery Colored Conservative Club in Mobile *Register* (weekly), September 12, 1874.
[28] Selma *Southern Argus*, March 6, 20 and *passim* April-July, 1874.
[29] Montgomery *Journal*, August 1, 22, September 18, 19, and *passim* August-October, 1874.

Democracy" of emphasizing the race issue in an attempt to restore the old slave-holding aristocracy's control over the state. It claimed that disfranchising the Negro would inevitably lead to the disfranchisement of poor whites.[30]

The Radicals also made much of the school question, asserting that Democrats had consistently opposed free public schools and emphasizing the fact that their own party was committed to a policy of separate schools for white and black. In answer to Democratic charges of misgovernment, Republicans declared: "The gibberish about 'redemption from the rule of rogues and spoilers' is simply the meanest of slanders. There is not a man connected with the present State government against whom any honest man has dared to allege dishonesty!" They also accused the Democrats of being so vague on the bond question as to imply "premeditate and deliberate repudiation."[31]

As to the conduct of the campaign, both sides have subsequently been accused of employing questionable tactics. The Democrats widely publicized the distribution of 200,000 pounds of army bacon in communities far distant from any stream, although the avowed objective was flood relief.[32] They also accused Republican officials of unnecessary arrests and mistreatment of prisoners for violation of the Enforcement Acts.[33]

The Republicans, on the other hand, protested loudly against what they considered a widespread spirit of violence, especially among the whites of the Black Belt. The Radical newspaper depicted the clashes between whites and Negroes in Choctaw, Greene, and other counties as the work of "white leagues" and "Ku Klux Democracy." At the request of Congressman Hays and Senator Spencer, the United States attorney general early in September ordered energetic action on the part of federal officials in Alabama, and troops were stationed at strategic points.[34] In requesting such steps, Hays stated that in the preceding two

[30] Florence *Republican* quoted in Montgomery *Journal,* July 31, 1874.

[31] Montgomery *Journal,* June 4, 13, September 18, November 6, 1874.

[32] Troops in Alabama, January 19, 1875, *House Executive Documents,* 43 Cong., 2 Sess., no. 110, pp. 7-15; Hilary A. Herbert (ed.), *Why the Solid South?* pp. 61-62.

[33] Mobile *Register,* September 26, October 17, 1874.

[34] Montgomery *Journal,* September 9-11, 20, 21, 23, and *passim* October, 1874.

and one-half months thirty-six Republicans had been killed and many others wounded, beaten, or driven away. A Congressional investigation, however, later revealed that only two of these alleged murders had been verified, those of Walter P. Billings, a white Republican, and Thomas Ivey, a Negro political leader. The Republican majority of the investigating committee reported that the troops were "absolutely necessary" and that previous to their arrival, Alabama Republicans had been unable to make any progress in the campaign. The Democratic minority, on the other hand, stated that calling in troops could not be justified on the grounds of lawlessness or violence. There did exist a widespread "spirit of social ostracism and political proscription" against Republicans.[35] Both sides undoubtedly made the most of every incident in an attempt to prove the opposition guilty of contemplating or inciting violence.

On election day considerable turbulence existed at some of the polls, with actual riots in Eufaula and Mobile.[36] The Congressional investigating committee reported that the riots usually began when stories of imminent Negro "risings" were circulated. Groups of whites would then roam the countryside, frightening Negroes away from the polls and intimidating those that appeared. The committee also found evidence of extensive frauds, failure to open polls, voting by non-residents, and other irregularities. The minority of the committee stated that the riots could not be blamed exclusively on either party or race; it admitted that the troops did not actively participate in the fighting. As to fraud and manipulation, the minority found considerable evidence that such practices were common on both sides.[37] In their zeal to redeem the state, Democrats undoubtedly resorted to many of the same devices employed by Radicals in winning and maintaining control of the black vote. A Negro student has described the Democratic victory in 1874 as "the climax to an ordeal of fraud, intimidation, and, in some instances, of murder."[38] A Democratic participant later admitted that his party overthrew the Radicals through the use of fraudulent voting and

---

[35] Affairs in Alabama, *loc. cit.*, pp. xvi-xvii, lv-lix, and *passim.*
[36] Montgomery *Journal,* November 4, 5, 1874.
[37] Affairs in Alabama, *loc. cit.*, pp. xxix-xxxiii, xvl, lxiii, lxvii.
[38] Williams, *op. cit.*, p. 58.

counting.[39] The results of the election showed that the Democrats had won both houses of the legislature and had cast 107,118 votes for Houston as against the Radicals' 93,928 for Lewis.[40] As compared with the figures for 1872, this shows an increase in the total vote of 29,797, practically all of which went to the Democrats.

INTERLUDE OF UNCERTAINTY

On November 24, 1874, Houston took the oath of office as governor amid scenes of celebration and rejoicing such as Montgomery had not seen in many a year; the inaugural ceremony was held in the morning, a barbecue dinner at noon, a dress parade in the afternoon, and grand balls and receptions at night. Hounton's address contained a great many generalities along with a plea for wiping out all bitterness and acrimony engendered by the recent contest.[41]

In spite of all the rejoicing, Democratic leaders did not feel entirely secure. At first they feared that the Radicals might attempt to barricade themselves in the capitol, establish a rival legislature, or follow some procedure similar to the aftermaths of the 1870 and 1872 elections.[42] But they soon realized that they had nothing to fear from the disrupted Republican party in Alabama. The Radical members of the legislature, of whom twenty-six were Negroes, could do little more than obstruct the Democratic program by insisting on strict parliamentary rules and by employing dilatory tactics in general.[43]

The real danger lay in the possibility that the Federal government, still controlled by Radicals, might decide to overthrow the Democratic regime in Alabama and re-establish military rule such as that existing in Louisiana. Congressman Charles Hays succeeded in having Congress carry out an extensive investigation of the recent election in the hopes of establishing a basis

[39] Hilary A. Herbert, "Grandfather's Talks about His Life under Two Flags" (unpublished manuscript), p. 278.

[40] *Senate Journal*, (1874-75), p. 29. For composition of the legislature see maps in the Appendix, pp. 218-219.

[41] J. W. DuBose, *op cit.*, pp. 1029-1030; Montgomery *Advertiser*, November 25, 1874.

[42] Mobile *Register* (weekly), November 14, 28, December 5, 1874.

[43] Selma *Southern Argus*, January 29, 1875; Mobile *Register*, January 17, 24, 31, 1875; John W. Beverly, *History of Alabama*, pp. 204-205.

for some kind of forceful action. The two Democrats on the investigating committee, however, brought forth considerable evidence about the election that was injurious to the Republican cause.[44]

In December, 1874, a convention of Negroes in Montgomery memorialized President Grant to interfere in their behalf.[45] Another memorial addressed to Congress, signed by the Republican members of the Alabama legislature, and dated February 15, 1875, denounced at great length the Democrats and their legislative program and requested the passage of some kind of force bill applicable to Alabama.[46] A later investigation by the legislature revealed that most of the Radical members had signed the document either without reading it or under false impressions as to its contents.[47]

When the Forty-third Congress finally adjourned on March 3, 1875, without having taken any action against Alabama, the state Democratic leaders breathed more easily and proceeded with less apprehension in making secure their control over the state government. "The agony is over," said one newspaper, "and Alabama still remains a state."[48] The legislature remained in session almost a month after the adjournment of Congress in an effort to push through legislation that earlier might have brought down upon the state the wrath of the congressional Radicals. The next legislature was audacious enough to address a memorial to the United States Senate requesting that Senator Spencer's seat be declared vacant on the grounds that he had not been elected to the senatorial seat by a legally constituted body.[49]

[44] Affairs in Alabama, *loc. cit.;* Mobile *Register,* January 3, 6, February 4, 25, 1875; New York *Tribune,* February 2, 5, 23, 1875.

[45] Memorial . . . from Convention of Colored Citizens, December 22, 1874, *House Executive Documents,* 43 Cong., 2 Sess., no. 46.

[46] Memorial of the Republican Members of the Legislature of Alabama, February 15, 1875, *Senate Miscellaneous Documents,* 43 Cong., 2 Sess., no. 107; Montgomery *Advertiser,* March 6, 1875.

[47] *Report of the Committee on the Memorial Addressed by Members of the General Assembly of Alabama,* pp. 3-5; *House Journal* (1874-75), pp. 450, 659-660.

[48] Mobile *Register,* March 5, 1875.

[49] *Acts of the General Assembly of Alabama* [hereinafter cited as *Acts*] (1875-76), pp. 407-410; *Senate Journal* (1875-76), pp. 31-73; Spencer Investigation, May 20, 1876, *Senate Reports,* 44 Cong., 1 Sess., no. 331.

CONSTITUTION OF 1875

The end of the long struggle between Radicalism and its opponents came with the adoption of a new constitution for Alabama embodying the more conservative ideas of those in power
after 1874. Such a project had to await the adjournment of
Congress which displayed a hostile attitude toward Democratic
governments in the South. From the very beginning of the
1874-1875 legislature a number of resolutions were introduced
looking toward the alteration of the 1868 constitution either by
amendment or by a new convention. The parts causing the
greatest criticism included the educational system, the policy of
public support for private enterprise, and the generally extravagant structure of the government.[50]

For some time opinion throughout the state remained divided
on the necessity or feasibility of such a change. Although some
sentiment for summoning a convention came from the press of
the larger towns, the weekly rural press opposed any change at
that particular time. "Really," said one Black Belt editor, "there
is but little to quarrel about in the present constitution; truly
the people as a mass are not quarrelling about it at all . . . . "[51]

Beginning about the middle of January, 1875, however, sentiment in favor of a new constitution began to grow rapidly. More
and more newspapers advocated calling a convention, and it
was reported that by February the Democratic press unanimously supported the movement.[52] Although the threatening attitude
of the Radicals in Washington had somewhat subsided, not
until the Forty-third Congress had adjourned on March 3, did
the legislature dare call an election for the early part of August.
The people would at that time vote on the question of summoning a convention and would also choose delegates. The convention would consist of ninety-nine delegates, with every
senatorial district and every county except Mobile sending one
delegate, Mobile County being granted two delegates.[53]

[50] *Report of the Joint Committee in Regard to the Amendment of the
Constitution*, pp. 6-10; Mobile *Register*, December 12, 1874, February
25, 1875.
[51] Willis Brewer to Robert McKee, February 13, 1875, McKee Papers.
[52] Mobile *Tribune*, January 31, 1875.
[53] *Acts* (1874-75), p. 109; Elections in Alabama, March 3, 1877,
Senate Reports, 44 Cong., 2 Sess., no. 704, pp. viii, 659.

Throughout the summer of 1875 the campaign progressed, with the Democrats supporting, and the Radicals opposing the call for a convention. The Radicals employed a seemingly divided strategy. One committee under Alexander White, supported by Spencer, Sheets, and others, advocated voting against the convention but did not nominate Radical delegates. The other committee, under Datus E. Coon, nominated Radicals from the Black Belt in the hope of controlling the convention. The Democrats saw in this apparent schism a clever plan. White's committee would create the impression in the white counties that no contest existed for seats in the convention, thereby causing a small attendance at the polls. This strategy would enable the large Negro vote in the Black Belt either to defeat the call or to gain a majority in the convention.[54]

The Republicans opposed calling a convention on the grounds that the time was inappropriate and the expense unwarrantable. They conceived of the effort as another attempt to "wipe out the results of the war" and to assure control for "the old leaders of Secession." They also considered the apportionment of delegates "grossly unfair" to Republican counties and warned that a convention under Democratic control would result in complete destruction of the public school system, reduction of the existing guarantees of exemptions from executions of judgments, and reestablishment of imprisonment for debt. Granting that certain parts of the 1868 constitution needed changing, the Republicans argued that it would be much safer and cheaper to amend specific clauses than entrust full power to delegates who might produce a constitution contrary to the interests of the common people.[55]

Although the Democrats denounced the extravagance and corruption prevalent under the 1868 constitution, they spent a great deal more time in denying charges made by the Radicals. They pointed out that the convention would cost only about $60,000, and the elimination of useless officials and functions would save

<hr/>

[54] Selma *Echo* quoted in Mobile *Register,* July 9, 1875; *Address of the Democratic and Conservative State Executive Committee* (1875), p. 6. See resolutions of Republican State Executive Committee in Mobile *Register,* June 18, 1875.

[55] Montgomery *Journal,* February 11, August 3, September 26, and *passim* July, 1875; Mobile *Register,* June 18, July 20, 1875.

the state some $81,000. They vehemently denied that exemptions would be reduced or that the public schools would be crippled.[56] Democratic speakers altered their arguments according to their locality, emphasizing the specific changes that would appeal particularly to the interests of the group addressed. For example, the north Alabama leaders emphasized the changes that would prevent a recurrence of Negro-Black Belt rule, while in south Alabama the speakers denounced the constitutional clauses permitting state aid in developing mineral and transportation interests.[57]

The election produced far less excitement and a smaller vote than that of 1874. The returns showed 77,763 in favor of the convention and 59,928 opposed. Nearly all the Black Belt counties and five others voted against the convention; Mobile voted affirmatively by only a very narrow margin. Of the delegates elected, eleven were Radical and seven independent.[58] But Sam Rice, leader of the opposition, could count on the consistent support of only twelve of these delegates.[59]

The convention assembled on September 6, 1875, and after simple ceremonies proceeded immediately to the business of organization. By having specified only one delegate from each county and senatorial district, the Democrats avoided the possibility of strong Republican representation from the heavily populated black counties. Among the delegates there was no one from the 1867 convention, seven from the 1861 convention, and two from the 1865 convention. By and large, the delegates were well advanced in age and long-time residents of the state.[60]

[56] *Address of Democratic Committee*, pp. 2-3; Mobile *Register*, July 17, 22, 29 and *passim* June - July, 1875; Montgomery *Advertiser*, July 18 and *passim* June - July, 1875.

[57] See speech of George Houston at Athens in Montgomery *Advertiser*, May 18, 1875, and of Levi Lawler at Mobile in Mobile *Register*, July 6, 1875.

[58] Montgomery *Advertiser*, September 5, 1875. See maps in the Appendix, pp. 220-221.

[59] *Journal of the Constitutional Convention of the State of Alabama* [hereinafter cited as *Convention Journal*] (1875), p. 166; Mobile *Register*, September 8, 23, 25, 1875.

[60] Malcolm Cook McMillan, "Constitutional Development in Alabama, 1819-1901" (unpublished Ph.D. thesis, University of North Carolina, 1948), pp. 293-294; Mobile *Tribune*, September 14, 1875; Mobile *Register*, September 8, 1875.

The convention contained four Negroes, but none of them played a prominent role.[61]

As its presiding officer, the convention unanimously elected Leroy Pope Walker, a prominent secession and Confederate leader and a lineal descendent of the presiding officer of Alabama's first constitutional convention. During the first few sessions some disagreements arose over the exact powers of the convention and the proper method of procedure; these were ultimately settled by restricting activities exclusively to constitution making and by working on all problems through committees. Most of the important questions were agreed upon in the Democratic caucus, which met each morning from nine until twelve o'clock.[62] The Republicans protested against this domination by "King Caucus," but their small minority could do little more than heed the warning from their newspaper organ to be "vigilant and watchful."[63]

During the first week the committees worked diligently preparing first drafts of the proposed articles, and the convention referred numerous matters without discussion to appropriate committees. Fully half of these propositions dealt with the troublesome question of exemptions.[64] Some difficulty arose in connection with the wording of the clause stating Alabama's position on secession. Ultimately a compromise was adopted, which said: "The people of this State accept as final the established fact, that from the Federal Union there can be no secession of any State."[65] The Democratic press of the state generally denounced this clause as unnecessary and needlessly self-effacing, while the Radical organ rejoiced over its passage.[66]

Other questions such as the public school system, aid to internal improvements, reduction of salaries and number of offices,

[61] J. W. DuBose, *op. cit.*, p. 1077; Williams, *op. cit.*, p. 58.
[62] McMillan, *op. cit.*, pp. 295-297; *Convention Journal* (1875), pp. 8-10, 16-17; Mobile *Register*, September 9, 11, 1875.
[63] Montgomery *Journal*, September 7, 1875.
[64] *Convention Journal* (1875), pp. 12-35.
[65] *Ibid.*, pp. 50-54; McMillan, *op. cit.*, pp. 290-300.
[66] Mobile *Register*, September 19, October 17, 1875; Mobile *Tribune*, September 22, October 5, 1875; Tuscumbia *North Alabamian*, September 23, 1875; Montgomery *Journal* quoted in Mobile *Register*, September 26, 1875.

and rate of taxation produced heated debates in the caucus and
on the convention floor. In regard to the extremely controversial
question of exemption from executions of judgments, there existed a wide divergence of opinion. The committee considering this
matter did not believe that any mention of it belonged in a
constitution, but in order to maintain harmony in the party it
recommended preserving the existing exemptions, $1,000 of per-
sonal property and eighty acres of land. The convention adopted
this recommendation but, as had been decided in caucus, added
a supplemental provision allowing the waiver of exemptions by
an instrument in writing.[67] Thus supporters of the new constitution could claim that the common man's rights had been
preserved, while others said that the supplemental provision in
effect nullified the entire exemption clause.

The proposed document was put into final form by the "committee on the order, harmony, and consistency of the whole
constitution." This committee suggested numerous changes most
of which met with approval from the floor. Although no vote
was taken on the completed constitution, a regulation approving
the work of the convention passed eighty-one to six, all of the
latter being Republicans.[68]

The convention adjourned on Saturday, October 2, having
completed a session of twenty-seven days. The address to the
people, emphasizing the improvements of the new constitution
over the 1868 document, pointed to such provisions of economy
as the elimination of the office of lieutenant governor, the substitution of biennial for annual sessions of the legislature, reduction of per diem and salaries of legislative members and all state
officers, and similar provisions. One clause strictly prohibited
the granting of financial aid by the state or local governments
to any individual or corporation. For the first time, moreover,
a maximum was placed on the rate of taxation that could be imposed by state and county governments. The article on education reorganized the public school system by eliminating the
board of education as well as some of the constitutional guarantees of financial support. All of these changes were cited as

[67] *Convention Journal* (1875), pp. 143-152; *Constitution of* 1875, Art.
XIV.
[68] *Convention Journal* (1875), p. 165; McMillan, *op. cit.,* p. 317.

improvements over the existing constitution, and the voters were urged to ratify the new document.[69]

Although the new constitution accomplished most of the principal Democratic objectives, it did not satisfy all of the diverse elements in the party. One Democrat declared: "It is far from being such a Constitution as I desire the State to have, but perhaps it is the best that could be ratified under the circumstances which now surround us."[70] The Selma *Argus* expressed similar sentiments, and the Montgomery *Advertiser* employed most restrained language in evaluating the work of the convention.[71] As a matter of fact, the new constitution preserved far more of the 1868 constitution than it changed. Both the general form and such Radical innovations as a completely elective judiciary, Negro suffrage, and general incorporation provisions remained unchanged.

The campaign for ratification of the constitution produced hardly any excitement. A number of prominent Republicans actively supported the new document; in this group were Ex-governors Parsons and Lewis and Auditor Robert T. Smith.[72] Other Republicans had difficulty organizing an opposition movement, and the party newspaper did not openly oppose the constitution until the last of October. Sam Rice, Ex-governor Smith, and others that were in opposition concentrated their attack on the school question, impeachment provisions, and dangers of repudiation. "Our position," said the *Journal*, "is NO REPUDIATION; no starvation of public schools."[73]

In the ratification election, November 16, 1875, the proposed document won a rather easy victory. Of the total vote (about half as large as that in the 1874 election) 85,662 favored the constitution and 29,217 opposed it. Only four counties, all in the Black Belt, showed majorities against adoption.[74] The act

[69] *Convention Journal* (1875), pp. 169-174.
[70] William C. Oates quoted in Mobile *Register*, October 5, 1875.
[71] Selma *Southern Argus*, October 8, 1875; Montgomery *Advertiser*, October 2, 5, 1875.
[72] Montgomery *Journal*, November 6, 11, 1875; Mobile *Register*, November 3, 4, 10, 1875.
[73] Montgomery *Journal*, October 31, November 6 and *passim* November, 1875; McMillan, *op. cit.*, pp. 321-326.
[74] Montgomery *Advertiser*, December 2, 1875; Montgomery *Journal*, December 2, 4, 1875.

calling the convention had required that the governor proclaim any new constitution in effect within ten days after the results of the ratification election became known; Governor Houston set the effective date as December 6, 1875.[75]

In 1874 the Democrats in Alabama seized their opportunity to end completely Republican control of the state government. Taking advantage of the economic depression, the declining prestige of the national administration, and growing disagreement among their opponents, they waged a strenuous campaign based almost exclusively on the race issue. The result was a smashing victory for the Democratic ticket; the election, like the campaign, was accompanied by considerable violence and irregular practices. After a decent interval the Democratic party consolidated its position with the adoption of a new state constitution. The party leaders were then in a position to manage state affairs free from any serious, organized opposition.

[75] *Acts* (1874-75), p. 109; Governor's Message, *Senate Journal,* (1875-76), p. 6.

CHAPTER THREE

Organization and Operation of the Democratic Party

EVER since overthrowing the Radical Republicans in 1874, the Democratic party has retained exclusive control over Alabama's state government down to the present day. To insure this supremacy the party formulated after 1874 methods of organization and control that have had a lasting effect. An examination of some of these should shed light on the political upheaval of the 1890's and on more recent political developments.

The Democratic and Conservative party, as already shown, brought together various elements that united in the common cause against Radicalism and Negro rule. From this mixed personnel and leadership there often arose discord and seeming contradictions in policy. When one Democratic newspaper complained that it was impossible to define Democracy, another explained the situation as follows:

> The Democratic party . . . is composed of men of all shades of opinion upon what to us are non-essential questions . . . . All of this heterogeneous crowd came together into the national Democratic party in 1868, not because they agreed upon any two of these [questions], but because we agreed upon the one great essential question, the preservation of State Government here in Alabama in the hands of the white race.[1]

[1] Mobile *Register*, February 5, 1887.

The party did not rely for leadership on figures prominent in the secession or war periods. Of all the delegates to the Constitutional Convention of 1875 only six had attended the 1861 secession convention. Many prominent ante-bellum leaders had passed from the picture. William Lowndes Yancey died in 1863. Two prominent governors, John Gill Shorter and John Anthony Winston, died in 1872 and 1871 respectively. Justice John Archibald Campbell of the United States Supreme Court left the state to continue his practice in New Orleans, and J. L. M. Curry turned from politics to the field of education. The only elder Democratic statesman prominent in the post-bellum party was Leroy Pope Walker, Secretary of War in the Confederate cabinet. Although some former Whig leaders such as C. C. Langdon and Thomas Hill Watts figured prominently in the Democratic and Conservative party, by and large the direction of affairs fell to a group of younger men, men who had not been too closely involved in the bitter struggle over state rights and secession. James H. Clanton, a former Whig, was practically a novice in the political field. Although Governor Houston had figured prominently in Congress until 1861, he took no part in political matters during the war period.

PARTY MACHINERY AND POLITICS

Final authority in all party matters rested with the state convention that met once every two years. County conventions selected delegates to this state meeting which always assembled in Montgomery. Delegates to county conventions were usually chosen by local meetings, but there was an increasing tendency during this period to use local primary elections for this purpose.[2] In 1878 Walter L. Bragg, chairman of the state executive committee, recommended the extended use of local primaries, and by 1880 some candidates for county offices were being chosen by primaries.[3] No one, however, as yet considered this method as desirable or proper for nominating candidates to state offices.

In organizing these biennial conventions, there usually arose considerable controversy over the apportionment of delegates

[2] Maggie Burgin, "The Direct Primary Election System in Alabama" (unpublished M.A. thesis, University of Alabama, 1931), p. 1.
[3] Montgomery *Advertiser*, May 31, June 15, 1878, January 26, 1879.

to the various counties. The usual method allowed each county one delegate for every two hundred Democratic votes cast in the last gubernatorial election. For the first few elections after 1874 this system worked fairly well. Plans for the 1880 convention, however, aroused violent criticism on the ground that the Democratic candidate in 1878 had run unopposed and thus the results would not represent the full Democratic strength of most counties. After heated discussions, the convention itself so altered the apportionment as to give larger delegations to all counties that would have benefited by using the 1876 vote as a basis.[4]

This compromise did not end the controversy over apportionment, and throughout the 1880's the white counties looked with suspicion upon the large delegations from counties in the Black Belt. After the Democrats had secured control over local governmental officials who managed the polls, they were able to swing a large part of the Negro vote. The white Democratic counties complained that such voters were in reality Republicans, and their numbers should not increase the power of counties in Democratic affairs. One newspaper pointed out that Montgomery and Dallas counties had forty-three delegates in the convention, while a dozen north Alabama counties did not have as many.[5] There seems to have been some sound basis for this complaint. In the 1876 convention 16 Black Belt counties sent 144 delegates, 26 per cent of the total number. In 1880 these same counties sent 182 delegates, 31 per cent of the whole, and in 1888 the proportion had increased to 34 per cent.[6] At the same time the ratio of total population in these counties to that of the whole state decreased from 38 per cent in 1870 to 32 per cent in 1890. During the same twenty-year period the ratio of white population to total population in the Black Belt counties decreased from 21 per cent to 14 per cent.[7]

In 1889 the controversy over apportionment flared up in a

[4] Montgomery *Advertiser*, March 19, May 25, June 3, 1880; Troy *Enquirer*, May 15, 22, 29, 1880.

[5] Huntsville *Advocate*, November 9, 1881. See also Troy *Enquirer*, September 6, 1884; Mobile *Register* quoted in Montgomery *Advertiser*, June 2, 1886.

[6] Montgomery *Advertiser*, May 31, 1876, May 25, June 3, 1880, March 8, 1888.

[7] *Compendium of the Eleventh Census* (1890), I, 475.

heated journalistic duel between two leading Democratic newspapers. The Birmingham *Age-Herald* contended for representation in the convention on the basis of white Democrats only, and
the Montgomery *Advertiser* assumed a defensive position. "The
handful of white men in the Black Belt," said the *Age-Herald,*
"cannot make the misfortune of heavy negro population . . . a
means of unduly increasing their strength and influence in the
party counsels."[8] Although the *Advertiser* agreed that some
change in the existing system was imperative, it favored making
the apportionment on the basis of representation in the legislature or on total population without any discrimination between
the races.[9] In spite of strong feelings engendered between Black
Belt and other Democrats, the method of apportionment remained unchanged for the momentous 1890 convention.

As the Democrats became more confident and secure in their
control over state politics, the party's organization became looser
and looser; confronted by no serious threats, the leaders failed
to see the need for a strong organization. A private secretary
under two governors described the condition of the party as
follows:

> The party organization in this state is only on paper, and
> exists by suffrance . . . . The chairman of the committee
> is practically the committee; and when a campaign is on,
> he goes through a form of work that is without plan, with-
> out intelligence, without effect, but that serves . . . him
> as a pretext for claiming to himself the credit of a suc-
> cess won by the people kept in line by pressure from
> without. The county organization is a shallow and more
> transparent pretense in most cases than that of the State.[10]

Indifference on the part of party constituents made it possible
in an increasing number of instances for cliques and "court
house rings" to take over the direction and execution of party
affairs. One observer stated that it was an "easy matter for a
few aggressive, resourceful men to control a county."[11] Another

[8] Birmingham *Age-Herald,* January 2, March 27, April 3, 1889.
[9] Montgomery *Advertiser,* March 19 and *passim March,* 1889.
[10] Robert McKee to John T. Morgan, January 8, 1882, McKee Papers.
[11] R[obert] H[enry] W[alker], *Alabama Politics from 1890 to 1938:
As Viewed by a Country Editor,* p. 3. See similar accusations in J[oseph]
C[olumbus] Manning, *Politics of Alabama,* p. 20.

remarked that the will of the people never prevailed in conventions but that the strings were always pulled by politicians.[12]

In the state campaign after 1875 the Democrats utilized as their one all-important argument the necessity of retaining control in the hands of native whites. Speakers and writers constantly alluded to imminent danger of a resurgent Negro-Republican coalition. "The downfall of Democracy," said the Democratic newspaper organ, "means the restoration of Negro rule."[13] Party platforms were phrased in the most general terms possible and seldom mentioned any controversial issues. If any individual or group proposed to discuss other issues, party leaders would raise the cry of treason and would accuse the offenders of endangering white, Democratic supremacy.[14] Although some Democrats genuinely resented what they considered undue emphasis on white supremacy,[15] this issue successfully prevented any serious split in the party before the decade of the 1890's. Because of the diverse composition of the Democratic party, the discussion of controversial issues would almost inevitably have led to serious intra-party disagreements.

At the same time, party leaders felt safe in emphasizing some few principles and ideas. Above all they were proud to point out the economical operation of the state government and to contrast it with the extravagance of Reconstruction regimes. Democratic speakers and writers constantly praised the Jeffersonian tradition of a vigorous but frugal government. One politically astute correspondent wrote Edward A. O'Neal's campaign manager as follows: "I would urge him [O'Neal] to stand on his record and commit himself to nothing in the future . . . . Rigid economy should be his sole committal."[16]

On the matter of friendship between sections of the country there was growing unanimity among Democrats. Beginning in

[12] A. H. Brittin writing in Huntsville *Advocate,* May 29, 1878.

[13] Montgomery *Advertiser,* August 2, 1882.

[14] Lauderdale *News* quoted in Montgomery *Advertiser,* February 27, 1880; Montgomery *Advertiser,* February 24, 1878, July 16, 1880.

[15] Robert McKee to L. W. Grant, October 22, 1882; Chappell Cory to Robert McKee, November 19, 1883, McKee Papers.

[16] R. B. Rhett to Emmett O'Neal, April 17, 1882, O'Neal Papers. See also S. S. Scott, *The Political Situation,* pp. 2-4; Montgomery *Advertiser,* May 13, 1876.

the 1870's and increasingly during the 1880's they openly expressed their loyalty to the Union and their desire to preserve friendly relations with the North. Democratic leaders realized that the prosperity of Alabama and other Southern states depended upon co-operation between influential groups in both sections. Raphael Semmes wrote in 1873 that he knew of no one in the South who did not believe that antagonisms had been settled and that the two sections would treat each other "with mutual respect."[17] A prominent Alabama Congressman described himself as "devotedly attached to the Union of the States, which I have for many years now believed to be essential to the happiness and prosperity of the American People."[18] Of course many Alabamians still revered the Confederate cause, but it would have been political suicide to advocate openly a return to slavery or the right of secession.

METHOD OF CONTROL

After the defeat of the Radicals in 1874, the primary problem facing the Democrats was that of maintaining a control efficient enough to guarantee further victories in succeeding elections. The condition of the Republican party both locally and nationally made this task easier. After 1876 the Republicans in the state offered little serious opposition, and after 1877 the national administration refrained from interference in state affairs. Nevertheless, Alabama Democrats remained constantly on the alert and developed through various devices a seemingly impregnable organization.

Control in the Black Belt and sometimes in the state at large depended on either eliminating or controlling a large number of Negro votes. While party leaders continued after 1874 to emphasize white supremacy in counties with small Negro populations, in other sections they played down the race issue. Indeed, Black Belt Democrats attempted in some instances to win Negro voters away from their traditional Republican allegiance by posing as the only reliable party upon which freemen should rely.

[17] Raphael Semmes to Frederick G. Bromberg, November 6, 1873, Bromberg Papers (Library of Congress).
[18] Herbert, "Grandfather's Talks," p. 4.

Thus, before the late 1880's there was little, if any, outspoken sentiment for disfranchising the Negro. Instead, many newspapers and leaders in the Black Belt put themselves and the party on record as favoring the Negro vote. "The enfranchisement of the colored race," said one paper, "whatever may have been the motives of the dominant party when accomplishing it, has resulted well for all our people."[19] The attitude toward Negro suffrage in other parts of the state varied from acceptance as a necessary evil to condemnation of its fraudulent use by Black Belt politicians. The Mobile *Register* accepted the Negro voter as one of the inevitable results of the war but looked upon him as a nuisance.[20] A Birmingham newspaper in criticizing Bourbon Black Belt control condemned the large majorities rolled up for the Democratic party by Negro voters in Black Belt counties.[21]

The primary problem for the Democrats, however, was not courting the Negro vote but controlling it. At the same time, this feat had to be achieved without alienating white support in non-Negro counties. The key to control generally rested with the sheriff and other local officials responsible for the conduct of elections. The sheriff, along with the probate judge or circuit clerk, appointed all inspectors and returning officers for the various precincts. Thus it was absolutely essential for the Democrats to control as many of the county and local governments as possible. In 1874 and later years they won control of these by elections in most counties, but in some Black Belt counties they had to resort to certain extra-legal devices. One method called for the legislature's placing the bonds of public officials so high that no local Republican could sign them; the legislature then prohibited anyone who lived outside the county from becoming a surety. If the bond could not be met, the office would be declared vacant, and the Democratic governor could make his own appointment.[22] Where Republicans could not be driven from office by election, intimidation, or prohibitive bonds, the

[19] Montgomery *Advertiser*, April 6, 1879.
[20] Mobile *Register*, February 22, 26, 1870, June 4, 1875.
[21] Birmingham *Alabama True Issue*, August 21, 1880.
[22] Memorial of the Republican Members of the Legislature of Alabama, February 15, 1875, *Senate Miscellaneous Documents*, 43 Cong., 2 Sess., no. 107, pp. 7-8; Elections in Alabama, *loc. cit.*, pp. v-vi; *Acts* (1874-75), p. 50.

legislature in some instances arbitrarily abolished the county or city government and substituted therefor one appointed by the governor. Seven such instances in the Black Belt can be cited.[23] The Republicans denounced such actions as flagrant denials of the will of the people.

With Democrats safely in control of election machinery, the legislature could afford to continue many of the centralized and arbitrary election laws inaugurated by the Radicals. Indeed, the Democrats favored strengthening the laws in some instances. The first two election laws after 1874 made no complete revision of the Radical legislation but did institute a few significant changes. Where the Reconstruction laws had allowed a voter to ballot in any precinct in his county, he was now required to cast his ballot in the precinct in which he had been residing for at least thirty days. As required by the new constitution, the time of state elections was changed from the November national election date to August, in order to lessen the danger of Federal interference.[24] The Democrats also instituted public challenging of voters at the polls, where formerly this right had been possessed only by the inspectors. These challengers could ask embarrassing and confusing questions designed to intimidate Negro voters.[25]

Another legal device that deprived many Negroes of the ballot was the inclusion of the word *larceny* in the disfranchising section of the constitution. While previous constitutions had disfranchised anyone guilty of a penitentiary offence such as *grand* larceny, the new constitution was interpreted as withdrawing the ballot from those guilty of *petit* larceny.[26] A Negro in Bullock County recounted how he cautioned a farmer to call in two turkeys sitting on a fence dangerously close to a public road. "Now . . . ," he said, "jest by . . . telling 'em to drive them turkeys

[23] *Acts* (1874-75), pp. 215, 220, 513; *ibid.* (1875-76), pp. 379, 381, 387; *ibid.* (1876-77), p. 156; New York *Tribune,* July 24, 1880; Elections in Alabama, *loc. cit.,* pp. vi, 134.

[24] *Acts* (1874-75), p. 76; *ibid.,* (1875-76), p. 103; *Constitution of 1875,* Art. VIII.

[25] Elections in Alabama, *loc. cit.,* pp. x-xi; *Acts* (1876-77), p. 122.

[26] *Constitution of 1875,* Art. VIII, sec. 3; *Anderson* v. *State* (1882), 72 Ala. 187; *Washington* v. *State* (1884), 75 Ala. 582; Elections in Alabama, *loc. cit.,* pp. 670-671.

off that road, I saved two Republican votes."[27] The process of registering voters rested safely in Democratic hands, because all registrars were appointed by the Secretary of State in Montgomery. Although the voter could register on the day of election, the Democratic registrar often failed to appear at the heavily Republican polling place.

In 1879 the legislature completely revised the election law and made two important changes ostensibly in the interest of ballot secrecy but actually designed to strengthen the hands of the Democrats in controlling the elections. The first specified that the ballot must be "a plain piece of white paper, without any figures, marks, rulings, characters or embellishment thereon, not less than two nor more than two and one-half inches wide, and not less than five nor more than seven inches long."[28] Since the government printed no official ballot, the act was supposed to bring about uniformity and a greater degree of secrecy. At the same time, however, the ignorant or the non-observant could be deceived by minor alterations that would invalidate his ballot if the inspectors felt so inclined. The second change amended the Code so as to eliminate the requirement of placing on the ballot the number corresponding to the voter's number on the poll list.[29] Again the supporters of this measure contended that it was fashioned in the interest of ballot secrecy, but it actually removed all possibility of conducting an accurate probe into an election suspected of being fraudulent.

For a number of years opposition to these changes remained strong, particularly in the non-Black Belt counties. One state senator ridiculed the argument of secrecy by saying: "There is too much secrecy now, for I fear some ballots that are cast are so secret they are never heard of again."[30] The Huntsville *Advocate*, anti-Democratic paper, led the fight against the new

[27] Union Springs *Herald* quoted in Montgomery *Advertiser*, August 19, 1876.

[28] *Acts* (1878-79), p. 72. Two years later these requirements were made slightly more liberal. *Ibid.* (1880-81), p. 29.

[29] *Ibid.* (1878-79), p. 7.

[30] George Robert Farnham quoted in Huntsville *Advocate*, February 16, 1881. See also speech of William Yates Titcomb quoted in Montgomery *Advertiser*, February 13, 1881.

election law, which it described as "giving impunity to fraud."[31] A Negro Republican journal, the Greenback platform, and the Republican platform denounced the existing law and advocated one that would give "a free ballot and a fair count."[32] Even a Black Belt Democrat denounced the system. "Laws are enacted," he said, "that facilitate fraud on the ballot-box; and the precedents set by the 'fools and thieves' during the reconstruction era are used to justify acts that merit no better defense."[33] Such Democratic papers as the Tuscaloosa *Clarion*, Scottsboro *Citizen*, Selma *Argus*, Gadsden *News*, and Lauderdale *News* added their protests. "It is worse than ridiculous;" said the Troy *Enquirer*, "it is mischievous in its results."[34]

The legislature almost re-instated the ballot numbering system in 1881, but Black Belt representatives successfully blocked this move instigated by members from north Alabama. Similar efforts in succeeding legislatures likewise met with failure.[35]

Although provision for Negro suffrage remained on the statute books during the period under consideration, a number of attempts were made to restrict or end it. Such suggestions as a literacy test or the presentation of a poll tax receipt were often considered but never passed by the legislature.[36] In the later 1880's sentiment for the elimination of the Negro from politics became so strong that the governor recommended a new constitutional convention for the specific purpose of settling the election and suffrage questions.[37] In 1889 the legislature seriously considered but finally tabled the Lawson Bill, which would have imposed intricate directions and specifications for voting. It

[31] Huntsville *Advocate*, March 19, 1879, December 8, 1880 and December, 1880 - January, 1881, *passim*.

[32] Huntsville *Gazette*, March 11, 1882; Montgomery *Advertiser*, June 27, 1880, July 7, 1882.

[33] Robert McKee to Rufus K. Boyd, February 3, 1882, McKee Papers.

[34] Troy *Enquirer*, May 15, November 20, 1880, January 1, 1881: Huntsville *Advocate*, Janurary 5, 26, 1881.

[35] *Senate Journal* (1880-81), p. 342, *ibid.* (1886-87), p. 793; *House Journal* (1884-85), p. 915; Jacksonville *Republican* quoted in Montgomery *Advertiser*, March 1, 1881; Huntsville *Advocate*, December 8, 1880.

[36] *House Journal* (1874-74), p. 731; *ibid.* (1886-87), p. 782; Mobile *Register*, February 21, 1887; Montgomery *Advertiser*, November 28, 1886, November 21, 1888.

[37] Governor's Message, *Senate Journal* (1890-91), pp. 32-34.

was generally understood that the primary purpose of this measure was to defeat Negro majorities by prescribing an educational qualification for voting.[38]

The election laws merely made control by the Democrats possible. Actual success depended upon the manner in which the laws were carried out in conducting elections. One lesson that the Democrats had learned well from the Radicals was that best results could be obtained by resorting not so much to violence and intimidation at the polls as to manipulation, deceit, and fraud. Even the Republicans admitted that little actual violence or intimidation existed in Alabama after 1874. They did, however, accuse the Democrats of "unblushing frauds" under cover of law and of carrying out all too literally the Democratic taunt, "You can out vote us, but we can out count you."[39]

In a number of elections after that of 1874, Democrats in border counties continued the practice of importing white voters from neighboring states, a practice that had been employed by Republicans during Reconstruction elections.[40] Critics of Democratic methods also reported numerous instances where pressure was applied to Negroes by their employers, landlords, or advancing agents. They complained that on occasion Negroes had been forcibly withheld from the polls by being thrown into jail and that Democratc officials bought up registration certificates from Negroes at two dollars apiece.[41]

One of the most common devices employed at election time simply called for the absence of Democratic inspectors and registrars from polling places where heavy Negro or other opposition vote might be expected. Although the law provided that in the event no election officials appeared at a designated polling place, the voters could improvise the necessary machinery, Negroes were usually too ignorant to do so, or the county canvassers could easily find some excuse for rejecting all votes cast under such a

---

[38] *Senate Journal* (1888-89), pp. 667, 754; Birmingham *Age-Herald* (weekly), February 13, 1889, February 12, 1890.

[39] Address of the Republican State Convention, Montgomery *Advertiser*, July 7, 1878; Elections in Alabama, *loc. cit.*, pp. ii-iii.

[40] Elections in Alabama, *loc. cit.*, pp. 458-459, 638.

[41] *Ibid.*, pp. 133, 636-637; New York *Tribune*, October 2, 13, 1880; Huntsville *Advocate*, July 24, 1878, October 5, 1881.

procedure.[42] The law also stipulated that at least one inspector had to belong to a party different from that of the others. But the Democrats usually appointed Negro Republicans who were too ignorant to detect fraud or who could be easily intimidated.[43] Inside the polling places the Democrats resorted to innumerable devices to deceive the unwary Negroes. In one instance the ballot boxes were placed so high up, nearly six feet at times, that the voter could not see what happened to the ballot when he reached up to put it in.[44]

Between 1875 and 1891 the United States House of Representatives heard a total of ninety-two contested election cases; ten of these originated in Alabama.[45] Most of these Alabama contests resulted from Republican efforts to unseat Democrats sent to Congress from the Fourth District. Although this district consisted entirely of Black Belt counties, it returned a Democratic congressman in every election after 1874. Republicans argued that only through fraud or other illegal practices could such results be explained.[46] The testimony published in these contested cases throws considerable light on Democratic election methods. Democratic canvassers threw out thousands of Republican votes because they failed to meet the minute and exact specifications of the election law or because of other "frivolous pretexts." The evidence also pointed to innumerable cases of gross miscounting and flagrantly false returns.[47]

Republicans complained that no indictments, much less convictions, in election fraud cases could be obtained because of Democratic control over courts and juries. "Swift is the punish-

[42] New York *Tribune*, December 27, 1882, December 5, 1884; Elections in Alabama, *loc. cit.*, p. 135.

[43] Huntsville *Gazette*, November 26, 1881.

[44] New York *Tribune*, July 7, 1879, November 16, 1882.

[45] Chester H. Rowell (ed.), *A . . . Digest of all the Contested Election Cases in the House of Representatives of the United States, 1789-1901*, pp. 11-12.

[46] In every contest except one, the Republican contestant was seated. *Ibid.*, pp. 364, 394, 411, 424, 454.

[47] See testimony in such significant cases as Smith v. Shelley, June 27, 1882, *House Miscellaneous Documents*, 47 Cong., 1 Sess., no. 21; Lowe v. Wheeler, May 17, 1882, *House Miscellaneous Documents*, 47 Cong., 1 Sess., no. 22; Craig v. Shelley, July 5, 1884, *House Miscellaneous Documents*, 48 Cong., 1 Sess., no. 30; McDuffie v. Turpin, May 7, 1890, *House Reports*, 51 Cong., 1 Sess., no. 1905.

ment of imprisonment . . . for the larceny of an ear of corn," read an address from the Republican state convention, "but for miscounting or destroying or refusing to receive the ballots of hundreds of electors . . . there is no punishment."[48] The sharp decline in Republican votes in state elections between 1874 and 1876, especially in the Black Belt, indicated to Republicans the prevalence of corruption and manipulation. Ex-governor William H. Smith complained about frauds in the 1880 elections and recounted as a typical example how a Democratic inspector "accidentally" knocked the light out during the counting; when it was restored, a sizeable Democratic majority had appeared in the ballot box.[49]

The more candid Democrats admitted that elections were often won by dishonest means but salved their own consciences by stressing "high ends" in justification of "low means." One prominent politician reflected in later years:

> It is lamentable that the whites of the South, trained to love honest elections, could not, as soon as they recovered control, return at once to fair elections; but the negro was still on hand to vote solidly against the white man, and it was not human nature that Southern Democrats, who in part by false counting had now restored honest and economical government, should allow it . . . to be endangered by fairly counting the ballots of those who had demonstrated their utter incapacity as suffragans.[50]

A Democratic congressman expressed similar ideas when he said:

> If the negroes all voted and their votes were counted . . . they would soon begin to scheme again to resume control of the county and State governments . . . . I assure you that the masses of the white people in the South do not want to be violators of the law, but when you put the alternative to them of abandoning their homes they will violate the law every time.[51]

In maintaining their political dominance, Alabama Democrats relied primarily on their control of election machinery. They

[48] Quoted in Montgomery *Advertiser*, July 7, 1878. See also *Address* . . . *by the Republican State Executive Committee* (1892), pp. 1-2.

[49] Letter in Montgomery *Advertiser*, August 18, 1880. See similar report of Paul Strobach in *ibid.*, September 5, 1880; New York *Tribune*, November 16, 1882.

[50] Herbert, "Grandfather's Talks," p. 278.

[51].William C. Oates interviewed in the New York *Herald* reprinted in Montgomery *Advertiser*, Januray 18, 1889.

employed innumerable devices for intimidating or confusing unwanted Negro votes. In some instances they even resorted to fraud and false counting, always justifying such actions as necessary in preventing a return to Republican-Negro control. These tactics might have precipitated intra-party discord, especially between Black Belt and white counties. To forestall such tendencies, Democratic leaders consistently avoided discussions of election laws, apportionment, or other controversial topics. They insisted that the sole and exclusive issue in any campaign should be the maintenance of a "Democratic, white-controlled" government.

CHAPTER FOUR

Threats
to Democratic Supremacy

PRIOR to the Negro disfranchising constitution of 1901, the hegemony of the Democratic party in Alabama was threatened from time to time by disagreements within the party and by opposition from other parties or groups. The most serious crisis developed with the Populist revolt in the 1890's. Between 1875 and 1890 discord and opposition did not reach dangerous proportions, but an examination of these movements should shed some light on the origins of Populism in the state.

INTERNAL STRIFE

In spite of its united front in opposing the Reconstruction Radicals, the Democratic party during the fifteen years after 1874 was by no means free from discord that sometimes became serious enough to cause open splits and defections from party ranks. This internal difficulty varied over the years and was much more noticeable in some elections than in others. For four or five years after the election of 1874 the chief threat to unity arose from violent disputes over financial matters, especially the problems of adjusting the Reconstruction debt. Indeed, Robert McKee and the Selma *Argus* went so far in denouncing Governor Houston and the debt adjustment that many party leaders feared an open break in the ranks. "Governor Houston," said McKee, "is no more the democratic party of Alabama now than Gov. Lindsay was in 1871-2 . . . . Our duty is to the party, not to those whom it elevates to office."[1] In spite of strained feelings in 1876, the party averted an open split, and two years later the Selma paper actually praised some accomplishments of the Houston administration.[2]

During the early 1880's there was some evidence of party discord resulting from the Greenback movement, which had encouraged a fairly strong independent feeling in northern Alabama. As one Democratic newspaper described the situation, "Discontent is the order of the day. Factions are raising up . . . . The great cry is that of 'rings' and star chambers and some argue that the Democratic Party is composed only of tricksters and demogogues."[3] The Troy *Enquirer* criticized particularly the dominance that the Black Belt maintained by controlling the Negro vote.[4] In Birmingham the *Alabama True Issue* spoke out more bitterly. "There must be," it said, "some opposition, or there will be no reformation."[5] The Selma *Times*, another Democratic paper, advocated the establishment of two opposing parties in the state, each taking advantage of the Negro vote.[6]

These isolated voices of protest, however, seem to have had little effect, and during the governorships of Rufus Wills Cobb, 1878-1882, and Edward Asbury O'Neal, 1882-1886, the party remained on the whole harmonious. Considerable differences of opinion did arise over the railroad commission question, and Governor O'Neal was criticized by a number of Democrats in 1884 because of his financial, military, and penitentiary programs. One newspaper described him as lacking "force of mind and character, sagacity, self-reliance and nerve," and a contemporary public figure criticized his "general love of fuss, pomp and parade."[7] Nevertheless, the strong tradition that a governor

[1] Selma *Southern Argus*, March 24, 1876.
[2] *Ibid.*, November 22, 1878; J. W. DuBose, *op. cit.*, pp. 1126-1127. See below, pp. 74-75, 83-85.
[3] Birmingham *Observer*, June 10, 1880.
[4] May 15, August 28, 1880.
[5] June 19, August 7, 1880.
[6] November 25, 1881.
[7] Selma *Times* quoted in Montgomery *Advertiser*, February 27, 1884; Joseph F. Johnston to Frederick G. Bromberg, September 11, 1883, Bromberg Papers (University of North Carolina).

should serve two terms prevailed, and O'Neal was renominated unanimously in 1884.

By the middle of the 1880's certain fundamental cleavages in the Democratic party were evident. One more or less constant source of disagreement centered around the party's leadership, management, and policies. Some ante-bellum political rivalry carried over into the post-war arrangement. Both "Old-Line" Whigs and "Old-Line" Democrats accused each other of exercising too much influence in the reformed Democratic and Conservative party; some of the same rivalry also existed between former secessionists and former unionists. Criticism arose over the absence of any specific or clearly defined Democratic party policy. As one newspaper pointed out, better unity and spirit could have been achieved with a platform more definite than mere opposition to Republicanism.[8]

Considerable dispute arose over the performance of Democratic office holders. Some newspapers and individuals felt that the public officers were carrying out their functions about as well as could be expected considering their meager salaries. Others were more outspoken in denouncing the inefficiency and laxness pervading the capitol; they frequently complained that politicians and their "rings" controlled the offices and thus prevented a good, "businesslike" government. A Birmingham paper, campaigning for new life in the Democratic party said:

> The Democrats have been in power for twelve years and we cannot hold up clean hands to the people . . . . There is a widespread belief that the state's business is conducted by many of its officers in a shamefully slipshod way.[9]

One of the best appraisals of the state government came from Robert McKee, who was in a position to know the situation. In 1882 he wrote:

> Our democratic adminitrations since 1874 have been slipshod and weak—very much weaker in all their details than any outsider supposes. They have been honest and economical. They have not squandered the people's money. They have stolen nothing. They have reduced taxes and sustained

[8] Montgomery *Advertiser*, January 5, 1876; Mobile *Tribune*, January 15, 1876; Tuscumbia *North Alabamian*, April 12, 1878.
[9] Birmingham *Chronicle*, March 28, April 11, 1886. See also Selma *Southern Argus*, March 22, June 7, August 9, 1878; Troy *Enquirer*; April 6. 1878. Brewton *Escambia Banner*, June 2, 1883.

the public credit.   But they have been conducted without
order, system, plan, design, or purpose; without method, or
checks, or safeguards other than the personal integrity of
the several heads of departments and the clerks therein.[10]
One of McKee's correspondents wrote in a similar vein:

> The reins are passing into the hands of schemers and cliques
> whose whole object is to attain power and to parcel out
> the places and raid the treasury.[11]

Some intra-party friction developed over certain sectional
disagreements.   Much of the feeling here grew out of the long-
standing controversy between north and south Alabama.   Just as
in the ante-bellum period and during Reconstruction, those in
the northern counties resented the strong influence of Black Belt
politicians.   Although the Black Belt had made many concessions
to north Alabama Democrats when attempting to overthrow the
Radicals, Black Belt Bourbons still retained a strong, and some
thought unduly influential, position in party and government.
"The people about the capital city," said one north Alabama
newspaper, "have begun to believe that this part of the State
will remain true to the party just for the glorious privilege of
voting the Democratic ticket, but we are afraid that our office-
loving friends of the South will tempt this part of the State
too far."[12]   Another paper, which described itself as residing in
the "live part of the State," said: "The chief idea of the men in
the sleeping part of the State is to hold office . . . . It is not so
up here.   We prefer to stay in the ranks and help make Alabama
what she should be."[13]

The sectional rivalry often broke out when nominations to
office and legislative seats had to be apportioned.   In 1875 the
seats in the legislature seem to have been fairly apportioned according to total population.   By 1890, however, because of the
rapid increase in population in north Alabama, nine of the eleven
counties in the mineral area were under-represented and eleven
of sixteen Black Belt counties were over-represented.[14]   North
Alabamians resented this inequality, especially since Black Belt
representation was based largely on Negro population.   An in-

[10] Robert McKee to John Tyler Morgan, January 8, 1882, McKee Papers.
[11] R. K. Boyd to McKee, February 26, 1883, McKee Papers.
[12] Florence *News* quoted in Hunstville *Advocate,* March 23, 1881.
[13] Birmingham *Chronicle,* June 28, 1885.
[14] *Constitution of 1875,* Art. IX, secs. 6-7; *Acts* (1880-81), p. 117.

dependent paper ridiculed this sectional discord in the Democratic party as follows: "The Bourbon of the south saith unto the Bourbon of the north this state is *our* state, (WE OF THE BLACK BELT) and the fat offices thereof, even from generation unto generation, we fixed it with our little election 'AND DON'T YOU FORGET IT'."[15]

Closely related to this sectional rivalry was a latent antagonism between rural-agrarian elements and those urban groups interested in the development of commercial, mining, and industrial enterprises. In 1885 a new boom in the mineral region of northern Alabama accentuated this controversy and precipitated the question of how far the state government should go in making concessions and giving encouragement to this type of development. North Alabama newspapers, especially those in Birmingham, described Alabama's government as having suffered under the hands of "old fogies" for fourteen years, and they felt that the time was ripe for younger men to steer a more progressive course. The argument assumed the form of a contest between traditionalists and progressives, with the former on the defensive.

One Birmingham paper stated its case as follows:

> We have due respect for age and experience. But the trouble is the experience of this element is not worth so much to this day and generation as might be imagined. The carpet-baggers and scallawaggers are dead and buried . . . . New issues are arising . . . . The bald-head element have done noble work for the Democracy of this State, all honor to them. They have had their reward. Now let the young men have a chance.[16]

Another paper commented:

> There exists a strong prejudice against the industrial interests in the agricultural parts of the state . . . . The people . . . have been made to believe that diversified interests are hurtful to the State . . . . Let the State pension the Confederate soldiers, but not by giving them state offices. We want a Governor who knows that a smokestack in the mountains doesn't injure corn and cotton in the prairies.[17]

[15] Huntsville *Advocate*, March 23, 1881. See also March 30, 1881; Mobile *Register*, January 14, 1887.

[16] Birmingham *Age* quoted in Montgomery *Advertiser*, August 15, 1885.

[17] Birmingham *Chronicle*, July 5, 1885. See also January 30 and February 1, 1885.

The Birmingham *Chronicle* assumed leadership of the forces advocating a more liberal program of expenditures and the ignoring of past issues. Among other things, it recommended increased school funds, state money for internal improvements, higher salaries for state officers, encouragement for immigration, and development of natural resources. It condemned the "Traditionists" for looking backward and never forward and for accusing unjustly the manufacturing cities of undermining the economic prosperity of the agricultural districts.

> It is a peculiar feature of the argument of traditionists, [said the Birmingham paper] that they put so prominently forward the fact that the northern republicans and negroes who managed our affairs . . . just after the war . . . were thieves. What earthly bearing can that undeniable fact have on the argument that our state should begin to improve her condition. The fact that money was stolen from the state during that period of misrule, is no argument for her remaining forever as she is.[18]

The progressive faction often attacked Robert McKee as a typical Bourbon or "traditionist." One newspaper said of him.

> He wants no immigration . . . wants no enterprise; wants no nuthin' but the dry-rot of taxation, and the dead eddy of bourbonism![19]

Although their program sounded strangely similar to that of Reconstruction leaders, the progressives vehemently denied any connection with Republicanism, but did admit that two parties would be beneficial to the state if the Negro vote could be evenly divided. In order to accomplish their aims, the progressives advocated drafting a new constitution or drastically amending the existing one, which they described as a guarantee against robbery and nothing else with no provision for the future growth of the state. So strong was this sentiment that in 1889 one branch of the legislature passed a bill calling for a new constitution.[20]

The rural elements just as loudly denounced what appeared to them an increasingly favorable attitude of party and state leaders toward industrial progress. Some resentment from agrarian groups arose over the preponderant influence of lawyers in

[18] *Ibid.*, October 4, 1885. See also February 22, 1885, November 28, 1886.
[19] Huntsville *Advocate*, September 7, 1881. See also Birmingham *Chronicle*, December 16, 1886.
[20] Birmingham *Chronicle*, October 24, 1886; Montgomery *Advertiser*, December 4, 1888; *House Journal* (1888-89), pp. 511, 1168.

the government. Although the first two legislatures after 1874 contained so many farmers that they were called "Grange Legislatures," by 1888 eighty out of the one hundred thirty-three members of the legislature were lawyers.[21] When a bill to raise the qualifications of justices of the peace was under consideration, one writer complained that lawyers had already taken too many offices away from the "horny handed tiller of the soil."[22] Robert McKee feared that Alabama was following the example set by Georgia where "Corporations, and capital, and the lawyers they own, govern to enrich the few at the expense of the many."[23]

Much of the agrarian opposition was directed against the rapidly growing city of Birmingham, where promoters were loudly advocating a New South movement for Alabama similar to the one in Georgia sponsored by Atlanta promoters. The Black Belt counties felt that the growing city was luring away too many agricultural laborers for work in the mines and mills and also complained that the industrial city did not benefit the farmer because it had not lowered the price of clothes, farm implements, and other necessities. One newspaper went so far as to assert that Jefferson County would be better off if all its furnaces were torn down, its mines filled with dirt, and its inhabitants put to planting cotton.[24] Another Black Belt paper, dubbed by a Birmingham rival as "that Rip Van Winkle of the crop lien belt," urged its readers to be true to the memories of Washington, Jefferson, and Lee and to be "no bastard heirs of the New South," a phrase of "Yankee invention."[25] Numerous state papers warned the people against shifting in large numbers to the Birmingham area.[26] The Democratic organ considered the controversy as purely an argument between those favoring economy in government and those favoring liberal expenditures.

[21] Z. M. P. Inge, "Lawyers in Politics," *Proceedings of the Alabama State Bar Association* (1888), p. 49.

[22] Montgomery *Advertiser*, February 29, 1880.

[23] McKee to R. W. Cobb, August 23, 1883, McKee Papers. See similar sentiments in *Proceedings of the . . . Alabama State Agricultural Society* (1887), pp. 7-11.

[24] Selma *Times* quoted in Birmingham *Chronicle*, June 27, 1886.

[25] Hayneville *Examiner*, quoted in Birmingham *Iron Age*, January 22, 1885.

[26] Birmingham *Chronicle*, November 8, 1885.

We agree [it said] that the government can and should
foster the industries of a state and can do much to develop
its resources. But we contend . . . that the very best way
to do this is not the expenditure of tax money . . . . The
prosperity of Alabama does not depend on what her government shall spend to enrich her people, but on what those
people shall do to enrich themselves.[27]

In an effort to minimize the effects of these disagreements
between urban and rural groups, party leaders and newspapers
attempted to point out the benefits of a well-balanced and
diversified economy. They emphasized the economic interde-
pendence between the business-manufacturing groups and their
farmer neighbors. "The agricultural must feed and clothe the
mineral district," stated one paper, "and the mineral district
furnish the needed articles made of iron or steel to the agricultural district."[28] An outstanding north Alabama leader said:
"The man who disembowels its [the earth's] minerals works in
harmony with the man who cultivates its surface . . . . The man
who manufactures cotton is the friend and not the foe of the
man who raises it."[29]

The election of 1886 brought much of the intra-party discord
to a head. The strongest candidates for the gubernatorial nomination, John W. McKleroy, N. H. R. Dawson, and Henry D.
Clayton, became dead-locked, and the convention chose a "dark
horse" candidate, Thomas Seay of Hale County. The choice
proved acceptable to all factions, because Seay had the ability
to get along with almost everyone; one contemporary described
the 1886 convention as a "victory of the young men . . . against
their elders."[30] During his four years in office Governor Seay
incurred less unfavorable criticism than his predecessors. Although the Governor generally sided with the more progressive
faction, Robert McKee described him as "thorough, exacting,
laborious," and the Montgomery *Advertiser* approved his pro-

---

[27] Montgomery *Advertiser*, January 29, August 15, 1885.
[28] Eutaw *Mirror* quoted in Warrior *Advance and Guide*, July 11, 1885.
[29] L. P. Walker, *State and National Affairs*, p. 10. See similar sentiments
in Montgomery *Advertiser*, December 28, 1887; *Proceedings of the . . .
Alabama State Agricultural Society* (1887), pp. 5-6; Samuel Noble to John
T. Morgan, March 5, 1886, Morgan Papers.
[30] J. W. DuBose, *op. cit.*, p. 1415.

gram as progressive but "tempered with that wise and prudent regard for economy and financial safety."[31]

Nevertheless, unity and agreement still did not characterize the Democratic party. In 1889 the controversy over apportionment in the state convention reached its height, and one of the Birmingham papers continued to denounce certain Black Belt senators as "Anti-Progress Alabamians." The same paper early in 1890 took the Montgomery *Advertiser* to task for opposing the political activities of the Alliance movement and Commissioner of Agriculture Reuben F. Kolb.[32] Thus the lingering rivalry between intra-party factions began to figure in the mounting agrarian unrest that was soon to culminate in open revolt against traditional party leadership and policies.

REPUBLICAN OPPOSITION

The only continuous, organized opposition to the Democrats came from the Republican party. Its strength varied from election to election, and in numerous instances it was overshadowed or absorbed by independent movements. The election of 1874 did not destroy the party but did considerably weaken it. Some Republican leaders hoped to make a comeback with support from former Whigs and others opposed to the ultra-conservative, Bourbon policy that they expected the Democrats to pursue. The actions of the Houston administration, however, especially its failure to adopt a policy of outright repudiation on the debt question, upset this particular piece of Republican strategy.

In 1875 the Alabama Republican party was split in two apparently irreconcilable factions. The principal Republican newspaper in the fall of that year ran a series of articles describing the dissensions and emphasizing the point that party harmony was the *sine qua non* of success in the coming election.[33] One faction, under the leadership of Warner, Rice, and Ex-governor W. H. Smith, hoped to win support from dissatisfied Democrats. At a convention on May 16, 1876, it nominated Judge Thomas

[31] McKee to John Tyler Morgan, December 31, 1886, McKee Papers; Montgomery *Advertiser*, November 15, 1888.
[32] Birmingham *Age-Herald* (weekly), February 20, 1889, January 1, 29, 1890.
[33] Montgomery *Journal*, October 6, 8, 9, 12, 1875, February 22, 1876.

M. Peters for governor.[34] Later in the month the other faction, led by Senator Spencer and Congressman Hays and relying primarily on Negro votes, held a convention and nominated a slate of candidates headed by James S. Clarke. When the latter refused to run, C. C. Sheets was given the gubernatiorial nomination.[35]

Republican leaders exerted every effort to reconcile the two factions and at the same time made overtures to Democrats that were dissatisfied with Governor Houston's administration. A conference between Republicans and independents at Blount Springs in July resulted in a compromise ticket, entitled "Independent State Ticket." As its candidate for governor, this coalition group selected Noadiah Woodruff, a successful merchant and prosperous planter of Selma. He had an excellent business and civic record with no political ties except a professed standing as "independent with democratic proclivities."[36] Both factions and the Republican organ supported Woodruff; the *Journal* stated that it preferred an independent ticket to "Houston tyranny."[37]

Democratic newspapers sternly warned voters against being misled by Republican factions or independent groups. "Radicalism means ruin, whether you spell it *Republican* or *Independent*."[38] One Democratic editor, however, privately commented on the dangerous situation: "Woodruff is a small potatoe, and is hardly worth the powder. But I tell you what is the fact; if a different man had been put in the field say a man like Patton, Houston's election would have been extremely doubtful!"[39] The results in the August elections dashed the hopes of the Republican coalition. The vote for governor stood 99,255 for Houston and 55,528 for Woodruff. Although the total vote was much smaller than in 1874, the Democrats had more than trebled their lead over the Republicans because of the large increase in Negro

[34] New York *Tribune*, May 18, 1876; Montgomery *Advertiser*, May 17, 24-26, 1876.

[35] Montgomery *Journal*, May 25, 27, July 11, 1876.

[36] J. W. DuBose, *op. cit.*, pp. 1135-1136; Selma *Southern Argus*, July 21, 1876; Montgomery *Advertiser*, May 23, June 23, July 18, 1876.

[37] Montgomery *Journal*, November 20, 1876.

[38] Montgomery *Advertiser*, July 18, 1876. See also July, 1876, *passim*.

[39] Horace Hood to Robert McKee, July 29, 1876, McKee Papers.

votes counted for the Democrats. The Republicans lost seventeen seats in the House and eight in the Senate; only one Negro sat in the new legislature.[40]

In the years following 1876 many prominent Republicans deserted the party. Some of the Northerners left the state, while others, such as Willard Warner, retired from politics and began business enterprises.[41] Some native whites continued to work in the Republican party; others, such as Ex-governor Lewis and John White, went over to the Democrats for various reasons; while still others, such as Sam Rice in 1882, ran as independents.[42] In 1881 a Negro Republican newspaper complained loudly about the desertion of white leaders from the party: "How many of those who called themselves Republicans in the days of the party's prosperity have . . . denied the faith because there were no spoils of office, leaving the Negro and the faithful few of white Republicans to uphold the Republican banner."[43]

The Republicans also lost strong newspaper support. The central party organ at Montgomery, the *Alabama State Journal,* ceased publication in April, 1877. In November, 1879, the first issue of the Negro-edited Huntsville *Gazette* referred to itself as the only Republican journal in Alabama, but in 1881 it mentioned three or four others, all Negro.[44] Some Democrats referred to the Huntsville *Advocate* as Republican, but technically it was a Greenback or independent paper. Although a white Republican paper, the Montgomery *National Union,* had been established in 1882, only one such paper, the Huntsville *New South,* begun in January, 1885, existed in 1887.[45]

The Republican party remained divided in two rival factions, each of which held separate conventions in 1878 and again in

[40] *Senate Journal* (1876-77), p. 43; Beverly, *op. cit.,* p. 206. See maps in the Appendix pp. 222-223.

[41] See interview with Willard Warner in New York *Tribune,* February 24, 1879.

[42] Montgomery *Advertiser,* June 8, August 31, 1876; Herbert, "Grandfather's Talks," pp. 261-262.

[43] Huntsville *Gazette,* June 25, 1881.

[44] Next to the Huntsville *Gazette* the most prominent Negro paper was the Mobile *Gazette,* edited by Phillips Joseph. Huntsville *Gazette,* June 25, 1881.

[45] *Ayer's American Newspaper Annual* (1887), pp. 200-205; Huntsville *Gazette,* December 16, 1882.

1884. These opposing groups came more and more to represent the rivalry between Negro and white Republicans. The Negroes always preferred a separate state ticket, while the whites usually advised co-operation with the Greenbackers and independents. The latter program prevailed, and for four elections after 1876 no Republican state ticket appeared. The state executive committee explained this lack of activity by saying that it would be futile to participate in a "mere mockery of an election" where Democrats would "cast their ballots to the winds and laugh in their faces."[46] On the other hand, a Northern observer asserted that Republican inaction was due to the generally poor quality of party members in Alabama, who were primarily interested in holding federal jobs.[47] Alabama Republicans in turn accused Northern Republicans of failing to support them.

In 1880 the Republican State Executive Committee advised support of the Greenback-Independent-Labor party, and in the next election the state convention endorsed the Greenback ticket.[48] Although Republicans could not approve the basic monetary principles of the Greenback movement, they hoped to take advantage of any potential threat to the practically complete control exercised by Democrats over the Alabama government. "The Independent and Greenback parties," said the Republican executive committee, "have declared for honest elections. This is all we ask. Because without this all else is nothing."[49]

By 1886 Alabama Republicans began to assume a more aggressive role in state politics. In national politics their party was now on the defensive, and Alabama leaders, hitherto inactive, desired to prove their zeal and fitness for possible future appointments. At the same time there existed in the state no widespread or organized undercurrent of opposition to the Democrats to which the Republicans could give their support. The 1886 Republican convention gave the executive committee authority to approve the nominees of the Prohibition party, but the com-

---

[46] Quoted in Montgomery *Advertiser*, July 7, 1878.
[47] A. K. McClure quoted in *ibid.*, December 24, 1880.
[48] Montgomery *Advertiser*, July 24, 1880, July 7-8, 1882; J. W. DuBose, *op. cit.*, pp. 1283-1285.
[49] Quoted in New York *Tribune*, August 2, 1880. See similar statements in Huntsville *Gazette*, March 11, 1882.

mittee decided that John T. Tanner, Prohibition candidate for governor, was "too much of a Democrat." Instead, the committee named a slate of its own headed by Arthur Bingham, prominent editor and officeholder of Reconstruction times. They did not, however, put out any local tickets for legislative or other positions.[50]

In 1888 the Republican convention nominated for governor Whitley Thomas Ewing, a mild Reconstructionist who had attended the 1867 constitutional convention, and county conventions nominated a number of Negroes for the legislature. The Republican platforms emphasized the rights of labor, demanded abolition of the convict lease system, and favored the Blair education bill, protective tariff, new election laws, and the temperance movement.[51] In neither election did the Republicans win any legislative seats. Bingham's vote was smaller than that of any previous Republican gubernatorial candidate, and Ewing won only a few thousand more.[52]

By the end of the 1880's the rivalry within the party between Negroes and whites had became quite serious. Earlier in the decade Negroes had bitterly criticized the whites for monopolizing practically all of the lucrative appointive positions. The Negro newspaper stated that there were only two colored Federal officials in north Alabama in 1881 and none in 1883. President Arthur in 1883 openly admitted in an interview that in the future he would appoint "but few colored men" to office in the South.[53] Negroes, however, largely managed and supported the 1888 campaign. One explanation of this situation could be found in the comparative popularity of the Seay administration in north Alabama, a situation unlikely to produce co-operation between Republicans and the whites of that region.

In 1889, with Republicans once again in control of the na-

---

[50] Huntsville *Gazette*, July 10, 1886; Birmingham *Chronicle*, August 15, 1886; Montgomery *Advertiser*, June 24, July 8, 1886.

[51] Montgomery *Advertiser*, July 17, 1886, July 19, 1888; Huntsville *Gazette*, July 24, 1886.

[52] Birmingham *Chronicle*, August 15, 1886; *Appleton's Annual Cyclopaedia*, XXVIII (1888), 10. For specific election returns see the Appendix, p. 213.

[53] Huntsville *Gazette*, November 12, 1881, January 20, February 10, 1883; Mobile *Register*, January 30, 1883.

tional government, the controversy between black and white factions in Alabama became intense. In January a Negro convention in Montgomery considered a resolution that only Negroes should hold Federal offices in Alabama.[54] In April two Republican gatherings met in Birmingham, one for whites and one for Negroes. The white convention, to which one thousand carefully selected individuals had been invited, declared that its purpose was "to advance the interests of the Republican party, and enlist in its upbuilding the new men and forces now developing the material interests of the State."[55]

The Negro meeting delivered to the Republican party an ultimatum declaring that if Negroes were not recognized in the distribution of Federal patronage as well as in citizenship, they would no longer consider themselves bound to the party. The Democrats considered both of these meetings as mere scrambles for spoils and the Negro meeting as a natural reaction to "the evident desire and intent of the administration to snub the negro and old time carpet-bagger and scalawag."[56] By 1890, to all intents and purposes, two Republican parties existed in Alabama, one relying on the Negro vote and the other anxious to divorce itself from Negro support and to co-operate with whatever dissatisfied white groups might wage political war on Democracy.

INDEPENDENT AND GREENBACK OPPOSITION

The Republican party by itself did not seriously threaten Democratic control because the voters, constantly reminded by Democratic orators, generally identified Republicanism with all the hardships, fraud, and corruption of Radical Reconstruction. A more serious threat to Democrats came from the Greenback and other independent movements.

From both Democrats and Republicans came at times expressions of a desire for party realignments. Some Democrats resented the dominant policy of their party that called for the avoidance of all controversial questions. Many Republicans complained of the lack of interest and divided counsels within

[54] Montgomery *Advertiser*, January 10, 1889.
[55] *Ibid.*, March 28, 30, April 11, 1889; Birmingham *Age-Herald*, April 3, 1889.
[56] Montgomery *Advertiser*, April 9, 11, 1889.

their own party. A prominent Republican lawyer, Chancellor Anthony W. Dillard, commented on the similarity of party conditions in the North and in the South in the following statement:

> Demagogues at the South strain every nerve and resort to every artifice and clap trap, to keep the people in a *fusible* state and turn them into the mold as a 'Solid South.' Demagogues at the North take equal pains to unite the North against the Solid South . . . . It is clear to all reflecting men, that both the old parties are now so organized, systemized, and methodized, as to leave the people nothing to do but to register the edicts of the caucus.[57]

An anonymous newspaper correspondent declared:

> It would greatly benefit the people as well as the government to disband existing parties and organize new ones on new and vital issues . . . . I am for organizing a Peoples Party that shall be guided by patriotic impulses more than by mere party machinery.[58]

The principal obstacle in the path of party reorganization was the fear of Negro political domination. Previous to the decade of the 1890's, few individuals seriously considered or recommended elimination of the Negro vote. As long as Black Belt Democrats could control the voting Negro they were not desirous of depriving him of the ballot; and many outside the Black Belt realized that laws designed to curtail Negro voting might also be used against unwanted white votes. Considerable sentiment did exist for party realignments with a more equitable division of the Negro vote. A north Alabama newspaper stated: "We should like to see the colored vote holding aloof from both parties . . . and voting for the best men presented. Then the white Republicans could bid for our vote and we could both bid for the colored votes."[59] "We need two parties," said another paper, "with white leaders and an equally divided Negro following in this state, the one to serve as a check upon the other."[60] A prominent Democrat observed that if the radical program of the Republicans had not forced a fusion of the anti-Negro groups,

[57] Quoted in Huntsville *Advocate*, August 28, 1878.
[58] *Ibid.*, July 24, 1878.
[59] Birmingham *Chronicle*, July 25, 1886.
[60] Birmingham *Alabama True Issue*, August 21, 1880. See also Selma *Times*, November 25, 1881.

there undoubtedly would have arisen two white parties in Alabama.[61]

Such expressions of dissatisfaction with existing party alignments and practices at times led to the formation of independent movements. It is difficult to evaluate the importance of some of these movements because they often grew out of purely local quarrels. The editor of the Montgomery *News-Item* in 1880 supported the national Democratic ticket, the state Greenback ticket, and a combination Democratic-Republican county ticket, and in the same year a Birmingham paper supported an independent ticket for the county and the Democratic ticket for state offices.[62]

Democratic leaders condemned any evidence of independency and denied participation in the legislative caucus to any legislator who had campaigned against an official Democratic nominee. In spite of this stand every legislature contained a sprinkling of independents. Some of them undoubtedly were not Democrats but ran as independents in order to conceal their true political preferences. In addition to numerous north Alabama counties, Jefferson and Tuscaloosa elected independent legislators in 1880 and 1886 respectively.[63] In 1884 Frederick G. Bromberg, former prominent Republican, led an independent movement in Mobile and said, "Let us show to the world that the race issue in Alabama is a thing of the past . . . that we of Mobile belong . . . to the new progressive South." In spite of strong opposition, the Mobile independents succeeded in winning the Senate seat and three of the four House seats.[64] In 1888 the Democratic caucus questioned the eligibility of legislators from ten counties.[65] By the late 1880's this threat from independents bore evidence of becoming serious.

The strongest third-party movement in Alabama during this

[61] Herbert, "Grandfather's Talks," p. 243.

[62] Troy *Enquirer*, August 7, 1880; Birmingham *Alabama True Issue*, August 19, 1880.

[63] Montgomery *Advertiser*, July 27, 1878; Montgomery *Dispatch*, October 20, November 10, 1878. For the total number and constituences of independents in the different legislative sessions, see maps in the Appendix, pp. 214-231.

[64] Mobile *Register*, July 6, 8, 15, 20, August 6, 7, 1884.

[65] Montgomery *Advertiser*, November 14, 1888.

period was that which centered around the Greenbackers in the late 1870's and early 1880's. Almost all of the groups dissatisfied with or opposed to the Democrats tended to co-operate with the Greenbackers. These groups did not agree on the fundamental financial and currency demands of the national Greenback party, but they realized the importance of connections with a nation-wide organiation.

In the 1870's the Alabama Democratic party had shown certain tendencies toward favoring currency expansion. "All the time since 1865," said one staunch Democratic journal, "a brutal contraction of the currency has been going on . . . . The 'dollar of the daddies' must be restored. The resumption act must be repealed."[66] The Montgomery *Advertiser* saw no need for a Greenback party in Alabama, because it felt that the Democratic party had always stood for the same currency principles.[67] In an effort to win Democrats to the Greenback cause, William Manning Lowe said, "The Democratic party, rank and file, is essentially a greenback people's party."[68]

The Mobile *Register,* however, spoke for a considerable portion of Alabama Democracy in its consistent opposition to inflationary measure.[69] In 1878 and 1880 the party successfully avoided a definite stand on the matter and thus opened the road for the Greenback party to organize in Alabama. In advocating the Greenback cause, an independent newspaper said that both the Democratic and Republican parties "espouse and champion the cause of the money power, the bondholders, the usurers, the railroad corporations and the monopolies."[70]

In the election of 1878 Alabama Greenbackers were not strongly enough organized to put out a state ticket, but they did assist in the election to the legislature of a small number of independents. Before the national elections in November, the party improved its organization and backed two congressional candidates, James P. Armstrong of the second and William M. Lowe of the eighth district; Lowe alone won a seat in Congress.

[66] Selma *Southern Argus,* November 30, 1877, September 6, 1878.
[67] August 21, 1878.
[68] Lowe to L. H. Brewer, Montgomery *Advertiser,* August 2, 1878.
[69] September 24, 30, October 8, 1875.
[70] Birmingham *Alabama True Issue,* July 31, 1880.

By this time the Greenbackers were beginning to win support from Alabama Republicans. One Republican explained his position as follows:

> There are questions of more vital importance in Southern politics than banking and currency . . . . They are issues such as fair elections, and honest count, free thought, free speech, free government itself. Upon these Col. Lowe and the Greenbackers were with us.[71]

An Alabama Republican newspaper believed Republican adherence to the Greenbackers necessary "under the existing state of affairs."[72] The Democrats attacked this "puny political orphan" as a threat to the solidarity of the white man's party and listed its two chief motivating influences as greed for office and socialistic appeal to the masses.[73]

In 1880 the Greenbackers held a state convention in Montgomery, and in their platform denounced the Democrats for changing the election laws, providing an inadequate school system, and continuing the convict lease system. They chose as their nominee for governor the Reverend J. M. Pickens of Lawrence County.[74] The party campaigned strenuously in north Alabama, but succeeded in electing only five representatives to the legislature. Pickens polled only 42,363 votes, against 134,908 for Governor Cobb.[75] Republicans and Greenbackers vigorously denounced the Democrats for counting out opposition votes by fraudulent and corrupt methods.[76] Congress substantiated some of these charges when it decided a contested election case in favor of Congressman Lowe instead of Joseph Wheeler, the Democratic candidate. Greenback influence also assisted James Q. Smith, Republican, in winning the fourth district Congressional seat in a similar contested case.[77]

[71] A. W. McCullough quoted in Huntsville *Advocate*, May 4, 1881. See also New York *Tribune*, September 22, 1879.

[72] Huntsville *Gazette*, July 15, 1882.

[73] Montgomery *Advertiser*, July 12, October 9, 13, 1878; S. S. Scott, *op. cit.*, pp. 10-11.

[74] Montgomery *Advertiser*, June 25, 27, 1880; Birmingham *Observer*, July 1, 1880.

[75] Montgomery *Advertiser*, July 1, November 23, 1880.

[76] New York *Tribune*, August 11, 14, 24, 25, 1880; Birmingham *Alabama True Issue* quoted in *ibid.*, September 13, 1880.

[77] Lowe v. Wheeler, May 17, 1882, *House Reports*, 47 Cong., 1 Sess.,

In 1882 the Greenbackers won even more active support from Republicans for their state ticket headed by James Lawrence Sheffield of Marshall County. At the behest of its white leaders, the Republican convention on July 6 ratified the action of a Birmingham Greenback-Independent-Labor Conference held the previous day and approved those portions of the platform that conformed to Republican demands for Alabama.[78] As a result, the Greenbackers made a better showing than in any other state campaign; they elected twenty-two members to the legislature, practically all from north Alabama, and in the gubernatorial contest won 46,386 votes to 100,591 for the Democrats.[79] The death of William M. Lowe in October, 1882, removed the most prominent Greenback leader; his Democratic opponent, Wheeler, succeeded him in Congress. By 1884 the Greenback party had practically disappeared. Independents and Republicans attempted to agree on a "People's Anti-Bourbon Party" for the state election in that year, but their nominee for governor, Charles Paul Lane of Huntsville, refused to run.[80]

A minor third-party movement in Alabama during the decade of the 1880's came from the Prohibition party. After 1880 temperance and prohibition forces in Alabama began to assume significant proportions. In 1881 the Woman's Christian Temperance Union entered the state, and the first state-wide temperance convention brought together all groups interested in the cause.[81] After successive legislatures had failed to satisfy the demands of prohibition forces for a local option law and other regulatory measures, the more radical prohibitionists deserted the Democratic party and joined forces with the National Prohibition party. The 1886 convention in Birmingham was the first to nominate Prohibition candidates for state offices, with the slate

---

no. 1273; Smith v. Shelley, June 27, 1882, *House Reports*, 47 Cong., 1 Sess., no. 1522.

[78] Montgomery *Advertiser*, July 7, 8, 1882; Huntsville *Gazette*, July 22, 1882.

[79] *House Journal* (1882-83), p. 63. See maps in Appendix, pp. 228-229.

[80] Huntsville *Gazette*, July 19, 1884; Montgomery *Citizen*, June 28, 1884; Huntsville *Democrat*, July 23, 1884.

[81] James Benson Sellers, *The Prohibition Movement in Alabama*, pp. 53, 74-75.

headed by John Thomas Tanner.[82] Most Alabama prohibitionists,
however, looked askance at this bolt and preferred to work within the Democratic party. Since the Prohibition party failed to
win support from Alabama Republicans, their third-party threat
proved harmless. Tanner polled only 576 votes, and their candidate in 1888, J. C. Orr, received less than half that number.[83]

The threat from such organized groups as Republicans or
Greenbackers did not give Alabama Democrats particular cause
for alarm in the fifteen-year period before the Populist revolt of
the 1890's. They generally spoke contemptuously of Republicans
for maintaining an organization solely to obtain Federal patronage, and described the Greenback or any other independent
movement as Radicalism in disguise. Disagreements and rivalries
within the Democratic party itself gave the leaders more cause
for concern. In spite of the arguments over apportionment, taxation, election laws, and other critical matters, the Democrats
preserved their unity by concentrating exclusively on the issue
of maintaining a native, white, economy-minded state government. By 1890, however, a number of developments indicated
that this particular argument was wearing thin and that a serious
breach in party unity was imminent.

[82] Huntsville *Advocate*, February 15, 1884; Birmingham *Chronicle*, July
11, 1886.
[83] *Senate Journal* (1886-87), p. 60; *ibid.* (1888-89), p. 46.

Debt Adjustment

THROUGHOUT Reconstruction and especially in the election of 1874, the Democrats severely criticized the financial policies of the Republican-controlled government of Alabama. They accused their political opponents of waste and extravagance and of adopting policies far beyond the means of a state economically impoverished as the result of the late war. Alabama's financial problems had already become acute when the nation-wide panic in 1873 further complicated the situation. Thus, when the Democrats assumed control in 1874, they were obligated to consider immediately this most critical of all government problems.

The sad condition of Alabama's governmental finances was apparent in a number of different situations. Tax collections declined sharply and in some places almost disappeared. Money on hand was inadequate to meet current expenditures. The most critical problem of all, however, was the large debt; payment of the interest would have consumed the major portion of the state's revenue. When interest went unpaid and rumors of repudiation circulated, Alabama's whole credit structure, both public and private, became insecure.

ORIGINS OF THE DEBT

The state debt existed largely in the form of bonds incurred for ordinary governmental expenses and to aid in railroad construction. A smaller floating debt consisted of unpaid interest, obligations to the school fund, and tax certificates. On the eve of the Civil War the bonded debt of the State of Alabama amounted to $3,445,000. In spite of considerable opposition, the Convention of 1865 repudiated the war debt and declared the 1861 figure the only valid debt of the state.[1] Immediately after the war Alabama authorized the issuance of bonds totaling $1,500,000 to meet ordinary government expenses. In November, 1866, Governor Robert M. Patton reported that Alabama's total bonded debt amounted to $4,186,490, and in July, 1868, just before the Republicans took control of the state, it amounted to $4,838,400, with $109,350 additional in the form of temporary loans.[2]

The trust funds for education, amounting to about $2,800,000, were generally considered part of the state debt. These funds had been lost when the state bank failed in 1846, but the state continued to raise by taxation a sum equal to the interest that would have been received if the funds had still been invested. Counting in the educational trust funds, an unofficial source estimated Alabama's total indebtedness at the beginning of Radical Reconstruction as $7,904,399.[3]

The actual bonded debt incurred for ordinary operations of the Alabama state government increased during Radical Reconstruction by about $2,500,000. In 1869 bonds for this purpose totaled $5,270,400 and by 1874, $6,619,800.[4] By adding in $1,000,000 of outstanding eight per cent obligations and $2,800,000 of educational trust funds the total debt for state purposes would be over $10,000,000 in 1874 when the Democrats took over the government.[5]

The largest part of the Reconstruction debt, however, resulted from the state's policy of encouraging railroad building by under-

[1] *Tenth Census* (1880), Valuation, Taxation, and Public Indebtedness, p. 592; McMillan, *op. cit.*, pp. 158-160.

[2] *Acts* (1865-66), pp. 40, 41; Governor's Message, *House Journal* (1866-67), p. 11; testimony of William R. Noble, chief clerk in auditor's office, in Ku Klux Report, *loc. cit.*, IX, 1055.

[3] New York *Tribune*, August 30, 1879.

[4] *Report of the Treasurer of the State of Alabama* [hereinafter cited as *Treasurer's Report*] (1869), p. 113; *ibid.* (1874), p. 61.

[5] *Report of the Auditor of the State of Alabama* [hereinafter cited as *Auditor's Report*] (1875), p. 53.

writing and granting funds to railroad projects. The Alabama legislature inaugurated this policy in 1867, prior to the beginning of Radical Reconstruction. The Republicans after 1868 extended the state-aid laws and granted state funds and credit liberally to a number of railroads beginning or extending their lines.[6] When this state-aid policy contributed to the virtual collapse of Alabama's financial structure, Democrats blamed the Radicals for carelessness, fraud, and waste in administering the program. Republicans, on the other hand, pointed out that a Democratic legislature had originated the idea, that Democratic railroad builders had profited from it, and that the Democratic administration of Governor Lindsay had also been lax in administering the law. One Democrat analyzed the situation as follows:

> It must be remembered that the State-aid policy was inaugurated by a Legislature composed of white men, before the Radicals in this State, as a party had any existence . . . . The inception was unfortunate, very wrong . . . but the practical operation of the policy has been outrageous . . . . The Conservatives or Democrats can be justly held responsible for the establishment of the State-aid policy and for thereby offering the Radicals an opportunity of swindling.[7]

Records on the state's endorsement of railroad bonds were kept by the governor's office rather than by the auditor, and considerable uncertainty, leading to violent political charges and counter charges, existed over the amounts endorsed. A special committee of the Alabama House of Representatives reported in 1872 that railroad bonds endorsed by the state totaled $13,600,-000. The auditor reported that these endorsed bonds amounted to $16,386,000 previous to an adjustment act in 1873 and $9,193,-000 in 1875.[8] Governor Lewis' financial agent estimated endorsed bonds for the same dates as $19,006,000 and $11,351,000 respectively.[9] The Democratic debt commission in 1876 finally recognized $8,847,000 as the amount of outstanding railroad bonds endorsed by the state.[10]

[6] See below, p. 127.

[7] Levi W. Lawler to Robert McKee, December 13, 1873, McKee Papers. See also Montgomery *Journal*, August 8, 1873.

[8] *Report of the Special House Committee Appointed to Investigate Railroad Matters*, p. 7; *Auditor's Report* (1873), p. 109; *ibid.* (1875), p. 54.

[9] Analysis of Financial Condition, Montgomery *Journal*, January 15, 1875.

[10] *Report of the Commissioners to Adjust and Liquidate the Indebtedness*

William Hugh Smith, first Republican governor, executed most of these endorsements, and criticism of his methods contributed materially to his defeat for re-election in 1870. Soon after Governor Lindsay and the Democrats took control, a crisis developed over the endorsement policy; the Alabama and Chattanooga Railroad, whose bonds to the amount of over $5,000,000 had been endorsed by the state, failed to meet interest payments. Under authority of a legislative act known as the Steele Bill, Governor Lindsay in 1871 met the interest payments out of the state funds and took over the railroad, thereby involving Alabama directly in the railroad business.

In addition to endorsing railroad bonds, Alabama also granted bonds as direct aid to two railroads. In 1870 the legislature authorized the issuance of $2,000,000 in state bonds to the Alabama and Chattanooga Railroad and $300,000 to the Montgomery and Eufaula.[11] In 1873 the Republican legislature, congnizant of the state's precarious financial position, authorized the exchange of endorsed railroad bonds for direct state bonds. The measure was criticized as being conceived in the interest of the railroad lobby, but nevertheless passed. Under its terms railroads could exchange bonds endorsed at the rate of $16,000 per mile for state bonds at the rate of $4,000 per mile. Three companies took advantage of the act and exchanged $5,103,000 of endorsed bonds for $1,156,000 of state bonds.[12] Thus, by 1875 the liabilities of the state resulting from its railroad-aid program amounted to $3,456,000 in direct bonds and $8,847,000 in endorsed bonds.

In its report of 1876, the debt commission declared that the total indebtedness of the State of Alabama amounted to $30,-037,563.[13] This figure included the trust funds for education, a miscellaneous contingent debt of over $2,000,000 and $4,654,-000 of unpaid interest. An analysis made at the same time by the

---

of the State of Alabama (1876) [hereinafter cited as *Debt Commissioners' Report*], p. 19.

[11] *Acts* (1869-70), pp. 89, 376.

[12] *Ibid.* (1872-73), p. 45; Mobile *Register* (weekly), March 22, 29, April 12, 1873; *Debt Commissioners' Report*, p. 14.

[13] This figure is incorrect because of an error in addition on p. 19 of the Report; the correct total should read $30,017,563. *Debt Commissioners' Report*, p. 23.

financial agent of the last Republican administration placed the
debt, exclusive of unpaid interest at $25,895.000.[14] This same
figure was accepted as correct by a Congressional committee
investigating the subject; the leading New York financial journal
estimated Alabama's total debt, exclusive of unpaid interest, at
$27,253,593.[15] Using the figures accepted by the debt commis-
sion but omitting the unpaid interest because it was never recognized, the debt can be broken down as follows:

Bonded debt for state purposes	$ 6,766,800	
Obligations and certificates	1,040,000	
Trust funds for education	2,810,670	
Total direct debt for state purposes		$10,617,470
Miscellaneous contingent debt (questionable bonds, claims of South and North Railroad on account of two and three per cent funds, and other claims)		2,443,093
Straight bonds issued to railroads	$ 2,300,000	
Straight bonds exchanged for endorsed railroad bonds under 1873 act	1,156,000	
Endorsed railroad bonds	8,847,000	
Total liability on account of railroads		12,303,000
Total debt exclusive of interest		$25,363,563

DEBT AND POLITICS

Throughout the period of Radical Reconstruction almost constant controversy centered around the financial problems of the
Alabama government. The Democrats accused the Republicans
of carelessness, extravagance, corruption, and other faults that
resulted in a debt far in excess of the state's ability to pay. The
Republicans contended that much of the increased expenditures
and debt resulted from expanded governmental and educational
activities.

The panic of 1873, however, made it apparent to both parties

[14] Montgomery *Journal*, January 15, 1875.
[15] Affairs in Alabama, *loc. cit.*, p. 1303; *Commercial and Financial
Chronicle*, XX (1875), 581.

that the state government was approaching bankruptcy. Alabama state and endorsed bonds declined on the market to less than half of their face value, and the state had to suspend all interest payments. One newspaper correspondent said:

> The financial condition of Alabama is absolutely deplorable and appalling. In truth, it really seems to be hopeless .... No one can tell what application has been made of the taxes that have been paid in since Nov., 1872, or even whether any taxes at all have been paid in. The treasury is ... as empty as a sucked orange and as flabby as a collapsed baloon.[16]

Governor Lewis stated that the whole financial system of the state was in a crippled condition, and the treasurer, unable to meet the ordinary expenses of government, was forced to issue thousands of dollars worth of state warrants. At the end of the fiscal year, disbursements so far exceeded receipts that balances owed and claims against the state totaled $823,454.[17] Further borrowing was out of the question; the governor reported: "This department has been unable to sell for money any of the State bonds during the present administration."[18]

The opposing political parties no longer argued over the merits or defects of Alabama's financial structure but rather attempted to fix the responsibility for the near bankruptcy of the state government. Republicans incurred most of the blame but defended themselves by contending that Alabama had been living beyond her income and resources before the Republicans took control, and that a large part of the debt had been incurred before 1868 and during Democratic Governor Lindsay's administration.[19] The Republican party, always attempting to encourage business and industrial development, was vitally interested in preserving the state's credit. Thus, the party never supported any proposal that implied the slightest repudiation, and the legislature of 1873 defeated two bills aimed at debt adjustment.[20]

---

[16] Mobile *Register* (weekly), August 16, 1873.

[17] Governor's Message, *Senate Journal* (1874-75), p. 7; *Auditor's Report* (1873), pp. 3-4.

[18] Governor's Message, *House Journal*, (1873), p. 7.

[19] Montgomery *Journal*, February 8, September 18, 1874.

[20] *Senate Journal* (1873), pp. 115, 176; *House Journal* (1873), p. 237; Mobile *Register* (weekly), November 29, December 13, 1873.

The fierce partisan rivalry previous to the 1874 election precluded any possible agreement on debt adjustment. After that year the victorious Democrats might be expected to take quick action. Their party, however, had never been in complete agreement on questions of financial policy. Ever since the end of the War, one segment of the party had approved in principle the encouragment and subsidies extended by the state government to railroad, business, and industrial enterprises. Opposed to such a policy were conservative Bourbon party members from the Black Belt and other rural regions. This schism became quite evident during the administration of Governor Lindsay, who approved the policy of lending money and credit to railroads.[21] But a storm of protest from the opposing faction of the party met his policy. Ex-governor John A. Winston, brother-in-law of Governor Lindsay, condemned the latter for giving in to pressure from railroad interests. "I fear," he wrote, "the Govr. is not the man for the occasion . . . he wants nerve—backbone—and those who look to him to face the issue lean on a shaken reed." Another Bourbon called for "uncompromising opposition to everything which tended remotely to the recognition of the validity of the bonds straight and endorsed issued under the free-booting legislation of the Radical Legislature . . . ."[22] The Selma *Southern Argus,* Bourbon newspaper, consistently and loudly advocated the repudiation of Alabama and Chattanooga straight and endorsed bonds, which it considered fraudulent.[23]

Other Democratic leaders, however, avoided any discussion of repudiation, because of the danger to Alabama's public and private credit standing outside the state. By 1871 Eastern and foreign creditors were becoming suspicious of Alabama's intentions or ability to support the shaky Alabama and Chattanooga Railroad. The London *Times* called the report of the railroad's bankruptcy and subsequent seizure by the state "a deplorable memorandum, relating . . . to a leading state of the American Union, which was at one time in high repute for its integrity."[24]

---

[21] Governor's Message, *House Journal* (1873), pp. 292, 295-297.

[22] John A. Winston to Robert McKee, February 21, 1871; Rufus K. Boyd to McKee, April 2, 1872, McKee Papers.

[23] January 12, February 9, 15, 23, 1872.

[24] January 1, 1873.

A leading Alabamian received in answer to his request for credit and advances the following statement: "There is no disposition to invest South. The credit of the Southern States is considered precarious . . . . Public repudiation is considered the forerunner of private repudiation."[25]

The two leading Democratic newspapers consistently reiterated the necessity of maintaining public credit. "Loss of state credit," said the Mobile *Register*, "means loss of capital and vice versa." The same paper suggested that the legislature pass a resolution pledging the government to pay every dollar on every bond legally issued.[26] The Montgomery *Advertiser* stated that the only two alternatives were imposition of higher taxes or resort to further borrowing; the credit of the state had to be resuscitated. It accused the opposing group within the party of attacking Lindsay's railroad policy in an attempt to put through repudiation.[27] To charges of this nature the accused repudiators replied: "We intend neither to abandon the party . . . nor to allow that party to be betrayed into the ranks of the republican enemy . . . . A few democrats have followed Governor LINDSAY into alliance with the fraudulent-bondholders."[28]

The intra-party controversy over the Lindsay administration contributed to the Democratic defeat in the election of 1872. By the time of the election of 1874, however, the critical financial condition of the state impelled the Democrats to subordinate their own disagreements and attack the Republicans' inability to cope with the situation. Thus, Democrats could blame their opponents for the financial muddle without running the risk of splitting their own ranks over the question of repudiation or adjustment. One newspaper well illustrated the Democratic attitude when it said:

> There is no doubt about the source and the causes of this sad and disgraceful state of affairs. It is the slime of the Radical serpent, the fruit of carpet-bag rule. These plunderers have simply ruined the State and there's an end of it.[29]

[25] W. W. Boyce to Clement C. Clay, January 10, 1872, Clay Papers.
[26] Mobile *Register* (weekly), February 11, 1871, May 30, 1874. See also March 14, 21, April 4, 1874.
[27] May 1, November 17, 1872.
[28] Selma *Southern Argus*, March 1, 1872.
[29] Mobile *Register* (weekly), November 22, 1873.

Democratic leaders successfully avoided any definite statements of financial policy. The platform pledged the party to make good every dollar justly owned by the state, a statement general enough to satisfy both repudiators and non-repudiators. The Republicans attempted to pin the badge of repudiation on the Democrats because of their "lack of explicitness and directness."[30] By nominating George Smith Houston, the Democrats avoided any real danger of repudiation. Although Houston did not come out clearly against repudiation, most people realized that with his north Alabama business background he would favor some kind of adjustment satisfactory to the state's creditors. One prominent Bourbon said of him:

> He is not the *kind* of man we want for Governor *now,* and I am sure he is not with us on the bond question.

Another said:

> I have never been willing to take Houston for Governor, unless he would declare upon the Bond payment question and that he will not do . . . . The nomination of any man merely because it is hoped he is popular with the Tory element in North Alabama and will be able to carry them, is quite too conciliatory to suit my taste. . . . [31]

The Selma *Argus,* in opposing the nomination of Houston, pointed out that it did not favor complete repudiation but did oppose those who would lump both valid and invalid claims together and scale down all alike. It estimated the total valid debt of Alabama at about $5,500,000.[32] Although the Democrats won the election of 1874 by subordinating all other issues to that of white supremacy, they employed the bankrupt condition of state finances as a secondary argument against the Republicans.

DEBT COMMISSION

Governor Houston in the fall of 1874 attacked with characteristic vigor the critical financial problem. He promised to restore the credit of the state but at the same time to protect the people against "excessive, unjust, and improper taxation." In addressing the legislature, he concluded that the only reason-

[30] *Ibid.,* August 1, 1874; Montgomery *Advertiser,* July 31, 1874; Montgomery *Journal,* September 18, 1874.
[31] C. C. Langdon to Robert McKee, May 16, 1874; Rufus K. Boyd to McKee, May 17, 1874, McKee Papers.
[32] February 20, April 10, June 12, August 7, 1874.

able course was for the state to seek an "honorable compromise" on its liabilities.[33] The legislature in December, 1874, authorized him to appoint two commissioners who would serve along with the governor in investigating the state's indebtedness and recommending to the legislature a compromise agreement. Houston appointed as commissioners Levi Welbourne Lawler of Talladega and Tristam B. Bethea of Montgomery.[34]

The commissioners spent a year in ascertaining the valid debt, with General Lawler working in New York and the other two in Alabama. They reported that their task was extremely difficult because of the absence of official records of bond sales, interest payments, and similar necessary statistics. Thus, they had to rely in part on unofficial evidence such as the records of New York and London financial agencies and even advertised through newspapers in an attempt to locate all possible creditors.[35]

While the work of the commissioners proceeded, those who opposed Houston's policy kept up a running fire of criticism. The Selma Southern Argus printed a series of long editorials in support of limited repudiation, stating that such action "when confined to claims invalid in law or equity" was not so terrible a thing except to financial adventurers.[36] Robert McKee, editor of the paper, received letters from Commissioner Lawler explaining the necessity of compromise and urging the paper to desist from its attacks on the commissioners. The secretary of state, a supporter of McKee's position, urged the editor to come to Montgomery and "fortify" Bethea who seemed to be wavering on his previous views concerning the bond question.[37]

The debt commissioners could not propose compromises with the creditors until the constitutional convention, meeting in the fall of 1875, adopted a definite policy on taxation. Unless the tax rate were fixed at a sufficiently high figure, the state could not hope to meet interest payments even on a debt materially scaled

[33] Senate Journal (1874-75), p. 42; ibid. (1878-79), p. 13.

[34] Acts (1874-75), p. 102; Mobile Register (weekly), November 28, December 12, 19, 1874.

[35] Debt Commissioner's Report, pp. 7-9; London Times, March 24, 1875; Commercial and Financial Chronicle, XX (1875), 570.

[36] May 28, July 2, June 18, 1875.

[37] Levi W. Lawler to McKee, June 12, 1875; Rufus K. Boyd to McKee, January 13, 1875, McKee Papers.

down. A heated debate on the bond question occurred in the convention, with George P. Harrison and William C. Oates leading the fight for repudiation. The delegates, however, defeated a proposal to prohibit the use of tax money for the payment of interest or principal on railroad bonds. The convention at the last moment also set the maximum tax rate at three-fourths of one per cent, the figure in effect during Radical Reconstruction.[38] This rate would be sufficient to meet interest payments on an adjusted debt, but would not possibly build up a sum sufficient to pay interest or principal on the entire debt at its face value. Thus, the action of the convention assisted the commissioners in their efforts to convince Alabama's creditors of the necessity of compromising.

The commissioners in December, 1875, made public the general plan of settlement, and in January of the following year the governor transmitted their official report to the legislature for enactment into law.[39] The report was divided into three parts. The first analyzed the entire debt of the state; the second discussed the resources of the state and its ability to pay; and the third contained detailed recommendations for adjustment. After studying the resources of the state, the commissioners estimated the government's future revenue at $1,040,000 annually. Of this amount about $500,000 would be needed for state expenses and $250,000 for school purposes, thus leaving about $290,000 for the payment of interest on the adjusted bonds and the state obligations.[40]

In order to reduce interest payments to something near this figure, the commissioners recommended a bond adjustment on the following terms. The bonded debt authorized for state purposes was to be recognized at its face value, but all past due interest up to July 1, 1876, was to be canceled. The bonds themselves, which had borne interest at the rate of five, six, and eight per cent, were to be exchanged for new "class A" bonds bearing interest at two per cent for the first five years, three per cent

[38] McMillan, *op. cit.*, pp. 313-314; *Convention Journal* (1875), pp. 64, 110-111, 163; Mobile *Register*, September 29, October 5, 1875.

[39] *Commercial and Financial Chronicle*, XXI (1875), 534; *House Journal* (1875-76), pp. 187-217.

[40] *Debt Commissioners' Report*, pp. 24-25.

for the following five years, four per cent for the next ten years, and five per cent for the last ten years.[41]

Of the straight bonds issued to railroads, the commission did not recognize the $300,000 issued to the Montgomery and Eufaula Railroad. The report stated, however, that holders of the $2,000,000 bonds of the Alabama and Chattanooga Railroad had a case "not entirely devoid of equity and one which should be settled by fair compromise." The commissioners reasoned that the state's seizure of the road in 1871 had been an admission of its obligation to the bondholders and that the damage to road and equipment resulting from state operation entitled the bondholders to some indemnity. Accordingly, an agreement had been entered into the T. W. Snagge, representing the English holders of the major portion of these bonds. The bondholders were to surrender their bonds, and the state in turn was to relinquish to them its claim to the railroad and title to all lands received by the state from Congress for the benefit of this particular railroad.[42]

Another part of the proposed compromise dealt with the endorsed railroad bonds that under the 1873 act had been exchanged for state bonds at the rate of $4,000 per mile. The commission recognized the validity of this exchange and recommended substituting for the state bonds new "class B" bonds at fifty cents on the dollar; these new bonds were to run for thirty years and bear interest at the rate of five per cent. The past due interest on the old bonds was to be offset by the unpaid taxes of the railroad companies.[43]

Of the endorsed railroad bonds, the commissioners advocated compromising only on those of the Alabama and Chattanooga Railroad. They argued that the state's relinquishing its lien on the other roads should be satisfactory enough to the creditors. In the case of the Alabama and Chattanooga, however, they felt that the state had become obligated when it paid interest on the railroad's bonds and seized the road. The agreement between the commissioners and Snagge provided that the endorsed bonds, estimated at about $4,720,000, could be exchanged for new

[41] *Ibid.*, p. 13.
[42] *Ibid.*, pp. 21, 34-40; London *Times*, September 8, 1875, June 27, 1876.
[43] *Debt Commissioners' Report*, p. 15.

"class C" bonds to be issued up to a total of $1,000,000. These new bonds would be distributed proportionately among the holders of the old endorsed bonds, would run for thirty years, and would bear interest at the rate of two per cent for the first five years and four per cent thereafter.[44]

The commission made no recommendations concerning the trust funds for education nor concerning the eight per cent obligations that had been issued in small denominations as an emergency measure beginning in 1873. It did express the hope that these latter liabilities, amounting to about $1,000,000 could be paid off with the surplus in the treasury during the first five-year period when the interest on the bonds remained low. Finally, the commission pronounced either invalid or outside its jurisdiction the miscellaneous contingent debt, which they listed as something over $2,400,000.[45]

It can be seen that approximately $18,000,000 of the public debt, as analyzed above, was recognized; this included some $7,500,000 of bonds issued for state purposes, $6,500,000 of railroad obligations, $3,000,000 of education trust funds, and $1,000,000 of floating obligations. This recognized debt was reduced to approximately $12,500,000. Unrecognized by the state were the $2,400,000 of miscellaneous contingent claims, something over $4,000,000 of bonds endorsed for railroads other than the Alabama and Chattanooga, and $2,300,000 of straight bonds issued to railroads. In settlement of this last item, however, valuable mineral lands held by the state had been transferred to the bondholders. A comparison of Alabama's old and new debt as made by a New York commercial journal follows:

	Old Debt	New Debt
Eight per cent certificates	$ 1,040,000	$ 1,040,000
Education trust funds	2,810,670	2,810,670
Class A bonds	7,416,800	7,127,709
Class B bonds	1,192,000	596,000
Class C bonds	5,300,000	1,000,000
Total acknowledged	$17,759,470	$12,574,379
Unprovided for except as explained:		
Alabama and Chattanooga RR.	2,000,000	

[44] *Ibid.*, pp. 20-21, 30-34.
[45] *Ibid.*, pp. 16-18, 29.

Other endorsed RR. bonds   4,705,000
Total old debt exclusive of
    interest . . . . $24,464,470[46]

The commission claimed to have reduced the debt from $30,-
000,000 to $10,000,000.[47] The Democrats wished this reduction
to appear as large as possible and thus included the $5,000,000
of unpaid interest as part of the original debt and neglected to
incorporate in the figure of settlement the funds held in trust for
educational purposes.

No proposal on the debt question could have satisfied all elements within the state. The newspapers of the larger cities and
some of the north Alabama papers approved the adjustment and
praised the beneficial efforts that it would exert on the development of the state.[48] In some agricultural regions, however, there
arose a storm of opposition headed by the same individuals and
groups who had opposed compromise from the very beginning.

The Selma *Southern Argus* and its redoubtable editor, Robert
McKee, led the fight against approval of the plan by the legislature. The paper did not consider valid all the debts the commission recognized at face value, and objected particularly to
compromising on the Alabama and Chattanooga bonds. In anger
it called the proposed plan "this thing of shreds and patches, this
device of inconsistencies miscalled a compromise, this vain attempt to bind freemen with legal withes and thongs to wrong-
doing, this ligature of straw."[49] A prominent north Alabama
Democrat denounced the plan in the following manner:

> Four fifths of the people of this County are opposed to
> this compromise . . . . This in my opinion is paying rather
> *too dear* for aid & assistance from rotten R. R. Rings . . . .
> We were promised economy and reduction in taxes by our
> democratic leaders, but to-day our people are more heavily
> taxed than they ever were under a Radical Administration.
> If this is Democracy I for one can see but little difference
> between the two parties.[50]

[46] *Commercial and Financial Chronicle,* XXIV (1877), 28.

[47] *Debt Commissioners' Report,* pp. 11, 27.

[48] Montgomery *Advertiser,* February 22, 26, 1876; Mobile *Register,* December 11, 14, 1875; Birmingham *Observer,* October 7, 1880; Birmingham
Alabama True Issue, September 18, 1880.

[49] February 18, 1876; *ibid.,* January 28, February 25, May 5, 12, 1876.

[50] Charles W. Raisler to Robert McKee, March 21, 1876, McKee Papers.

While the commission was at work, the Republican newspaper reported rumors of impending repudiation; but after the report was made public, the paper did not criticize the adjustment.[51]

In spite of opposition, the plan of the commissioners passed the legislature with comfortable majorities.[52] The opponents of compromise then turned their wrath upon the legislators, accusing them of submitting passively to the administrative machine. The feeling within the party became so intense that many Democrats feared for the essential unity of their party. General feeling, however, agreed with newspaper sentiment that admitted obvious defeats in the adjustment but did not consider them sufficient to justify a party split.[53] The year 1876 was a trying time for the Democrats and particularly for the Houston administration, which lost many of its former supporters over the debt question.

Outside the state the reaction toward the plan of settlement varied between a feeling of relief that complete repudiation had been avoided and dissatisfaction over the scaling down that had taken place. When first approached on the matter, the New York bondholders, protesting against repudiation of past interest and reduction of· future interest, attempted unsuccessfully to name their own rates.[54] After the adjustment the New York *Tribune*, true to its usual anti-Southern policy, described the Alabama Debt Commission's report as "not a pleasant document for Americans to read." It continued:

> It is always possible for a State to obtain relief from really fraudulent indebtedness . . . . But the refusal to pay interest on any part, because some part is deemed fraudulent, is not an honest performance . . . . The Southern voter . . . does not realize that the repudiation of a debt by a single State may be a robbery of the savings of half the laboring men and women of the North.[55]

[51] Montgomery *Journal*, November 14, 1875, and *passim*, December, 1875, January, 1876.

[52] *House Journal* (1875-76), pp. 465-466; *Senate Journal* (1875-76), p. 356; *Acts* (1875-76), p. 130.

[53] Tuscumbia *North Alabamian*, April 6, 1876.

[54] Mobile *Register*, December 23, 28, 1875; New York *Tribune*, December 15, 1875, January 10, 1876; *Commercial and Financial Chronicle*, XXI (1875), 590, 612; *ibid.*, XXII (1876), 110.

[55] New York *Tribune*, December 16, 1875, January 27, 1877, December 15, 1879.

The English bondholders referred to the adjustment as "a montsrous demand to which [we] were obliged to agree." At the same time they realized how valuable were the 500,000 acres of land transferred to them in exchange for the surrendered bonds.[56]

The debt commission made no specific recommendation in connection with the $1,000,000 eight per cent state certificates. These had been authorized in denominations of from $10 to $100 by the last Republican-controlled legislature in 1873, and were held largely by residents of the state. Although the debt commission had hoped that these obligations could be speedily retired, the lack of any surplus in the treasury made such redemption impossible. Thus, the legislature in 1879 provided that they could be exchanged dollar for dollar for new six per cent bonds to run for twenty years. These new bonds had a rapid sale; in 1887 they were exchanged for three and one-half per cent bonds running for thirty years.[57]

The debt adjustment effected a comparatively rapid restoration of the state's credit. In 1879 a New York paper headlined, "Alabama Solvent Again."[58] In 1886 "class A" bonds were reported to be slightly above par; the new four per cent bonds, which went on the market in 1889, were quoted at 101 1/10 per cent of par; and in 1890 Alabama bonds were held at a higher premium than any other Southern state securities.[59] In 1882 the governor reported that the exchange of bonds was practically complete and that those still unexchanged had probably been lost or destroyed. The total bonded state debt as of September 30, 1882, stood at $9,154,300, bearing an annual interest charge of $323,649. At the end of the fiscal year 1890, the bonded indebtedness totaled $9,249,900, and the interest charge had increased to $375,386.[60]

A sizeable county debt also faced the Democrats after 1874.

[56] London *Times*, February 18, 1874, June 27, 1876.

[57] *Acts* (1878-79), p. 17; Governor's Message, *Senate Journal* (1880-81), pp. 25-26; *Acts* (1886-87), p. 126.

[58] New York *Tribune*, December 30, 1879.

[59] Montgomery *Advertiser*, August 1, 1886, October 30, 1889; Governor's Message, *Senate Journal* (1890-91), p. 16.

[60] Governor's Message, *Senate Journal* (1882-83), p. 14; *Auditor's Report* (1882), p. 37; *ibid.* (1890), p. 9.

Most counties followed the lead of the state government in reaching some agreement with their creditors on the matter of adjustment. To facilitate this process, the Constitution of 1875 authorized the counties to levy a special property tax of one-fourth of one per cent to meet payments on debts existing at the time of the adoption of the constitution, and the legislature empowered courts of county commissioners to compromise the county debts incurred before November 16, 1875.[61] The state government had to give special assistance to five "strangulated" counties that found it impossible to make satisfactory adjustments. These counties, Chambers, Lee, Pickens, Randolph, and Tallapoosa, with aid from the state, succeeded in reducing their total indebtedness to about one-fifth its former size by 1890.[62]

As a result of its debt adjustment program Alabama preserved its public credit standing and brought its obligations down to a reasonable figure. Extremists attacked the adjustment from two directions, the ultra Bourbons desiring more repudiation and some creditors complaining of excessive repudiation. In reality Alabama repudiated or scaled down only its railroad debt, most of which was a contingent liability. Although Democratic leaders described the adjustment as a severe reduction in an effort to satisfy the conservative elements in their party, the state had not reduced any of its debt incurred for ordinary governmental purposes. In 1890 Alabama ranked sixth from the top among all states in its state debt per capita.[63]

It is true that the state did not incur any new debt during the period under consideration because of the strict limitations imposed by the 1875 constitution, but the constitution did allow county governments to float loans of restricted amounts to finance public improvements. In 1890 the total bonded debt of Alabama counties was only slightly less than it had been in 1870. This fact indicates that although the Reconstruction debts of the "strangulated" counties were considerably reduced, other counties increased their indebtedness after 1875. The municipal debt of Alabama towns increased by some eighty-three per cent be-

[61] *Constitution of* 1875, Art. XI, sec. 5; *Acts* (1875-76), p. 236.

[62] Owen, *History of Alabama,* I, 420-422; *Acts* (1882-83), pp. 45,47; *Auditor's Report* (1888), pp. v-viii.

[63] *Eleventh Census* (1890), Wealth, Debt, and Taxation, I, 146, 247.

tween 1870 and 1890, but Alabama remained considerably below
the national average in both its municipal and county debt per
capita.[64]

[64] *Ninth Census* (1870), III, 15; *Eleventh Census* (1890), Wealth, Debt,
and Taxation, I, 247, 287.

CHAPTER SIX

State Finances

ONCE the bonded indebtedness had been adjusted, the financial problems of the Alabama government largely centered about the task of maintaining public credit by meeting interest payments promptly. Thus it became necessary to maintain an adequate revenue and to restrict expenditures by operating the government economically.

The Democratic party was not always in complete agreement on the policy of low taxation and extreme economy. Immediately after the 1874 victory, however, the conservative Bourbon element began demanding severe reduction in taxation rates and in government spending. They were more successful in reducing expenditures than in reducing taxation, because the debt, even after adjustment, required sizeable outlays from the treasury.

EXPENDITURES

One of the principal accusations directed by Democrats against the Radical regime had been the excessively high cost of the state government. Thus, once in office, Democratic leaders were obligated to curtail governmental functions and reduce expenditures. Governor Houston and his successors constantly reiterated the necessity for economy and for cutting governmental costs to the bone. Within the short space of four years between 1873 and 1877 annual expenditures fell from $2,237,822 to $880,604.[1] In one year Republican Governor Lewis spent $12,471 from the governor's contingent fund, while for a comparable period Governor Houston spent only $2,537.[2]

Houston's successors in the governor's chair continued to emphasize the necessity for strict economy. In 1880 Governor Cobb said: "It only remains for us to pursue with unrelenting vigor the course of economy inaugurated by Governor Houston and approved and supported by contemporaneous legislatures . . ." The state auditor attributed Alabama's growing treasury balance to the "praiseworthy frugality now perceptible in every branch of the State government."[3] A policy of economy and reduced expenditures went largely uncontested during the last half of the 1870's but in the 1880's met with increasing opposition from some Democrats who believed that Alabama's progress depended on a more liberal financial program. Governors, auditors, and certain newspapers constantly found it necessary to warn legislators against departing from the "plain and simple ways" of an economical government.

The effects of the economy drive can best be illustrated by citing the reduced salaries paid Alabama officeholders after the Democrats established control. The Democratic Constitution of 1875 required a twenty-five per cent reduction in the salaries of all state officers and judges and prohibited any increase except by a vote of a majority of all elected members of the legislature.[4] In 1876 the salary of the governor was reduced from $4,000 to $3,000 per year and those of other elected officials as follows:

	Annual Salary 1869-1876	Annual Salary 1877-1890
Lieutenant Governor	$1,500	(Office eliminated)
Secretary of State	2,400	$1,800
Auditor	2,400	1,800
Treasurer	2,800	2,100
Attorney General	2,800	1,500

[1] *Auditor's Report* (1873), p. 3; *ibid.* (1877), p. 4.

[2] *Ibid.* (1873), p. 22; *ibid.* (1877), p. 20; Report of the Committee on the Contingent Fund, *Senate Journal* (1874-75), pp. 581-607.

[3] Governor's Message, *Senate Journal* (1880-1881), pp. 21, 23; *Auditor's Report* (1877), p. 4.

[4] Art. X, sec. 8.

| Superintendent of Education... | 3,600 | 2,250 |
| Commissioner of Industrial Resources | 2,500 | (Office eliminated)[5] |

Democratic legislatures created a number of new appointive positions with somewhat higher salaries: Penitentiary Warden, $2,000; Railroad Commissioners, $3,000-$3,500; and Commissioner of Agriculture, $2,100. The salaries for these new officers, however, came out of special funds provided for by the acts creating the positions.

The Democrats reduced the number and salaries of clerks and assistants in state offices. For the fiscal year ending in 1878 the state government employed only four permanent secretaries or clerks, two for the governor and one each for the auditor and treasurer; their total salaries amounted to $5,700. Five temporary clerks were also employed at a cost of $3,780.[6] During the next ten years, 1878-1888, the number of assistants gradually increased along with the growing duties of the state government. Governor O'Neal in 1884 cited the large sums being spent on temporary clerks and recommended increasing the permanent staff.[7] As a result, permanent clerks were added to the offices of education, agriculture, secretary of state, and an additional one to the auditor. In 1890 a total of twenty-one permanent and temporary assistants were employed in administrative departments at a total salary cost of $19,701.[8]

The economy drive resulting in reduced salaries for administrative officers went unchallenged neither in the Democratic party nor in the state at large. The two strongest Democratic newspapers consistently urged increases in salaries. The Montgomery *Advertiser* characterized the salaries as below a living wage, and recommended at least $4,000 and a house for the governor.[9] The Mobile *Register* believed in economy in government but felt that the legislature was carrying it too far in refusing to grant salary increases.[10] The Huntsville

[5] *Acts* (1876-77), pp. 29-30; *Auditors' Reports* (1869-1890), *passim.*
[6] *Auditor's Report* (1878), pp. 24-25.
[7] Governor's Message, *Senate Journal* (1884-85), p. 23.
[8] *Auditor's Report* (1886), pp. 38, 40; *ibid.* (1888), pp. 230-233; *ibid.* (1891), pp. 41-42.
[9] January 24, August 25, 31, 1877.
[10] December 5, 1884. See also Birmingham *Chronicle,* August 9, 1885.

Advocate, the most consistent critic of the Democrats, opposed increased salaries; it argued that salaries had been reduced in order "to sweeten the pill [the Constitution of 1875] and humbug the people" and that now the Bourbons were trying to raise them behind the scenes without making an election issue.[11] Some of the most conservative Bourbon papers also consistently opposed raising salaries as too great a deviation from their basic policy of strict economy.[12]

In 1887 the House of Representatives passed by a close vote a bill to raise the governor's salary to $4,000, but the proposal died in the Senate.[13] A number of persons recommended a more just equalization of salaries. Upon O'Neal's recommendation, such an equalization bill passed the House in 1887 but died in the Senate.[14] In the following session a similar bill unanimously passed the Senate but failed in the House by a very close vote.[15] Thus by 1890 the salary situation remained unchanged. In his last message to the legislature, Governor Seay reiterated the fact that salaries paid the governor and state officials were not sufficient to guarantee such services as the state was entitled to receive.[16] The $3,000 paid each of the governors of Alabama, North Carolina, and Georgia was the lowest figure of any Southern state, and lower figures were paid by only those of the other forty-one states with smaller populations.[17]

The Democrats also drastically reduced the expenses of legislative sessions. The Constitution of 1875 specified biennial instead of annual sessions and for the first time in the state's history prescribed a specific salary rate for members. Legislators were to receive $4.00 per day of attendance and ten cents per mile transportation; the presiding officers of both houses received $6.00 per day. Reconstruction statutes had granted legislators

[11] January 12, 1881.
[12] Selma *Southern Argus*, September 20, October 19, 1878, August 24, 1877; Troy *Enquirer*, October 26, 1878; Monroeville *Monroe Journal*, November 24, 1884, November 20, 1885.
[13] *House Journal* (1886-87), p. 972; *Senate Journal* (1886-87), p. 898.
[14] *House Journal* (1886-87), p. 1202; *Senate Journal* (1886-87), p. 895.
[15] *Senate Journal* (1888-89), p. 581; *House Journal* (1888-89), pp. 922, 936; Montgomery *Advertiser*, February 28, 1889.
[16] *Senate Journal* (1890-91), p. 22.
[17] *World Almanac* (1892), p. 293.

$6.00 per day and forty cents per mile.[18] The measures, along with the limitation of fifty days on legislative sessions, made possible a remarkable saving of money. The average cost of annual legislative sessions, including salaries of members, clerks, and other attendants, during Reconstruction times (1868-1873) had been $86,801. The average cost of each biennial session under the 1875 constitution and through the session 1888-89 was $46,506.[19]

The economy program also affected the judicial branch of the Alabama government. The Reconstruction salaries of supreme court justices had been $4,000 per year; the Democratic legislature reduced this figure to $3,600 in 1881. The number of circuit courts was reduced from twelve to nine and chancery courts from five to four. Circuit judges and chancellors received $2,250 ($2,500 after 1888) annually instead of the $3,000 paid during Reconstruction.[20] Alabama lawyers often denounced this economy move as deterimental to the quality of the judiciary.

TAXATION AND REVENUE

In spite of reduced governmental costs, Alabama's government still required considerable revenue, the largest part of which went to pay interest charges on the debt. Fairly strong sentiment in the 1875 convention favored writing into the constitution a low maximum tax rate. The advice of the debt commissioners, however, prevailed, and a maximum of seven and one-half mills on the dollar was adopted. This figure was the highest rate ever imposed during Reconstruction.[21]

In each legislature after 1875 the Bourbon Democrats made vigorous efforts to reduce the tax rate. In 1877 they succeeded in bringing it down to seven mills and in 1880 to six and one-half mills.[22] During this period the Selma *Southern Argus,* as it had on the debt issue, led the conservative forces demanding a lower

[18] *Constitution of 1875,* Art. IV, sec. 6; *Code of 1876,* Sec. 43; *Acts* (1878-79), p. 52.

[19] *Auditors' Reports* (1869-1889), *passim.*

[20] *Acts* (1880-81), pp. 13, 17; *ibid.* (1886-87), p. 134; *Code of 1876,* Secs. 650, 668; *Code of 1886,* Secs. 748, 757; *Auditors' Reports* (1869-1887), *passim.*

[21] See above, pp. 70-71.

[22] *Acts* (1876-77), p. 3; *ibid.* (1880-81), p. 3.

Alabama State Tax Rate and Assessed Valuations 1876-1890[1]

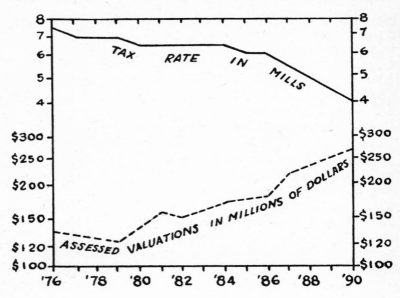

Receipts and Disbursements of the Alabama State Government
1869-1890[2]

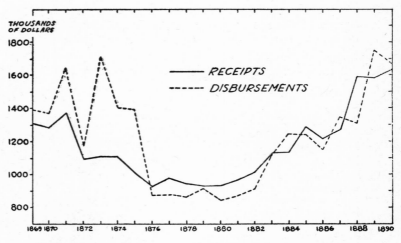

[1] *Auditor's Report* (1891), p. 6.   [2] *Auditor's Reports* (1869-1890).

rate. It insisted that a surplus existed in the state treasury, an argument supported by Willis Brewer, state auditor, 1876-1880.[23] A few other newspapers supported the *Argus,* and the question of tax reduction created a minor threat to Democratic party unity in the election of 1878.[24] Before 1882 the governors and most Democratic newspapers firmly opposed any reduction in the tax rate. The Montgomery *Advertiser* bitterly denounced the *Argus* and maintained that tax reduction was unthinkable while revenues were still low and interest payments were increasing.[25]

This agitation over tax rate and revenue laws reached a climax during and immediately after the 1882-1883 legislative session. Revenues had by that time increased somewhat, and by the end of the fiscal year in 1882 the treasury balance stood at $498,545.[26] Following the recommendation of Governor Cobb, the legislature reduced the rate of taxation but also passed a number of special appropriations amounting to over $200,000.[27] Although some believed that increasing tax values warranted both these actions, others felt that the legislature, in an effort to appease all groups, had attempted the impossible. After Treasurer Isaac Vincent early in 1883 embezzled a large part of the state funds,[28] it became clear that the decreased tax rate would not provide an adequate revenue for all of the increased appropriations. Fortunately for the supporters of economy and conservative government, the state Supreme Court declared the new revenue measure unconstitutional because a minor alteration had been made in the bill after enrollment.[29] In spite of considerable agitation for a special legislative session to correct the error, the old revenue law, with the rate of six and one-half mills, remained in effect.

[23] Selma *Southern Argus,* January 19, October 26, 1877, February 22, March 1, 8, 1878; *Auditor's Reports* (1877-1880), *passim;* Willis Brewer to Robert McKee, May 31, 1877, January 21, 1878, McKee Papers.

[24] Talladega *Mountain Home* quoted in Montgomery *Advertiser,* January 30, February 3, 1878; Monroeville *Monroe Journal,* February 10, 1879; Troy *Enquirer,* May 18, 1878.

[25] Montgomery *Advertiser, passim,* 1878. See also Tuscumbia *North Alabamian,* March 8, 1878.

[26] *Auditor's Report* (1882), p. 3.

[27] Governor's Message, *Senate Journal* (1882-83), pp. 19-21; *Acts* (1882-83), p. 67.

[28] See below, pp. 88-90.

[29] *State of Alabama* ex rel. *Moog* v. *F. C. Randolph* (1883), 77 Ala. 597; Montgomery *Advertiser,* April 13, 1883.

A controversy between advocates of tax reduction and advocates of increased spending continued throughout the decade of
the 1880's. Because of the rapidly mounting revenues the legislature could satisfy both demands to some extent by increasing
appropriations and reducing the tax rate at the same time. In
1888 rumors circulated concerning an $800,000 surplus in the
treasury, and by 1890 the total disbursements stood at a figure
double that of 1876.[30] At the same time the legislature had
gradually reduced the rate of taxation until by 1889 it stood at
four mills on the dollar[31] These reductions were not made without difficult legislative battles, and increases in other sources of
revenue had to be provided.

The amount of money received from general taxes did not
increase materially during the period under consideration; it
actually amounted to less in 1887 that it had in 1877. The growth
in total receipts resulted from other sources of revenue. Revenue
from license taxes increased from $65,000 in 1877 to $149,000 in
1890, and revenue from the hire of convicts grew from $14,000
to $109,000 over the same period of time. Additional income
came from the fertilizer tax earmarked for the agricultural commission and the railroad tax for the railroad commission.[32] The
legislature in 1884 imposed a special two per cent tax on the
gross receipts of telephone and telegraph companies, electric
light companies, express companies, and any person or company engaged in lending money on mortgage or lien. As a result
of the growing prohibition sentiment, the revenue law of 1887
almost doubled the license taxes on liquor.[33] The special tax on
the sale of liquor by the drink also received widespread public
approval but was never enacted by the legislature.[34]

Advocates of tax reduction often compared Alabama's state tax
rate with those of other states; only four other states had higher

[30] Montgomery *Advertiser*, June 24, October 5, 1888; *Auditor's Report*
(1876), p. 3; *ibid.* (1890), p. 3. See graph. p. 84.

[31] *Acts* (1884-85), p. 3; *ibid.* (1886-87), p. 31; *ibid.* (1888-89), p. 42.
See graph, p. 84.

[32] *Auditor's Report* (1877), p. 20; *ibid.* (1887), p. 5; *ibid.*, p. 20; *ibid.*
(1890), p. 21.

[33] Sellers, *op. cit.*, p. 70; *Acts* (1884-85), pp. 3, 14; *ibid.* (1886-87),
pp. 34-35.

[34] Montgomery *Advertiser*, March 1, 29, April 3, 1878; Tuscumbia *North
Alabamian*, April 5, 1878; Monroeville *Monroe Journal*, February 10, 1879.

rates.[35] Total taxation, however, remained exceptionally low, because county and municipal taxes were so small. In 1870 Alabama's total rate of taxation had been $1.92 on each $100. By 1890 this figure had declined to $1.15, the lowest of any state except North Carolina. In per capita taxation Alabama ranked third from the lowest in 1880 and next to the bottom in 1890.[36] With sentiment so strongly opposed to increased taxes, the Alabama government had no revenue adequate to expand materially its functions or activities. Both revenue and expenditures did increase between 1875 and 1890 but only in proportion to Alabama's general growth during those years.

FINANCIAL ADMINISTRATION

Because of the financial limitations of the Alabama government and the steady reduction of tax rates, a thorough collection and efficient administration of the revenues available became highly important. A fair assessment of property values was one phase of financial administration that caused considerable discussion and controversy. The Democrats had expected taxable values of property to increase rapidly from the low figures shown in 1875. Instead, there was constant decline in value through the year 1879, a development causing concern among both official and non-official circles.[37] "With increasing prosperity and increasing population," commented one newspaper, "the assessments go down—down. Nobody but an idiot can believe that the value of property in this State has diminished twelve millions of dollars in the past three years."[38] A number of explanations of this state of affairs were advanced, but no one seemed able to stop the downward trend before the 1880's. In 1880 Alabama per capita assessed valuation of $97.32 was the lowest of any state in the nation.[39]

After 1882 assessment values rose steadily because of improving economic conditions, lowering of the tax rate, and a

[35] *Statistical Abstract of the United States* (1889), p. 9.
[36] *Tenth Census* (1880), Valuation, Taxation, and Public Indebtedness, plate II; *Eleventh Census* (1890), Wealth, Debt, and Taxation, II, 61.
[37] See graph above, p. 84.
[38] Mobile *Register,* October 29, 1880. See also Montgomery *Advertiser,* December 12, 1880.
[39] *Eleventh Census* (1890), Wealth, Debt, and Taxation, II, 59.

concerted effort on the part of state officials to improve the methods of assessment. Under strong admonitions by governors and auditors, each legislature during the 1880's passed lengthly acts designed to improve the assessment machinery.[40] Governor Seay in 1890, at the end of his second term, could boast that the increase in valuation during the preceding four years had been "prodigious."[41]

Another troublesome problem centered around the conduct of the county tax collectors. The auditor and the governor warned that collectors were failing to turn over to the state treasury all money for which they were charged. In 1880 the auditor estimated that taxes which for one reason or another had never been turned over to the state amounted to "tens of thousands of dollars," and an unofficial estimate placed the figure at $605,588.[42]

The management of the state treasury itself was apparently above question until the sudden defalcation of Treasurer Isaac H. Vincent in 1883 threw the spotlight of attention on financial and other aspects of the Democratic administration. On January 30, 1883, Governor O'Neal transmitted to the legislature notice that Treasurer Vincent had disappeared leaving a shortage in his accounts of $230,569.[43]

Reaction throughout the state was spontaneous and immediate. The Democrats were naturally embarrassed over this official whom they could not disown, and their opponents delighted in emphasizing this glaring defect in a party priding itself on honesty and faithfulness. One paper said: "There is no excuse or palliation for this flagrant breach of trust." It blamed Vincent himself as well as the laws and regulations that made such a thing possible.[44] Other Democratic papers blamed the powerful Montgomery politicians for having selected Vincent in the first place and for allowing the gradual removal of public funds before their very eyes.[45]

[40] *Acts* (1882-83), p. 83; *ibid.* (1884-85), p. 21; *ibid.* (1886-87), p. 3.

[41] Governor's Message, *Senate Journal* (1890-91), p. 15. See graph, p. 84.

[42] *Auditor's Report* (1880), pp. 17, 18; Governor's Message, *Senate Journal* (1882-83), pp. 16-17; Mobile *Register,* November 27, 1886; Montgomery *Advertiser,* November 21, 1886.

[43] *House Journal* (1882-83), pp. 437-438, 460.

[44] Mobile *Register,* February 2, 1883.

[45] Huntsville *Democrat,* February 14, 1883; Birmingham *Chronicle,* February 21, 1886.

In 1879 the legislature had repealed the section of the Code requiring an examination of the treasurer's and auditor's books each year.[46] The only check over financial officials was the discretionary power of the governor to appoint a "competent person" to examine the books of the treasurer. Such action had never been taken, partly because four dollars per day would have been insufficient to obtain a qualified accountant.[47]

After investigation by a special joint committee, the legislature authorized the governor, auditor, and secretary of state to settle the claims of the state against Vincent's bond sureties on terms "for the best interest of the State."[48] Vincent's $250,000 bond proved to be inadequate, because only one signer, Merrill E. Pratt, could make good even a portion of the loss suffered by the state. Since the bond itself and even the copy of it had been lost, considerable sentiment developed for compromising in some way with Pratt. The special committee agreed that Pratt should pay $60,000, but the legislature later reduced the sum to $37,000.[49] Some newspapers and individuals disagreed with these compromises, because they believed that Pratt could have paid much more.[50] From three other signers of the bond the state ultimately obtained a total of $6,000. The attachment of Vincent's property produced $10,000 and $20,000 was realized from a judgement against Fred Wolffe, Vincent's New York agent. Thus of the total loss of over $230,000 the State recovered approximately $73,000.[51] As the facts came to light later, Vincent for some time had been using money in the state treasury to speculate on cotton futures in the New York market. He had left Montgomery for New York in order to "settle his affairs" when he read a newspaper account of the governor's order for his arrest. He then turned back at Cincinnati and headed for Mexico. Later

[46] *Acts* (1878-79), p. 68.
[47] *Code of 1876*, Sec. 104; Montgomery *Advertiser*, February 7, 1883.
[48] *Acts* (1883-84), pp. 141-142; *Report of the Joint Committee of the General Assembly Appointed to Investigate the Conduct . . . of Isaac H. Vincent* (1883); Montgomery *Advertiser*, February 18, 1882.
[49] Montgomery *Advertiser*, October 27, 1883; *Acts* (1884-85), p. 290.
[50] Monroeville *Monroe Journal* quoted in Montgomery *Advertiser*, September 13, 1885; Robert McKee to Edward A. O'Neal, August 3, 1883, McKee Papers.
[51] Governor's Message, *Senate Journal* (1884-85), p. 14; *Vincent v. State* (1884), 74 Ala. 274; *Acts* (1888-89), p. 639.

joined by his family, he remained in Mexico until his capture by
a Texas officer on March 13, 1887.[52] Vincent was tried in 1887,
found guilty on three counts, and sentenced to fifteen years in
the penitentiary. In 1893 Governor Thomas Goode Jones issued
a full pardon.[53]

The Vincent defalcation caused a re-examination of the administrative machinery and an attempt to bring its operations
more into conformity with provisions of the law. Governor
O'Neal described the situation as follows:

> It is found that some things had been done in disregard of
> law for so long a time that of late years no one had thought
> of questioning their legality, and that many irregularities
> had become custom so established that no one enquired
> into their reason or doubted their propriety.[54]

A number of steps were taken in an effort to correct this prevalent administrative laxness. Immediately after the Vincent
incident the legislature created the office of examiner of accounts. Although the salary of $1,500 was none too attractive,
the governor highly praised the work of the first examiner, J. W.
Lapsley. Lapsley found and corrected numerous errors and saved
the state thousands of dollars.[55] As an additional safeguard,
Governor O'Neal recommended that, in spite of the expense, the
treasurer should be bonded by a guarantee company; this action
was not taken until 1898.

Malcolm Clayton Burke, state auditor 1884-1888 also diligently exposed and corrected numerous irregularities in financial
machinery. A number of tax collectors were removed from office
and large amounts of back taxes were recovered. For the fiscal
year ending in 1886 all state taxes charged against tax collectors
were paid in with the exception of $50.[56] Auditor Burke investi-
gated shortages in the accounts of a number of probate judges,
one of whom, J. L. Powell of Butler County, had left a shortage
of $10,000 in his accounts of 1887.[57] Some irregularities in the

[52] Montgomery *Advertiser*, February 6-8, March 16, 1887.
[53] *Ibid.*, August 9-18, 1887; Owen, *History of Alabama*, II, 1324.
[54] Governor's Message, *Senate Journal* (1884-85), p. 15.
[55] *Acts* (1882-83), p. 184; *ibid.* (1884-85), p. 122; Governor's Message,
Senate Journal (1884-85), p. 16; *ibid.* (1886-87), p. 18.
[56] *Auditor's Report* (1886), p. 14; Governor's Message, *Senate Journal*
(1886-87), pp. 13-14; Montgomery *Advertiser*, August 22, 1886.
[57] Montgomery *Advertiser*, August 19, 1887; *Acts* (1888-89), p. 431.

handling of funds by county superintendents of education also came to light in this period.[58]

Alabama's financial structure after 1875 necessarily developed around the problem of paying interest on the adjusted debt. These payments prevented an immediate reduction in the tax rate. As increasing assessment values and other forms of taxation brought in more revenue, however, the tax rate was reduced to a point where Alabama ranked among the lowest of all states in per capita taxation. As a result, expenditures had to be cut to the bone by following a policy of strict economy. The administration of financial affairs improved considerably after the defalcation of Treasurer Vincent rudely awakened the Democrats to the dangers of laxness and inefficiency.

[58] See below, p. 153.

CHAPTER SEVEN

Agricultural Problems

ALABAMA was still predominantly a rural state, with only slightly more than ten per cent of the population listed as urban. Agricultural problems were thus uppermost in the thinking of a majority of the people, and discussions of them consumed much of the legislature's time. In the first two legislative sessions after 1874 the agrarian influence was so strong that the name of Grange legislature was often applied. The Reconstruction government had inaugurated a number of measures designed to benefit the small farmers. Since the Democrats in the 1874 campaign had won considerable support from the Grange and from the yeoman farmer class, they had to preserve an appearance of interest in the small farmers' welfare. At the same time the large farmer, ex-planter group wielded appreciable influence within Democratic party circles. Thus, a portion of the legislative discussions and agrarian difficulties grew out of the differences between these two interests. Other agricultural problems considered by the state government were common to both large and small farmers.

Although the Alabama Democratic party generally adhered to the traditional nineteenth-century doctrine of *laissez faire*, some of the farmers' grievances and problems imperatively demanded attention from the state government. In the middle 1870's Alabama agriculture still remained in the depressed condition in which the post-war years had found it. Although some of the white farmers had begun to prosper as a result of the break-up of the plantation-slavery regime, farming conditions in the Black Belt remained close to chaotic.

PROBLEM OF CREDIT

Time and again the statement was made that the two most pressing needs of Alabama farmers were adequate credit and more reliable labor. The chief source of credit for the average farmer was provided by the crop lien system, which had been inaugurated before the beginning of Radical Reconstruction.[1] After 1874 this system came in for a great deal of criticism and discussion; practically every session of the legislature debated at length its repeal or modification. Opposition arose from two quarters: some believed that such a lien harmed more than it benefited the small farmer; others felt that it interfered with the control large planters should rightfully exercise over their Negro tenants. The State Grange denounced the deterimental effects of the existing credit system and resolved that it should be discouraged. Worthy Master William Henry Chambers, however, opposed as a substitute any "visionary schemes" of co-operatives, and no state-wide co-operative movement was ever established.[2]

During the later 1870's and the 1880's, the strongest opposition to the crop lien came from landlords and large planters. As a result, the legislature strengthened the lien for advances that a landlord might hold on the crop of his tenant by making it paramount over all other liens, enforceable in the same manner as a lien for rent, and assignable to a third party with all remedies for enforcement.[3] Yet this did not end the landlord's efforts to abolish altogether a system that allowed tenants to obtain credit from merchants rather than from the owner of the land. Unsuccessful attempts to repeal sections 3286-3288 of the Code, the crop lien law, were made at each legislative session before 1884.[4] The

---

[1] *Acts* (1865-66), p. 44.

[2] *Proceedings of the State Grange of the Patrons of Husbandry of Alabama* [hereinafter cited as *Grange Proceedings*] (1874), pp. 10-11, 36-37, 39.

[3] *Acts* (1876-77), pp. 74, 112; *ibid.* (1878-79), p. 72.

[4] *Senate Journal* (1878-79), pp. 210-211, 562; *House Journal* (1880-81), p. 865; *ibid.* (1882-83), p. 391.

Montgomery *Advertiser* consistently and strongly advocated repeal, as did many agricultural leaders of the Black Belt. The
most outspoken advocate was William H. Chambers, former
Grange official, agricultural publisher, and professor at the Agricultural and Mechanical College, who introduced a number of
the repeal bills.[5]   A typical argument for repeal, written by a
newspaper correspondent, stated that Negro labor still could be
used profitably when directed and controlled by the planter.
It continued:

> But who can control or direct his labor with this law re-
> maining upon our statute books? Leaving out of consider-
> ation the towns and villages, there is a shantie at almost
> every fork of the road, whose occupant is ready, willing,
> and anxious to advance to the negro, if only he will get
> rent cheap, and buy supplies from him at from 125 to 150
> per cent.[6]

The State Agricultural Society in 1884 passed a resolution in
favor of repealing the crop lien law.[7]

Opposition to repeal came primarily from north Alabama; but
because of the dangers of its misuse, no one supported the lien
law too strongly. The most outspoken defense of the system came
from a Negro Republican newspaper that warned the legislature
against listening to the appeals of "agents and servants of capitalists." A Democratic newspaper in north Alabama openly
advocated repeal, while another admitted that a majority of the
state press favored repeal.[8]

The controversy over the crop lien law reached a climax in
the legislative session, 1884-1885, and resulted in the abolition
of the law except in twenty-three counties located in the extreme
northwest and the extreme southeast of the state; The next legislative session added thirteen more counties to the excepted list.[9]
In 1887 the State Agricultural Society held an open discussion on

[5] Montgomery *Advertiser*, August 27, November 3, 1883, November 14,
1882, November 26, 1884.

[6] *Ibid.*, December 29, 1878.

[7] *Proceedings of the First Annual Session of the Alabama State Agricultural Society* [hereinafter cited as *Agricultural Society Proceedings*]
(August, 1884), p. 167.

[8] Huntsville *Gazette*, December 16, 1882, November 28, 1884, January
13, 1885; Tuscumbia *North Alabamian*, February 10, 1876; Huntsville
Democrat, December 17, 1884.

[9] *Acts* (1884-85), p. 563; *ibid.* (1886-87), pp. 164, 165.

whether or not repeal of the crop lien had benefited agriculture in Alabama. Some expressed the opinion that repeal had not accomplished its purpose of taking the Negro out of the merchants' hands and putting him in the hands of the farmers. Others thought repeal beneficial, because "it is a very poor plan to do business on another man's money."[10] After an unsuccessful attempt in 1887, the legislature in 1889 made it lawful for farmers to mortgage unplanted crops. Although different in form and requiring registration, such mortgages served large planters in much the same fashion as a crop lien.[11]

Progressive farmers and writers on agricultural problems often emphasized the need for better credit resources that would not carry exorbitant interest rates or force the farmer into virtual economic bondage to his creditor. "I am continually striving," said one Black Belt planter, "to . . . make cotton at a profit to please my creditor. In a word *capital* in cash is necessary . . . ."[12] The state government, however, took no steps toward encouraging or providing such credit. Indeed one legislative session went so far as to impose a special two per cent tax on all foreign money brought into the state and secured by mortgages; after a loud outcry from the press, the next legislature repealed this act. The legislature also defeated a suggestion to memorialize Congress on the subject of small loans for Alabama farmers.[13] The crop lien, in some form or other remained the basic credit system, and it has been estimated that between eighty and ninety per cent of Alabama cotton growers used it in 1890.[14]

PROBLEM OF LABOR

Along with the problem of obtaining credit, Alabama agriculture was seriously handicapped by the lack of a dependable

[10] *Agricultural Society Proceedings* (February, 1887), pp. 39-41.

[11] Montgomery *Advertiser,* February 19, 1887; *Acts* (1888-89), p. 45; *Keyser* v. *Mass and Schwarz* (1895), 111 Ala. 390.

[12] J. W. DuBose to Robert McKee, September 3, 1881, McKee Papers. See also remarks of Sam Will John in *Agricultural Society Proceedings* (February, 1888), p. 78; "Retrogression in Alabama," *Nation,* XXXVII (1883), 372-373.

[13] *Acts* (1884-85), pp. 10-11; Mobile *Register,* January 14, 17, 1885; Birmingham *Chronicle,* January 10, February 22, 1885; *Acts* (1886-87), p. 38; *House Journal* (1888-89), p. 1168.

[14] Albert Burton Moore, *History of Alabama,* p. 567.

labor supply. Most large Black Belt planters preferred to use Negroes as wage laborers or tenants, and could not see the necessity of encouraging white immigrants to settle as independent farmers in the Black Belt or elsewhere. For some time after the Civil War, however, it proved difficult to control Negro labor.

Negroes also emigrated in fairly large numbers from the Black Belt westward to Mississippi and other states, lured by promises of higher wages and other attractions. Such movements were particularly noticeable following the panic of 1873 and after the Democrats won control of Alabama's government in 1874. Reactions to this migration by the blacks were mixed. Some welcomed Negro emigration in the hope that it would clear the way for white immigration. Others advocated some legislative measures to check the work of agents sent into Alabama by railroads and other groups to lure Negroes away.[15] An attempt to impose a $500 tax on such agents failed, but the legislature did authorize a $100 tax on agents operating in fourteen Black Belt counties.[16]

Emigration continued, however, during the 1880's, and in 1889 one newspaper still accused railroad agents of enticing Negroes from Alabama to Louisiana, Mississippi, Texas, and Arkansas.[17] During the late 1880's, however, the Black Belt was more concerned over the losses of both Negroes and whites to the booming urban and industrial centers in north Alabama. Newspapers and farm journals time and again deplored the seemingly universal desire to desert the farm for the $1.50 to $2.00 daily wages in the towns.[18] Between 1870 and 1890 Alabama's total population increased fifty-one per cent, but the population of sixteen Black Belt counties increased only twenty-one per cent; the increase of whites in these counties was only five per cent.[19]

When it became evident that immigrants from the North or

---

[15] Mobile *Register,* January 13, 17, 1874; Montgomery *Advertiser,* January 30, 1876, April 17, August 10, 1879; Selma *Southern Argus,* March 6, 1874, October 5, 1877.

[16] *House Journal* (1875-76), p. 391; *Acts* (1876-77), p. 225.

[17] Montgomery *Advertiser,* July 26, 1889; J. W. DuBose, *op. cit.,* p. 1234.

[18] Montgomery *Advertiser,* September 9, 1885, November 25, 1887; *Southern Plantation,* III (1876-1877), 24, 233.

[19] *Compendium of Eleventh Census* (1890), I, 475.

from foreign countries were not going to come in large numbers
to Alabama, farmers and editors, facing facts more realistically,
cast about for the best possible methods of managing the existent
labor supply. Although numerous systems of dealing with Negro
laborers had been advocated and attempted, most planters
preferred some form of share cropping. Practically every agricultural publication in the state, however, disapproved of the system and recommended instead either the payment of standing
wages or the stipulation of standing rent in cash or produce. The
official organ of the state Grange said:

> The system of renting lands to negroes or cropping with
> them on shares, in most cases does not pay, and unless
> speedily changed or modified will surely result in a decline
> in the value of lands and a steady decrease in the annual
> crop returns. The wages system, with proper oversight, is
> certainly the most remunerative both to the landholder and
> laborer.[20]

But the state Grange itself took no official stand or action on this
matter. The State Agricultural Society held a lengthy discussion
on the labor question, and a definite split of opinion appeared
as to the relative merits of the wage or cropping systems; all
agreed that the Negro made the best laborer if handled properly.[21]

In spite of the theories and efforts of agricultural reformers, a
steady decline began in the number of Alabama farms operated
by owners. In 1886 the state commissioner of agriculture deplored the tendency of so many landowners to desert their farms
and plantations for residence in the towns.[22] This increase of
absentee ownership left many Negro tenants in the Black Belt
without direct supervision; in such instances share cropping
proved to be the only logical arrangement.

The legislature spent considerable time discussing and enacting
measures to bring Negro laborers or tenants more directly under
the control of the landowners. During Reconstruction Black Belt
farmers had complained bitterly about the lack or authority or

[20] *Southern Plantation,* I (1874-1875), 136. See also *ibid.,* I, 169, III,
40; *Farm Journal,* I (1878), 102.

[21] *Agricultural Society Proceedings* (August, 1885), pp. 68-73; *ibid.*
(August, 1888), p. 20.

[22] *Report of the Commissioner of Agriculture of the State of Alabama*
[hereinafter cited as *Agriculture Commissioner's Report*] (1886), pp. 18-19.

restraint exercised over the freedmen. The widespread theft and depredations of agricultural products resulted in part from malice and in part from the ignorance of property rights on the part of newly liberated slaves. Republican-controlled legislatures discussed corrective legislation but did not adopt any for fear of strengthening the control of ex-planters over the Negroes.[23]

The first legislature after the 1874 Democratic victory, however, passed a series of measures designed to stop the thefts and at the same time to increase the control of land owners and merchants over their tenants. In spite of some opposition from white farmers in north Alabama, the legislature passed an act aimed at destroying "dead-falls," small temporary roadside stands, usually operated by dishonest whites, where Negroes or others could dispose of agricultural products under cover of darkness. The act prohibited anyone from buying, selling, or in any way dealing in certain agricultural products between sunset and sunrise. A few years later an amendatory act prohibited the transportation between sunset and sunrise of seed cotton except that to be ginned. At the same time the legislature made it a felony in nine Black Belt counties to sell cotton in the seed at any time or in any place.[24] Two other acts provided severe penalties for stealing. One declared that any person who stole a farm animal, outstanding crop, or personal property worth $25 or more would be guilty of grand larceny carrying a sentence of from two to five years. The other extended the definition of burglary to include the breaking into of any structure "within the curtilage of a dwelling."[25] When the Republicans complained that these measures were aimed at restoring Negroes to the status of slaves, the Democrats replied that they applied to both races alike and made the white receiver of stolen goods just as guilty as the thief.[26]

The Democrats also passed a number of measures aimed directly at giving the landlord a greater degree of control over his

---

[23] Montgomery *Advertiser*, November 17, 1872; *House Journal* (1873), p. 43; Mobile *Register* (weekly), April 19, November 29, 1873.

[24] *Acts* (1874-75), p. 241; *ibid.* (1878-79), pp. 63, 206; Mobile *Register*, February 11, 15, 1875; Montgomery *Advertiser*, January 28, 1879.

[25] *Acts* (1874-75), pp. 258, 259.

[26] Memorial of the Republican Members of the Legislature of Alabama, *loc. cit.*, pp. 2-4; Selma *Southern Argus*, February 26, 1875.

tenants and laborers. One, intended to protect goods and materials advanced to share croppers, provided in effect that any share cropper who, with intent to defraud, concealed or converted any property, including agricultural products, would be punished as if he had stolen the property. A later amendment made liable to the same punishment anyone who aided in removing or concealing such property.[27] Numerous remedies were proposed to guard against desertions by laborers or tenants in mid-year. Although Black Belt representatives and newspapers favored severe measures against farm laborers who broke agreements or contracts with owners,[28] the legislature in 1885 enacted a more moderate proposal. The act required proof that the laborer had entered the contract with intent to defraud and again with fraudulent intention had refused to perform the act or service for which he had contracted and refused to return or refund the property advanced to him.[29]

It would seem that most of the agricultural legislation during this period was directed toward improving the position of the landowner and planter rather than that of the small farmers. A proposal to exempt small farms, ten to eighty acres, from taxation for five years met a cold rebuff from the legislature in 1888.[30] The tax law, moreover, was revised to benefit large farmers. Instead of exempting $500 worth of property, as had been done under the Constitution of 1868, it exempted specified items that would be found in varying numbers on different farms. In order that most Negroes would have to pay some tax, the new tax law did not exempt mules and horses.[31] It was estimated that under this law some wealthy Black Belt planters exempted property worth $5,000 or more, while small farmers, mechanics, and laboring men could not exempt even $500 worth of property.[32]

---

[27] *Acts* (1875-76), p. 289; *ibid.* (1876-77), p. 138.
[28] *Senate Journal* (1878-79), pp. 377, 577; *House Journal* (1884-85), pp. 562, 957; Montgomery *Dispatch,* March 28, 1886; Montgomery *Advertiser,* February 10, 1885.
[29] *Acts* (1885-86), p. 142; Ex parte *Riley* (1891), 94 Ala. 82.
[30] *House Journal* (1888-89), p. 1005.
[31] *Acts* (1875-76), p. 43; Montgomery *Advertiser,* June 6, July 9, 1876.
[32] Selma *Southern Argus,* May 5, 1876.

FARMERS AND TRANSPORTATION

Another difficulty often cited by Alabama farmers as a major cause of depressed agricultural conditions was the lack of adequate transportation facilities charging reasonable rates. The state government spent considerable time listening to complaints from farmers and attempting to pass some remedial legislation. Most of the controversy centered around the railroads,[33] but other means of transportation also came up for discussion. The farmers at times displayed an interest in the improvement of Alabama's fine system of natural waterways. The real driving force, however, behind the improvement of waterways, as well as the development of railroads, was the expanding business, industrial, and mining interests of the urban centers.

Of more immediate concern to the farmers, particularly those living some distance from a railroad line, were the efforts to improve the country roads. In Alabama during the last half of the nineteenth century, as in most Southern states, the roads deteriorated into worse and worse conditions. Newspapers, commissioners of agriculture, and farmers' associations all deplored the condition of the roads and urged the legislature to take action.[34]

The state government, however, could do nothing toward building or improving roads because the Constitution of 1875 forbade the state from engaging in projects of internal improvement. Entire responsibility fell upon the counties and municipalities.[35] The road law, which had been changed only slightly since ante-bellum times, required every able bodied man between the ages of eighteen and forty-five to render ten days of labor each year on the public road to which he was assigned. This work was to be managed by three apportioners in each election precinct who appointed overseers for each road precinct and apportioned to each overseer a certain number of "hands." The

[33] See below, pp. 129-140.

[34] Montgomery *Advertiser*, June 19, December 27, 1883, August 4, 1885; Selma *Mail*, January 16, 1888; Birmingham *Chronicle*, April 12, 1885; *Agricultural Society Proceedings* (February, 1885), pp, 21-23; *Agriculture Commissioner's Report* (1886), p. 17.

[35] Leonard Calvert Cooke, "The Development of the Road System of Alabama" (unpublished M. A. thesis, University of Alabama, 1935), pp. 114-116.

court of county commissioners supervised this system and appointed the apportioners every two years.[36] The system failed to function properly because of inadequate financial support and lack of interest on the part of most overseers, apportioners, and workers. The fundamental conception of this law was based on the slavery system, and it could never operate smoothly by relying entirely on free labor. One newspaper correspondent complained that only about one-half of the road hands performed any labor, and these accomplished only about two hours of work in the entire year.[37]

During the 1870's the legislature made only minor changes in the road law in an attempt to control more closely the overseers and hands. As economic conditions improved in the 1880's, agitation increased for a more fundamental revision of the law. Some proposed that convict labor be utilized to work on public roads, while others emphasized the necessity of imposing road taxes to pay hired hands or, at least, to purchase adequate tools and equipment. It was pointed out that too much of the burden fell upon rural labor and that others, particularly property owners in towns, who would benefit from improved roads, should contribute toward road maintenance.[38]

The 1884-85 legislature passed special road acts for about fifteen different counties with varying provisions including a county road supervisor, road tax, and use of convicts.[39] This same legislature proposed for popular ratification an amendment to the constitution that would have allowed the legislature to levy in any county a special road tax not to exceed one-half of one per cent; this tax could be imposed in addition to the constitutional limitation of one-half of one per cent on general county taxes. In spite of support from the Montgomery *Advertiser*, the amendment was defeated at the 1886 election.[40] By 1890 the general

[36] *Code of 1886*, Secs. 1387-1441. Cf. *Code of 1852*, Secs. 1129-1188; *Code of 1867*, Secs. 1310-1380.

[37] Montgomery *Advertiser*, November 28, 1880. See also February 1, 1880, June 19, 1883, February 15, 1885.

[38] Montgomery *Advertiser*, April 15, 1880, June 19, 1883, August 4, September 25, 1895; Tuscumbia *North Alabamian*, March 22, 1878.

[39] *Acts* (1884-85), pp. 709, 937.

[40] *Ibid.*, p. 826; Montgomery *Advertiser*, July 30, 31, 1886; *Appleton's Annual Cyclopaedia* (1886), p. 8.

road law remained unamended, and the roads in most Alabama counties were left unimproved. Considerable work had been done in Jefferson, Madison, and a few other counties whose revenues allowed them to finance some road building without exceeding the constitutional tax limit. Governor Seay in 1890 stated, "We continue to work the public roads as our ancestors fought the savages."[41]

AGRICULTURAL ORGANIZATIONS

Agricultural clubs of local, county, or state-wide scope were often suggested as a means of solving or relieving the many problems besetting the farmers. The president of the State Agricultural Society explained the need for organizations as follows: "No wonder the farmer is made to bear the burden of taxation. It will ever be so until through organization we can be heard and felt as other enterprises and interests are recognized . . . ."[42] The farmers hoped to make known their demands and wishes more effectively and, when necessary, to unite against corporation, monopolies, or other forces considered injurious to their well being. They also hoped that the organizations would serve as media for exchanging information and education that would lead to more progressive farming methods.

During the decade of the 1870's the Patrons of Husbandry, or Grange, spread fairly rapidly over Alabama and served the agriculturists as a unifying force. The movement took root in Alabama with the organization of the first local Grange in July, 1872. In November, 1873, the first annual session of the state Grange met in Montgomery with representatives from 129 local Granges; by December of the following year the number of local Granges had grown to 650. The Patrons in Alabama reached the climax of their development in 1875, and both the number of local Granges and total membership gradually declined during the latter half of the decade.[43]

The Grange undoubtedly did significant work in organizing the Alabama farmers and emphasizing the common problems

---

[41] Governor's Message, *Senate Journal* (1890-91), p. 30.

[42] *Agricultural Society Proceedings* (February, 1888), p. 20.

[43] Owen, *History of Alabama*, I, 666-667; John B. Clark, *Populism in Alabama*, pp. 51-59.

confronting them. Its outstanding leader was William Henry Chambers, Worthy Master of the state organization from 1873 through 1877. By 1877 the Alabama Grange was beginning to suffer from the declining popularity of the national organization. A completely new set of officers took over in that year, and the official organ admitted: "The Grange today is making but little noise . . . ."[44] Although it continued in existence during the 1880's, the Grange exerted little influence and was soon overshadowed by the more active Alliance and other forerunners of Populism.

Although the Grange disclaimed any interest in politics, both the Alabama state and local Granges discussed at length what steps the government should take toward improving the farmers' plight and often sent to the legislature memorials and resolutions on these problems.[45] The growth of the Patrons organization in Alabama coincided with the campaign to overthrow Radical Reconstruction, and there is good reason to believe that the political connection between Grangers and Democrats was closer than openly admitted. In 1874 the Republican newspaper expressed concern over the support given the Democrats by Alabama Grangers.[46] By 1880 the Granger movement had spent its force but had caused Alabama farmers to realize the benefits to be derived from workable organizations.

Between 1880 and 1885 the state government, with the establishment of both the department of agriculture and a state agricultural society, assumed an active role in farmers' organizations. The agricultural department, which began operation in 1883, grew out of a variety of movements and suggestions made during previous years. Many farmers and editors had been advocating a bureau or inspector to analyze the numerous brands of fertilizers and supervise their sale in the state. Some felt that control over this matter should be vested in the state agricultural college at Auburn, while others wished to create a special state department modeled on that in Georgia and other Southern states. Considerable controversy developed in the 1882-83 legislature over a bill

[44] *Southern Plantation, III* (1876-1877), 6.

[45] *Grange Proceedings* (1874), pp. 9-10; Mobile *Register* (weekly), December 19, 1874.

[46] Montgomery *Journal,* August 13, 1873, February 1, 17, 1874, and *passim,* 1873-74.

to establish an agricultural department. Some opposed the measure as being of no practical value and too reminiscent of fertilizer inspection and the industrial commissioner of Reconstruction days; others protested that taxing fertilizers in reality imposed the burden of supporting a state-wide agency on the most unproductive sections of the state.[47]

When finally passed, the act created the office of commissioner of agriculture, to be appointed by the governor and to receive an annual salary of $2,100. Revenue to pay the commissioner's salary and other expenses of the department derived from the sale at fifty cents each of guarantee tags attached to each ton of fertilizer sold in Alabama and bearing an analysis of its contents. Although the tags carried the signature of the commissioner, the Agricultural and Mechanical College conducted the actual analyses and received one-third of the revenue from the tag tax. The commissioner was charged with numerous duties, the most important of which called for encouraging agriculture, collecting statistics, fostering experimentation, and encouraging immigration into the state.[48]

The department was first under the direction of Commissioner Edward Chambers Betts, a sixty-three year old lawyer and planter from Huntsville, who maintained an office at the Agricultural and Mechanical College. Here some confusion existed as to whether or not Professor William Stubbs, the state chemist who analyzed the fertilizers, and Professor James S. Newman, director of the experiment station, were working under the commissioner or under the college authorities. Professor Newman and Commissioner Betts evidently did not work well together, and in 1886 the new Code transferred the commissioner's office to Montgomery.[49] Criticism of Commissioner Betts came from a number of people, some of whom expressed the desire to have a more practically experienced agriculturist as head of the department.[50]

[47] Mobile *Register*, February 27, 1883; Huntsville *Democrat*, February 14, 1883; protest of three legislators in *House Journal* (1884-85), p. 632.

[48] *Acts* (1882-83), p. 190; *ibid.* (1884-85), p. 168.

[49] *Code of 1886*, Sec. 133; James S. Newman to William LeRoy Broun, October 30, 1883, Broun Papers; Edward C. Betts to John Tyler Morgan, February 10, 1887, Morgan Papers.

[50] Montgomery *Dispatch*, March 12, 1886; Hiram Hawkins to Robert

In 1887 Commissioner Betts resigned, and Governor Seay appointed in his place Reuben Francis Kolb of Barbour County. Shortly after taking over the office, Kolb expressed his surprise at how little the people of Alabama, even the farmers, knew about the agricultural department.[51] Under his direction the department began to play a much more important part in the agricultural life of the state and ultimately became involved in the Populist revolt of the next decade. The revenue of the department increased from $12,000 in 1886 to $47,000 in 1890; in the latter year the department turned over to the state treasury a surplus of $18,614.[52]

The act creating the department of agriculture called upon the commissioner to re-establish a state agricultural society. Such an organization had been founded in Alabama in 1855 and had sponsored agricultural fairs until 1861. As the Grange declined during the later 1870's, demands increased for some state-wide organization to take its place. Commissioner Betts in 1884 called a meeting in Montgomery to form an agricultural association for Alabama. Some one hundred and twenty delegates attended, founded the Alabama State Agricultural Society, and elected as its first president Professor James S. Newman, who had so strongly urged its organization.[53]

The legislature at first appropriated $2,500 annually to the society and later raised the amount to $5,000 with the understanding that this sum be used primarily for the operation of a state fair.[54] For a number of years the meetings, held twice each year, were well attended. The papers read and subjects discussed from the floor benefited farmers through the exchange of ideas and information and afforded a means of airing grievances and making demands. By 1889, however, the Alliance movement overshadowed the state society, and in spite of the optimism of its officers, the July convention of that year was the last of which

McKee, August 10, 1885, McKee Papers; *Agricultural Society Proceedings* (February, 1887), p. 36.

[51] *Agricultural Society Proceedings* (August, 1887), p. 16.

[52] *Auditor's Report* (1886), p. 23; *ibid.* (1890), p. 22; *Agriculture Commissioner's Report* (1890), p. 12.

[53] Montgomery *Advertiser,* January 30, July 29, August 2, 1884, June 20, 1885.

[54] *Acts* (1884-85), p. 124; *ibid.* (1888-89), p. 52.

any record is available. Commissioner Kolb reported that practically all of the local clubs and groups that had formed the state society had gone over to the Alliance with its more aggressive political program.[55]

During the latter part of the 1880's there sprang up in Alabama a number of agricultural organizations that outspokenly criticized agrarian conditions; they demanded reform and generally favored aggressive action through political channels. The status of the farmer in Alabama, as in the country as a whole, had failed to improve. The striking contrast between agrarian destitution and the boom in north Alabama towns afforded fertile grounds for the spread of militant farmer organizations that had sprung up in other Southern states.

The Agricultural Wheel entered Alabama early in the 1880's but was soon overshadowed by the Farmers Alliance, which first formed a local organization in the state in March, 1887.[56] Early in 1889 the legislature passed an act allowing all local Alliances to incorporate, and the state Agricultural Society in that year gave up its traditional August convention date to the State Alliance gathering.[57] The 1889 meeting attracted widespread attention and brought about the consolidation of the Wheel and Alliance in Alabama.[58] By 1889 Democratic leaders were already beginning to fear the vigorous political activities of Alliance men. A bitter dispute developed between Kolb and the Alliance on one side and the Montgomery *Advertiser* on the other. In the following year the *Advertiser* and the Birmingham *Age-Herald* exchanged violent journalistic blows over the political activities of the Alliance. The stage was being set for the momentous election in 1890 ushering in the Populist period.[59]

AGRICULTURAL PUBLICATIONS

As in the ante-bellum period, a number of publications appeared in Alabama in the post-war years devoted to improving

[55] *Agricultural Society Proceedings* (July, 1889), p. 38.
[56] Owen, *History of Alabama*, I, 563-567; J. B. Clark, *op. cit.*, pp. 71-73.
[57] *Acts* (1888-89), p. 42.
[58] *Farmers State Alliance of Alabama, Minutes of the Fourth Annual Session* (1889), p. 15.
[59] Montgomery *Advertiser*, August 9, 25, December 12, 1889, January, 1890; Birmingham *Age-Herald* (weekly), January 1, 29, 1890. For the

agrarian methods by disseminating and exchanging new ideas. Most of these magazines or newspapers were sponsored by some agricultural organization or by the department of agriculture. The earliest of the post-bellum publications was a magazine, the *Rural Alabamian,* published by Charles Carter Langdon of Mobile who had long been interested in agricultural reform. The first issue appeared in January, 1872, and the twenty-four monthly issues published contained a wide variety of information on farmers' problems with particular emphasis on the need for diversified agriculture. Although the magazine had no official connection with any organization, Langdon praised the Grange movement and hoped for its "speedy triumph."[60] The State Grange established as its official organ the *Southern Plantation,* a weekly publication first appearing in November, 1874, and continuing through April, 1877. In addition to articles and comment on agricultural problems, it published the proceedings of Grange meetings and the official directory of Grange organizations in Alabama.[61] The *Farm Journal,* a monthly magazine edited by William H. Chambers, past Worthy Master of the state Grange, was the unofficial continuation of the *Southern Plantation* and ran until 1880. The editor explained the change in title when he said: "In this section of the South . . . *farming* must take the place of *planting,* if we would become prosperous and independent."[62] Both the Wheel and Alliance had official state newspaper organs: the *Alabama State Wheel* published at Moulton and the *Alliance Advocate* succeeded by the *Alliance Herald* in 1890.

The act establishing the department of agriculture required the commissioner to publish information concerning Alabama's agricultural, mineral, and other industries. Commissioner Betts in 1884 issued a 144-page handbook, *A General Description of the State of Alabama,* which was devoted to an "almost literal transcription" of the 1883 report of the state geologist on Alabama's soil and mineral formations. The commissioner issued a

evolution of the Alliance into the Populist revolt, see J. B. Clark, *op. cit.,* pp. 78 ff.

[60] *Rural Alabamian,* II (1873), 543.
[61] *Grange Proceedings* (1874), p. 28.
[62] *Farm Journal,* I (1878), 2.

second handbook in 1887, but all copies were destroyed in a fire at the Agricultural and Mechanical College. The experiment station at Auburn between 1883 and 1888 published some thirty bulletins on various agricultural subjects, but almost all of these were destroyed by the same fire.[63] The 1884 handbook was not too popular because of its technical style. In 1887 the legislature appropriated $1,500 to print 5,000 copies of a handbook by Reverend Benjamin Franklin Riley entitled *Alabama As It Is: The Immigrant's and Capitalist's Guide Book to Alabama.* The book, written in a clear and simple style, consisted almost entirely of information on the individual counties obtained from probate judges. In 1888 Commissioner Kolb revised it and had 25,000 copies printed for distribution in this country and abroad.[64] A number of books published by private concerns attempting to stimulate interest in the state's resources contained some discussions of Alabama agriculture.[65]

Agrarian matters necessarily came in for a great deal of attention from Alabama legislatures and administrations. Legislation after 1875 on problems of agrarian credit and an adequate labor force generally benefited the large rather than the small farmers. The economic condition of Alabama farmers remained poor throughout the period under consideration, but the state government took no direct action to alleviate the distress. It did, through the formation of the department of agriculture and the state agricultural society, attempt to disseminate information on the agrarian resources of Alabama and on improved farming practices. By 1890, however, the more aggressive political tactics of the Farmers Alliance overshadowed the state government's activities. Some Alabama farmers were ready to demonstrate their dissatisfaction by revolting against existing Democratic party leadership.

[63] *Agricultural Society Proceedings* (August, 1887), pp. 16-17.
[64] *Acts* (1886-1887), p. 79.
[65] See below, p. 114.

CHAPTER EIGHT

Business
and Industrial Policies

THE ALABAMA Democratic government after 1874 generally proclaimed a hands-off attitude when the question arose of the connection between the state government and business or industrial development. Most party leaders realized that Alabama's mineral, water power, and other resources made possible extensive industrial enterprise. They felt, however, that their primary objective should be the establishment of a stable and economical government, and that industrial prosperity would ensue of its own accord. A newspaper editorial expressed the general sentiment when it said: "The world is governed too much. The governing power should seek to do no more than to regulate, facilitate and smooth the way for the processes of natural law."[1]

At the same time demands came from certain quarters for active intervention by the government in economic matters. Some agrarians urged the legislature to check the growth or regulate the activities of corporate enterprise. Other post-war Democrats, interested in the state's progress toward a more balanced economy, believed that Alabama should offer encouragement and definite inducements to attract capital and to foster industrial activity. This latter sentiment was dominant in the urban centers and growing north Alabama towns. Thus, in order to maintain

[1] Mobile *Register,* September 23, 1875.

its unity and harmony the Democratic party often played a dual role of simultaneously impeding and encouraging business and industry, all the while professing adherence to the theory of *laissez faire*.

DISTRUST AND REGULATION

For a number of years after 1874 those unalterably opposed to governmental encouragement of business and industry seemed to dominate the Democratic legislatures. Largely agriculturists, they often demanded that effective restraints be placed on what they considered harmful business practices. The Republican party in Alabama had advocated governmental assistance and encouragement to industrial enterprise. The Democrats in political campaigns had criticized this as a wasteful, extravagant policy, and thus after the 1874 victory were obligated to pursue a different course. The panic of 1873, moreover, wiped out much optimism as well as assets of mining, railroad, and other undertakings. Many people became disillusioned about Alabama's bright economic future and listened more attentively to accounts by agrarians and conservatives concerning the dangers of growing trusts and monopolies.

Typical of this anti-business sentiment was the statement of the presiding officer before the 1875 constitutional convention who declared that the growth of corporations was increasing and should be diminished.[2] A Black Belt newspaper stated:

> The people of the United States are rapidly passing under a yoke as galling and far more degrading than that of a military dictatorship.... A few giant corporations, rich, powerful, mercenary, and heartless, today, if united in interest, could control absolutely the policy and measures of the federal government and of a large majority of the state governments.[3]

Another typical Black Belt Bourbon declared:

> The possession of a million dollars is a crime in nine hundred and ninety-nine cases in every thousand .... Corporations are soulless. Capital is blind.[4]

The denunciations of business and corporate enterprise were generally leveled at those outside of Alabama or outside of the

[2] *Convention Journal* (1875), pp. 6-7.
[3] Selma *Southern Argus,* December 29, 1876.
[4] Robert McKee to Rufus W. Cobb, August 23, 1883, McKee Papers.

immediate locality of the writer. When the Montgomery *Advertiser* in 1886 criticized the efforts of a number of corporations to monopolize most of the coal lands in north Alabama, a Birmingham newspaper pointed out that the Montgomery paper had completely ignored the attempt of certain lumber men in Montgomery to monopolize timber lands in south Alabama.[5]

This dominant feeling of distrust of business-industrial enterprise was reflected in the Democratic Constitution of 1875. It eliminated the office of commissioner of industrial resources, prohibited the state from engaging in works of internal improvement or from lending money or credit to such projects, and specified that the property of private corporations, associations, and individuals should forever be taxed at the same rate.[6] The Democratic legislatures, especially the first few after 1874, also displayed suspicion of business and corporations. Some particular types came in for regulation or attempted regulation: railroads, fertilizer companies, loan agencies, and others directly affecting the farmers' welfare.[7]

The Democrats repealed the fertilizer inspection law passed during Reconstruction and incorporated in the new constitution a prohibition against creating any state office for the "inspection or measuring of any merchandise, manufacture, or commodity."[8] As a result, farmers continued to be deceived by spurious brands of fertilizers, and the state Grange attempted in vain to remedy the situation.[9] In 1878 there began a movement to vest powers of fertilizer inspection in the chemistry department at the Agricultural and Mechanical College, and this proposal caused considerable controversy during the two legislative sessions between 1878 and 1881. In the latter year the legislature passed a bill embodying this idea but failed to override a veto by Governor Cobb.[10] As noted previously, a provision for the inspection of

[5] Birmingham *Age* quoted in Montgomery *Advertiser,* March 16, 1886; Montgomery *Advertiser,* Februray 12, 20, 1886.

[6] *Constitution of 1875,* Art. IV, sec. 54, Art. XI, sec. 6.

[7] For a discussion of railroad regulation, see below, pp. 129-140.

[8] *Acts* (1874-75), p. 244; *Constitution of 1875,* Art. IV, sec. 38.

[9] *Grange Proceedings* (1873), pp. 6-7; *ibid.* (1874), p. 10; *ibid.* (1875), p. 21.

[10] *Senate Journal* (1880-81), pp. 327-332, 404; *House Journal* (1880-81), pp. 600, 723-30, 748.

fertilizers was incorporated in the 1883 act establishing the state department of agriculture.

The jute bagging industry, along with the railroads and fertilizer manufacturers, incurred the distrust and antagonism of farmers. Although the state government took no action to regulate this particular business, the Farmers Alliance in the late 1880's declared open war on the "jute trust." An increase in the price of jute bagging from seven to eleven cents per yard in 1888 precipitated this campaign by the Alliance, and the State Agricultural Society joined in advocating the substitution of some type of cotton bagging. In the following year an even more vigorous campaign by the Alliance forced the jute trust to reduce its prices.[11]

Another object of the farmer's suspicion and distrust was the commercial drummer who brought his fancy schemes and exaggerated guarantees into the rural area. The Grange legislature in 1876 imposed a $50 state tax on all drummers, and in 1884 a $10 county tax was added. In 1879 the legislature imposed a $100 tax on all agents of lightning rod companies operating in the state.[12]

Insurance companies had long been objects of concern to the Alabama government, and previous to 1875 the law required deposits from out-of-state companies and supervision of them by the state auditor. In 1875 the legislature passed a comprehensive insurance law pertaining to out-of-state companies, which required no specific deposit but an annual license tax of $100.[13] Between that time and 1890 numerous attempts were made in the legislature to impose stricter regulations on insurance companies. Opponents of the proposals predicted that such regulations would drive the companies from Alabama. Supporters declared: "The disposition of moneyed corporations . . . to get above the law, and to dominate the proceedings of legislative bodies . . . seems to be continually on the increase."[14] Although

[11] Montgomery *Advertiser,* August 2, September 14, 1888, September 13, 24, 1889; *Agricultural Society Proceedings* (August, 1888), pp. 47-48, 89-92; J. B. Clark, *op. cit.,* pp. 76-77.

[12] *Acts* (1875-76), p. 43; *ibid.* (1884-85), p. 3; *ibid.* (1878-79), p. 25.

[13] *Ibid.* (1874-75), p. 142.

[14] Mobile *Register,* November 24, 1880, February 24, 1881; Troy *Enquirer,* December 4, 1880; Montgomery *Advertiser,* February 1, 1881; Minority

none of the regulatory measures passed at this time, the agitation led the way to the creation in 1897 of the office of commissioner of insurance.[15]

Alabama also made a few feeble attempts during this period to regulate industries in the interests of industrial laborers. In 1887 Senator Daniel Smith of Mobile succeeded in putting through the legislature the first child labor act passed in any Southern state. It provided punishment for the following offenses: compelling a child under eighteen or a woman to work more than eight hours a day, permitting a child under fourteen to work more than eight hours, or working in a mine children under fifteen.[16] This act was only a prelude to the bitter controversy over child labor that raged in Alabama during the following twenty to thirty years. In the next legislative session the act was repealed for two counties where cotton mills were located, and in 1894 mill interests brought about repeal for the entire state.[17] Some unsuccessful attempts were made to improve the working conditions of miners, but these failed to pass the legisltaure.[18] The legislature passed two minor acts in the interest of labor; one defined the liabilities of employers when workmen were injured in service, and the other specified accommodations where female clerks were employed.[19]

SUPPORT AND ENCOURAGEMENT

The account of distrust and attempted regulation conveys only one aspect of the Alabama Democrats' attitude toward business and industry. Urban newspapers and party leaders constantly pointed out the benefits to be derived from an economy more evenly balanced between agriculture, business, and industry. They pointed to the industrial resources of the state and urged

---

report of insurance committee in *House Journal* (1880-81), pp. 651-657; *Auditor's Report* (1877), pp. 13-15.

[15] *Acts* (1896-97), p. 1377.

[16] *Ibid.* (1886-87), p. 90; Elizabeth H. Davidson, *Child Labor Legislation in the Southern Textile States*, p. 19.

[17] *Acts* (1888-89), p. 923; *ibid.* (1894-95), p. 18; Owen, *History of Alabama* I, 243-244.

[18] *House Journal* (1878-79), pp. 243, 847; *ibid.* (1888-89), p. 854; Montgomery *Advertiser*, November 21, 25, December 2, 1888.

[19] *Acts* (1884-85), p. 115; *ibid.* (1888-89), p. 81.

the influx of sufficient capital and labor to develop them. The Mobile *Register* in a typical editorial declared: "We *must* wake from our sleep of security and its delusive dream of cotton. We *must* shake the opiate of the 'good old times' from our eyelids, and open them on a practical and progressive present."[20] Even the Montgomery *Advertiser* said that the capital city would not grow as it ought simply by trading in dry goods, groceries, and cotton. "She needs," it continued, "new furnaces rolling mills and factories."[21] Practically all newspapers encouraged the establishment of local cotton mills.

Individuals, real estate concerns, railroads, and other interested groups made determined efforts to publicize Alabama's resources. Numerous books and pamphlets, many of a statistical nature, appeared in the post-war years to advertise the state. Four of these circulated widely: *Alabama Manual and Statistical Register* edited by Joseph Hodgson, Saffold Berney's *Handbook of Alabama,* John T. Milner's *Alabama: As It Was, As It Is, and As It Will Be,* and Benjamin F. Riley's *Alabama As It Is: The Immigrant's and Capitalist's Guide Book.* Railroad, real estate, and other developmental companies also published numerous pamphlets during the 1870's and 1880's describing the limitless possibilities and resources of their own particular areas. Typical of the railroad pamphlets were: Hiram Haines' *L'Etat d'Alabama;* Haines' *Report of the Traffic Resources of the South and North Alabama Railroad; Homes and Investments in the South . . . 600,000 Acres of Land in the Hill Country of Alabama on the Alabama Great Southern Railroad; Facts and Statistics Concerning Northeastern Alabama.* Typical of the real estate and town pamphlets were William Anderson's *The City of Mobile; Reliable Information as to the City and County of Tuskaloosa, Alabama; The Queen City of the South: Huntsville.* Birmingham and some other booming north Alabama centers also received publicity from the press outside the state.[22]

In an effort to stimulate business and industrial activity, pri-

[20] Mobile *Register* (weekly), July 26, 1873.
[21] Montgomery *Advertiser,* October 17, 1886.
[22] New York *The South,* April 5, 1873; Monroe Kirk, "The Industrial South: Birmingham, Alabama," *Harpers Weekly, XXXI* (1887), 213-216, 223; M. S. Hillyard, *The New South,* pp. 226-251; Alexander K. McClure, *The South,* pp. 96-108.

vate groups formed a number of associations or societies. One of the most active of these was the Alabama Industrial Association, organized by Colonel W. H. Chambers in September, 1877, at a meeting in Blount Springs. Invited to the gathering were two delegates from each county, two from each town, and one from each lumber interest, railroad, newspaper, college, and county agricultural association. Chambers, when elected president of the association, stated his belief that the time had come for Alabama to become alive to her vast potentialities through the formation of an "industrial public opinion." He continued:

> We are now prepared to consider the questions how we may best restore the shattered industries of the country . . . . The undue subordination of this industrial element was a defect, and an enfeebling defect, in the ante-bellum . . . South . . . . There is no disloyalty to the buried past in the hearts of those who are laboring for a new South.[23]

In the second annual meeting, held in Birmingham a year later, President Chambers made more specific recommendations:

> Gentlemen, the object of your Association is to promote the material prosperity of the State . . . by lending your influence to the formation of a sound public opinion; a public opinion which will so shape the policy of the government, as to make it work with you, in the accomplishment of your designs.[24]

Alabama was also represented at the numerous national and international exhibitions so popular during the late nineteenth century. During Reconstruction the legislature had appropriated money to send displays and commissioners to the Paris Exhibition in 1867 and to the Vienna Exhibition in 1873.[25] The Democratic legislature, however, refused to finance any exhibits or commissioners from Alabama to the Philadelphia Centennial celebration of 1876. This action provoked considerable criticism from the state press, but Alabama remained without representation or exhibits at the celebration of the one hundredth anniversary of the country's independence.[26] Alabama exhibits were

---

[23] Montgomery *Advertiser*, September 5, 1877. See also Selma *Southern Argus*, September 21, 28, 1877.

[24] Montgomery *Advertiser*, September 5, 1878.

[25] *Acts* (1866-67), p. 329; *ibid.* (1872-73), p. 544; *Report of the Commissioners of the State of Alabama to the Universal Exhibition at Vienna, Austria.*

[26] *Senate Journal* (1875-76), p. 632; Montgomery *Advertiser*, January

displayed at the Atlanta Exposition in 1881, the Louisville Exposition in 1883, and the New Orleans Exposition in 1885, but these were all subsidized by private interests.[27]

Although a majority of Democratic leaders and newspapers espoused the cause of industrial progress in Alabama, they refrained at first from advocating governmental assistance of any sort. The aid given to industrial development, especially railroad building, during Reconstruction had been so severely condemned by Democrats that they were obligated to avoid any appearance of favoritism to railroad, mining, or other industries. This non-aid sentiment remained strong during the 1870's while the memory of Reconstruction was fresh and the agrarian elements dominated the legislature. Governor Cobb warned the legislature against considering any schemes for the "development of latent resources" or measures of "fostering and encouraging special industries."[28]

The 1880's witnessed a general revival and expansion of business and industrial activity. During that decade the iron and steel industry in Alabama increased its production by 763 per cent. In 1884 Alabama invested more capital in new industries than any other Southern state and more than twice the amount invested in any other Southern state except Virginia or Texas.[29] During this same period the attitude toward governmental encouragement began to change in the booming north Alabama towns. A typical north Alabama newspaper editorial identified this development with "the redemption of the grand old state from sloth, stagnation, and general decay."[30] The Birmingham *Chronicle* in 1885 openly advocated amending the constitution so as to allow state aid to internal improvements. The paper stated that the mere fact that corrupt Radicals had begun and mismanaged such a policy should not prevent its being tried

---

13, 20, March 9, 1876; Mobile *Register*, August 24, October 12, December 5, 1875.

[27] Owen, *History of Alabama*, I, 216; Montgomery *Advertiser*, June 21, 1881, August 21, 1883, March 28, May 5, 1885.

[28] Governor's Message, *Senate Journal* (1880-81), p. 23; *ibid.* (1882-83), p. 21.

[29] *Abstract of the Eleventh Census* (1890), pp. 110, 127; *Manufacturers' Record* quoted in Montgomery *Advertiser*, January 11, 1885.

[30] Warrior *Advance*, March 5, 1885.

again. "The policy," it said, "was right, and Alabama, even though her substance was outrageously wasted and stolen, made more than she lost by her trial of a progressive policy."[31] Constant repetition by north Alabama Democrats of the need for governmental assistance and the determination of the Bourbon element to resist any such move led to a definite cleavage in the ranks of the party.

The Democratic government, however, never returned to the Reconstruction policy of open governmental assistance to railroad and industrial development, but the legislature did approve some measures beneficial to the introduction of capital, home industries, and general commercial welfare. The adjustment of the Alabama state debt avoided outright repudiation and thus in some measure reassured bankers and business men that might be interested in developing Alabama resources. The railroad and convict leasing policies of the Democrats, moreover, were often fashioned to the liking of certain business and industrial interests.

Almost everyone, including Republicans, approved at the time the prohibition in the Constitution of 1875 against granting state funds or credit to private enterprise.[32] The constitution, nevertheless, contained some less obvious points pleasing to business interests. One clause, not found in previous constitutions, prevented any corporation stockholder from being held individually liable for a greater amount than his own stock. A large manufacturer stated that this one measure was all that out-of-state capitalists desired from Alabama in the way of protection and immunity.[33] When informed that large investments awaited this change in corporation laws, the legislature passed a series of acts that brought the laws into conformity with the new constitution and granted the required immunity to stockholders.[34] The legislature passed another measure, requested by foreign capital and corporations, that enabled aliens to acquire, hold, and dispose of property just the same as citizens.[35]

[31] Birmingham *Chronicle,* October 4, 1885. See also October 24, 1886.
[32] Montgomery *Journal,* July 29, 1873.
[33] Art. XIV, sec. 8; Mobile *Register,* October 20, 1875.
[34] *Acts* (1875-76), pp. 244, 260, 261; Montgomery *Advertiser,* January 7, March 8, 1876.
[35] *Acts* (1874-75), p. 120; Mobile *Tribune,* March 2, 1875.

One of the first steps taken by the Democrats to remedy the effects of Reconstruction was repeal of the act granting ten-year tax exemptions to new manufacturing establishments. The 1875 constitutional convention, however, failed to adopt a proposal that would have prohibited the exemption from taxation of property belonging to any individual or corporation.[36] Under the Democrats few special corporation taxes existed, and individual communities made numerous exemptions from local taxation in an effort to encourage certain businesses and industries. The state auditor often complained about the general undervaluation of property and pointed out certain defects in the revenue laws that benefited corporations while depriving the state of income. One such defect allowed owners of capital to deduct all indebtedness before paying any tax.[37]

The Constitution of 1875 eliminated the office of commissioner of industrial resources that had been established under the Radical Reconstruction Constitution. It continued, however, the office of state geologist, which had been revived in 1873 after being dormant for fifteen years. Dr. Eugene Allen Smith, professor of geology at the University of Alabama, occupied the office and spent his vacation and spare time in continuing the state survey. The legislature increased slightly the appropriation to the geological survey in 1877, in 1883 raised it to $5,000, and in 1891 to $7,500.[38] Dr. Smith, helped at times by voluntary assistants, worked diligently on the survey, and between 1873 and 1890 published twelve reports covering in detail various aspects of the mineral and agricultural resources of Alabama.[39] In 1890 Governor Seay stated that much of the marvelous development of the mineral region of Alabama resulted from the work of the geological survey.[40]

One of the strongest inducements that Alabama could offer to

---

[36] *Acts* (1872-73), p. 72; *ibid.* (1875-76), p. 100; *Convention Journal* (1875), pp. 112-113.

[37] *Auditor's Report* (1886), pp. 7-8; Huntsville *Advocate*, June 22, 29, 1881.

[38] *Acts* (1876-77), p. 44; *ibid.* (1883-84), p. 57; *ibid.* (1890-91), p. 427.

[39] *Geological Survey of Alabama, Reports of Progress* (1873-1890); *History and Work of Geological Surveys and Industrial Development in Alabama.*

[40] Governor's Message, *Senate Journal* (1890-91), p. 18.

mineral and lumber interests was a liberal policy in the sale and distribution of land. Although the state itself during this period had no land for sale, the legislature urged the Federal government to pursue a liberal policy in disposing of public lands within the state. In 1883 Governor O'Neal stated that the United States government still held about 3,200,000 acres in Alabama, 400,000 acres of which were classified as mineral lands.[41]

During the 1880's the Alabama legislature took an interest in the disposition of some of these mineral lands. In 1879 the United States land commissioner, acting on reports made by geological investigators, classified a large area of the public domain in northern Alabama as mineral lands and thereby subject to disposition under the restrictive terms of the mineral and coal land laws. In the Forty-seventh Congress, 1882-1883, William H. Forney and Senator John Tyler Morgan advocated the withdrawal of these restrictions from Alabama mineral lands.[42] The legislature likewise petitioned Congress in favor of this proposed withdrawal.[43] Senator Morgan argued that the railroads could sell their large areas of coal lands more cheaply than the $10 to $20 per acre price imposed by the mineral land laws. He further argued that Alabama was only asking for the same concessions already granted to Kansas, Missouri, Nebraska, and Michigan. Opponents of the withdrawal bill stated that it was merely an attempt of the capitalists to obtain large tracts of extremely valuable land at the minimum price of $1.25 per acre. One government agent stated that it was the greatest land swindle ever perpetrated in the United States. As the measure finally passed Congress, it stipulated that all public lands within the State of Alabama, mineral or otherwise, would be disposed of as agricultural lands, provided that the mineral lands would be offered for sale first, rather than being open to homestead or other entries.[44] The law met with general approval from the state

[41] Interview with O'Neal in New Orleans *Time-Democrat* printed in Montgomery *Advertiser*, September 6, 1883.

[42] Report of Committee on Public Lands, April 20, 1882, *Senate Reports*, 47 Cong., 1 Sess., no. 454; Report of the Committee on Mines and Mining, March 2, 1882, *House Reports*, 47 Cong., 1 Sess., no. 614.

[43] *Acts* (1882-83), p. 667; *Congressional Record*, 47 Cong., 2 Sess., p. 3564.

[44] *Congressional Record*, 47 Cong., 2 Sess., pp. 3563-3570, 3572; 22 *United States Statutes at Large* 487.

press, but Robert McKee, typical Bourbon, vigorously expressed his disapproval. A few years later one newspaper reported a rumor that certain mining corporations were combining for the purpose of excluding all competition at the sale of public lands in Alabama.[45]

The question of annexing West Florida to Alabama received some attention during this period. Such a move was intended primarily to benefit Alabama's business and industrial life by providing additional outlets, principally Pensacola, to the Gulf of Mexico. This boundary change had been discussed ever since Alabama's admission to the Union and almost came about during Reconstruction.[46] In 1869 commissioners from Alabama and Florida, acting under authority from their respective legislatures, agreed on terms of cession, but the Alabama legislature failed to ratify the agreement. In 1873 the Alabama legislature appropriated $1,000,000 in bonds to pay for West Florida, but the Alabama commissioners this time failed to win any action from the Florida legislature.[47] In the late 1880's popular attention turned once again toward this project. The citizens of West Florida seemed anxious for annexation, and an annexation convention held at Chipley, Florida, was attended by some Alabamians. But the Alabama legislature in 1889 failed to pass a bill for the appointment of a negotiating commission.[48]

IMMIGRATION ENCOURAGEMENT

All the forces working in Alabama for economic progress believed that a more adequate labor supply was needed to build the railroads, open the mines, and serve in other industries. Newspapers, writers, and speakers urged the state to encourage

[45] Birmingham *Iron Age*, March 8, 1883; Mobile *Register*, March 13, 1883; Robert McKee to John Tyler Morgan, April 7, 1882, McKee Papers; Montgomery *Advertiser*, February 16, 20, 1886.

[46] Francis G. Caffey, "The Annexation of West Florida to Alabama," *Proceedings of the Alabama State Bar Association* (1901), pp. 108-133; Owen, *History of Alabama*, II, 1392-1395.

[47] *An Agreement Between Alabama and Florida Commissioners, Document Accompanying Governor's Annual Message; Acts* (1872-73), p. 125; Montgomery *Journal*, February 7, 1874.

[48] Montgomery *Advertiser*, February 3, 14, July 4, 1889; Pensacola *Commercial* quoted in Birmingham *Age*, February 18, 1886; *House Journal* (1888-89), p. 1169.

in every way possible immigration from abroad and from other sections of the country. For a number of years after the Civil War when Negro labor was in disrepute, agrarian forces also looked with favor upon plans to bring in labor from outside the state.

One Alabama planter in 1870 expressed a typical sentiment when he said: "I am preparing to get independent of the freedman. Until he is taught that we are or can make ourselves independent of him . . . he will be a poor and unreliable laborer."[49] Newspaper editorials and articles attempted to attract immigrants and to win public support for the cause of immigration. In a typical editorial the Mobile *Register* discussed the troublesome labor problem and declared: "There is one answer —*and one only*—WHITE IMMIGRATION!"[50] Even the rabidly anti-Radical Tuscaloosa *Monitor* admitted: "We are more than willing to encourage the immigration of *good* northern men."[51]

In spite of the general sentiment favoring immigration, Alabama, unlike Western states, took little effective governmental action to encourage the movement. During Reconstruction the commissioner of industrial resources had been entrusted with the task of encouraging immigration, but the only tangible result was the publication in 1869 of a small pamphlet, *Alabama, A Few Remarks Upon Her Resources, and the Advantages She Possesses as Inducements to Immigration,* for distribution in the North and in Europe. After the 1874 Democratic victory, both governors and legislatures professed sincere interest in the cause of immigration but regretted that the financial condition of the state treasury would not support an active program of encouragement.[52] The Constitution of 1875 stated in its bill of rights that "immigration shall be encouraged," and almost every session of the legislature discussed some plan to implement this policy.[53]

[49] Robert Jemison to Andrew Coleman Hargrove, January 3, 1870, Jemison Papers.

[50] Mobile *Register* (weekly), July 19, 1873.

[51] Quoted in *ibid.*, April 10, 1869. See also Montgomery *Advertiser,* April 5, June 8, September 7, 23, 1877; Tuscumbia *North Alabamian,* June 24, 1875; Montgomery *Journal,* January 5, 1873.

[52] Governor's Message, *Senate Journal* (1874-75), p. 43; *ibid.* (1876-77), p. 16; *ibid.* (1878-79), p. 27.

[53] *Constitution of 1875,* Art. I, sec. 31; Owen, *History of Alabama,* II, 726-728.

An 1875 Act provided for a commissioner of immigration assisted by an immigration board with immigration directors to be appointed for various communities of the state, but made no provision for financial support. An amendment in the following year provided two associate commissioners; still without salaries, the commissioners could contract to bring in immigrants and include in the agreement commissions for themselves.[54] C. F. Seivers served as commissioner, and while traveling as a commercial agent in the mid-West, studied the immigration agencies operating in other states. In 1878 he made a fairly complete report covering the possibilities of governmental action in the immigration field. He reasoned that since Alabama had no large landed corporation except the land-grant railroads, the state itself should do more than other states in gathering and distributing statistics on lands open to sale and settlement. More specifically, he proposed an integrated system of county agents working through a central office in Montgomery. After sufficient information had been collected, it would be synthesized, published, and distributed through various agencies in the North and West. Seivers believed that such an arrangement could be self-sustaining on a commission basis if the legislature would appropriate $5,000 for publications.[55]

By the 1880's considerable opposition to immigration was being voiced by conservative Democrats. Black Belt planters had brought the Negroes pretty well under control as laborers or tenants; thus they were not particularly anxious to upset the established agricultural labor pattern. One newspaper expressed this feeling when it said: "We don't want to depopulate Alabama of Negroes . . . . They are, in our opinion, the best laboring class in the world today . . . . We prefer them to foreigners."[56] In a legislative debate on the immigration question in 1889 a group of Black Belt senators contended that immigrants would bring in ideas of communism and anarchism.[57]

[54] *Acts* (1874-75), p. 121; *ibid.* (1875-76), p. 266; Mobile *Register*, January 19, 21, 30, June 6, 15, 1875.

[55] *Report of the Commisisoner of Immigration* (1878), *passim*.

[56] Montgomery *Dispatch* quoted in Montgomery *Advertiser*, January 13, 1889.

[57] Birmingham *Age-Herald* (weekly), February 20, March 6, 1889. See also Montgomery *Advertiser*, November 23, 1888.

Progressive elements, however, continued to push the immigration movement. Industrialists and railroad promoters in north Alabama and real estate interests in the towns argued that immigration of farmers as well as industrial workers would assist Alabama's economic growth. Most newspapers joined the demands and urged the legislature to establish some program co-ordinating the efforts of railroad, real estate, and privately incorporated immigration companies. Both Democratic and Republican platforms endorsed state action, and the Republican plank included the additional recommendation that the state enact laws that would "make it to the interest of immigrants to seek homes in Alabama." The State Agricultural Society also favored governmental action.[58]

The legislature made a number of changes in immigration legislation but never adopted an integrated program adequately financed as had been recommended by Commissioner Seivers. Although the immigration commission technically remained in existence until 1887, it does not appear to have functioned after 1880. The Code of 1886 omitted the provision for immigration officials, the code commissioners stating that the offices were unfilled and called "rather for the transaction of private than of public business."[59] The act establishing the office of commissioner of agriculture listed among his duties that of attracting immigration and capital to Alabama. No funds, however, were set aside to support an organized state immigration system, and the attorney general ruled that the agricultural funds could not be used for this purpose without legislative authorization.[60]

In the latter half of the 1880's advocates of an immigration program were divided between those who wished a separate department and those who thought that the commissioner of agriculture should be given sufficient funds to supervise such work. The commissioner in 1888 requested $50,000 for two years to encourage immigration, but the legislature refused.[61] Com-

---

[58] Montgomery *Advertiser*, July 7, 1882, June 6, 1884; *Agricultural Society Proceedings* (August, 1886), p. 45; *ibid.* (August, 1888), pp. 57-58.
[59] *Report of the Commissioners . . . to Revise . . . Code* (1886), p. 11.
[60] *Acts* (1882-83), p. 190; Montgomery *Advertiser*, December 19, 1886.
[61] *Agriculture Commissioner's Report* (1888), p. 12; *House Journal* (1888-89), p. 1198; *Senate Journal* (1888-89), pp. 518-519, 535-541, 548; Montgomery *Advertiser*, February 10, 21, 1889.

missioner of Agriculture Reuben Kolb, nevertheless, made a
spectacular bid for immigration in 1888 with his famous "Alabama on Wheels." In March he made a preliminary trip to
Chicago and the Northwest and in August and September he
and twelve other prominent Alabamians traveled through seven
mid-Western states in a special railway car displaying exhibits
and illustrations of Alabama's agricultural and industrial potentialities. Expenses were defrayed by private contributions and
the Louisville and Nashville Railroad, which furnished cars
and transportation.[62]

Although the state government never undertook an effective
program to encourage immigration, the railroads and other private concerns with lands to sell did bring in some new settlers.
The most famous of these was the colony of Germans who in
1871 came in via the South and North Railroad and established
the town and county of Cullman.[63] In spite of all the discussion
and private efforts, no great influx of settlers poured into Alabama. Foreign immigrants seldom went to the Southern states,
and Alabama's foreign-born population in 1880 amounted to
only 0.7 per cent. By 1890 it had risen to about 1 per cent. Of
native-born outside of the state, Alabama had 18.8 per cent in
1880 and 14.9 per cent in 1890, somewhat lower than the average
for the south central states.[64] The following table showing the
decennial percentage increases in total population for Alabama,
the United States, and sixteen Southern states shows that Alabama's rate of increase was below the average both for the country as a whole and for the South.[65]

	1870	1880	1890
Alabama	3.4	26.6	19.9
South	10.4	34.4	23.3
United States	22.6	30.1	25.5

Some Democrats would have liked to see the state government
lend encouragement and support to Alabama's young but prom-

---

[62] J. B. Clark, *op. cit.*, p. 64; *Agriculture Commissioner's Report* (1888),
p. 11; Montgomery *Advertiser*, March 29, June 2, August-September,
passim. 1888.

[63] John Clinton Bright, "Some Economic and Social Aspects of the History
of Cullman, Alabama" (unpublished M.A. thesis, University of Alabama,
1937); Saffold Berney, *Handbook of Alabama* (1878 ed.). pp. 87-88.

[64] *Compendium of the Eleventh Census* (1890), I, 472, III, 6.

[65] Lillian Worley, *Alabama's People*, p. 1.

ising mineral, railroad, and mining interests. But reluctant to imitate the Republicans in any respect, the Democrats officially maintained a hands-off attitude. Indeed, in some instances they pursued an outright anti-business, regulatory policy. In other less obvious ways, however, the legislature assisted business and industrial enterprise. The prosperity of the 1880's brought renewed pressure on the Alabama government to take positive action in such matters as immigration encouragement and other aids to business and industry. Although the thriving north Alabama towns spoke optimistically of the New South idea, the party leaders never admittedly departed from their avowed position of non-participation in private enterprise.

CHAPTER NINE

The State
and Railroads

THE ATTITUDE of Democrats toward railroads in the 1870's and 1880's was similar to their attitude toward other corporate interests: a mixture of sentiment for encouragement and support with demands to control unjust practices and monopolistic tendencies. The sentiment for railroad regulation was running strong in Alabama when the Democrats took over in 1874. This anti-railroad feeling led to the enactment of a number of regulatory measures and the establishment in 1881 of a railroad commission. During the latter 1880's, however, the attitude toward the railroads became much more favorable.

Immediately after the Civil War, Alabama, like other Southern states, felt the need of an expanded system of railway transportation in its efforts to recover from the devastation of the war and to encourage new industrial enterprises so badly needed to counterbalance the predominance of agriculture. One Alabamian wrote in 1876, and many others would have agreed, that by far the greatest need in the state was better transportation facilities and that all other economic progress depended on railroad extension.[1] Because of the heavy initial costs of railroads and the general benefits to be derived from them, governmental assistance to new projects had been urged in Alabama since an early

[1] John T. Milner, *Alabama As It Was, As It Is and As It Will Be,* p. 140.

date. Before the Civil War, however, no direct financial assistance came from the state government. A number of railroad projects in the 1850's did receive from the Federal government grants of public lands to be administered by the state.

A vigorous railroad-building program began as soon as conditions permitted after 1865. In 1867 the legislature, before it came under the control of the Radicals, passed the first state-aid law for the assistance of newly formed railroad companies. This act provided for state endorsement of railroad bonds under certain conditions, and its terms were liberalized by subsequent Radical legislation. The Radical legislature in 1870 also authorized granting some state bonds as direct assistance to two railroad projects; $2,000,000 in bonds went to the Alabama and Chattanooga road and $300,000 to the Montgomery and Eufaula.[2]

Since these state-aid laws were carelessly administered and the legislature subject to bribery and corruption, Reconstruction railroad development left a trail of fraud and manipulation that was exploited by the Democrats to the utmost in the 1874 campaign.[3] Some people hoped that the Democratic administration that came into office in 1870 would end the policy of state aid and close the door to further irregularities. Governor R. B. Lindsay, however, strongly approved of the policy, and put the state directly in the railroad business by seizing the Alabama and Chattanooga railroad, which had defaulted on the interest payments of its state-endorsed bonds.[4] Other defaults, coupled with the spreading financial panic and a depleted state treasury, placed both Alabama and the railroads in an embarrassing financial predicament. The story of this financial distress, which led to virtual state bankruptcy, and an account of the accompanying political implications have been treated previously.[5]

Irrespective of the drain on the treasury and injury done the government's reputation, it cannot be denied that state aid did stimulate the rebuilding of Alabama's destroyed railroads and

[2] *Acts* (1866-67), p. 686; *ibid.* (1868), p. 198; *ibid.* (1869-70), pp. 89, 149, 376.
[3] Albert Burton Moore, "Railroad Building in Alabama During the Reconstruction Period," *Journal of Southern History*, I (1935), 422-441.
[4] *Acts* (1870-71), p. 13; Governor's Message, *House Journal* (1871-72), pp. 16-21; *ibid.* (1873), pp. 292-293.
[5] See pp. 62-69.

RAILROADS IN ALABAMA, 1882

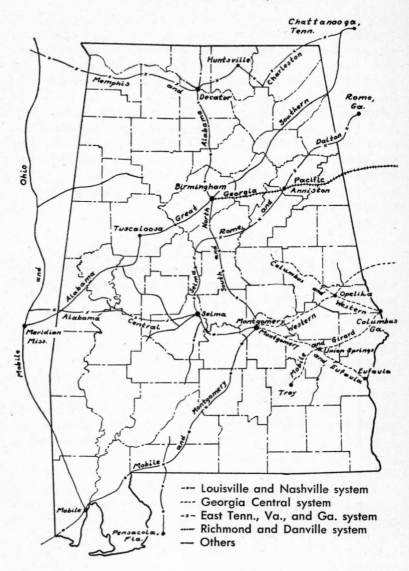

(Information from *Annual Report of Alabama Railroad Commissioners,* 1882)

the construction of new lines. A complete north-south link running from Nashville to Mobile through Birmingham and Montgomery was completed in 1872, and the north-east and south-west line between Meridian, Mississippi, and Chattanooga was completed in 1871 although it did not operate as a unit until after 1877. These two major lines materially increased Alabama's railroad facilities by connecting the northern and southern portions of the state. The four major lines, which had been completed either before or during the Civil War, were the Memphis and Charleston (running through the Tennessee Valley), the Selma, Rome, and Dalton, the Western Railroad (linking Montgomery and Atlanta), and the Mobile and Montgomery. In 1865 Alabama had 805 miles of railroad; by 1873 this had been increased to 1,793 miles.[6]

REGULATION

In spite of the enthusiasm for railroad construction and for state aid during Reconstruction, there existed also a growing sentiment for increased state control over the common carriers looking toward regulation in the public interest. Certain regulatory features accompanied the state-aid acts, and the legislature passed a few special regulations during the 1870's. From the very beginning of railroad construction, the state had exercised some control over individual railroads through provisions incorporated into their charters. As the railroads grew in size and influence after the Civil War, the legislature deemed it necessary to pass certain general laws that would apply to more than one road.

The state-aid act of 1867 contained no definite requirements concerning rates, but it did provide for loose supervision by the state, annual reports to the governor, and state representation on the board of directors of each road. The state-aid act of 1870 limited passenger rates on the roads affected to four cents per mile and prohibited freight charges in excess of twenty-five per cent above through-freight tariffs.[7]

Before the Radicals lost control of the Alabama government, sentiment for railroad regulation was growing. The chief Re-

[6] *Statistical Abstract of the United States* (1879), p. 156; *Auditor's Report* (1875), p. 4. See map, p. 128.
[7] *Acts* (1866-67), p. 686; *ibid.*, (1869-70), p. 149.

publican newspaper saw a definite need for railroad regulation
in all states.[8] The first regulatory law applying to all railroads
in the state passed in 1873. The bill as introduced would have
prohibited railroads from making a greater charge for local than
for through freight, but the act as finally approved limited passenger fares to five cents per mile and allowed a maximum rate
of fifty per cent more on local than on through freight. This
legislation did not arouse any particular excitement among the
people or the press. Evidently the original act was not rigorously
enforced; a subsequent act, in 1875, stated that any railroad or
employee violating the 1873 law would be guilty of a misde-
meanor and fined from $100 to $500.[9] The railroad attempted to
have the 1873 act repealed, but the agrarian-minded legislatures
of the 1870's refused. Although the Alabama supreme court
interpreted the 1873 act in favor of the shippers, the railroads
succeeded in simply ignoring it.[10]

With the advent to power of the Democrats in 1874, interest
in regulatory legislation increased. The railroads of the state
were suffering as the result of generally depressed economic
conditions; between 1873 and 1880 only forty miles of new railroad lines were constructed in Alabama.[11] The public became
suspicious of the promised economic boom the railroads were
supposed to bring about, and many people blamed the railroad
companies for the questionable financial transactions that had
brought the state so close to bankruptcy. Thus, attempts at
regulation increased in an atmosphere of distrust and suspicion.

To some extent this anti-railroad feeling was connected with
the country-wide work of the Patrons of Husbandry. The Patrons, or Grangers, in Alabama, however, never joined in any
concerted attack on the railroad. The leaders of the state organization felt too keenly the need of further railroad development in order to stimulate Alabama's economic recovery. The
Southern Plantation, official organ of the State Grange, reflected

[8] Montgomery *Journal,* February 11, 1874.
[9] *Senate Journal* (1872-73), p. 385; *Acts* (1872-73), p. 62; *ibid.* (1874-
75), p. 243.
[10] *State,* ex rel. *Harrel* v. *Mobile and Montgomery Railway Co.* (1877),
59 Ala. 321; James F. Doster, *Alabama's First Railroad Commission,*
1881-1885, pp. 10-16.
[11] *Aditor's Report* (1875), p. 4; *ibid.* (1880), p. 77.

no anti-railroad sentiment whatever. The strongest newspaper supporter of the Alabama Grangers did warn against the "overweening power of railroad corporations" but opposed outright regulation.[12] Some sentiment for restrictive legislation probably existed in the local Granges, and occasional proposals were made in the state conventions. The second annual session indefinitely postponed action on two resolutions, one favoring direct state legislation on passenger and freight tariffs and another demanding an outright reduction of freight rates.[13]

Occasional criticisms of railroad monopolies could be found in the public press, but such denunciation usually applied to railroads in general or to lines outside of Alabama. Most Alabamians either valued their local railroads too highly or were too much interested in the pressing political problems of the time to become disturbed over unjust railroad practices. Some of the strongest anti-railroad sentiment of the period came to light in the 1875 constitutional convention. The delegates showed decided hostility to the policy of fostering and encouraging industries, and one of their first actions was to impose a constitutional prohibition on the state's engaging in, or lending its money or credit to, works of internal improvement. Counties and municipalities were likewise prohibited from lending money or credit to such projects.[14] The legislature had already repealed the state-aid laws, but the public in general felt that some constitutional prohibition was necessary. One newspaper, urging such action, said:

> The development dodge has pretty nearly served its day. Burdened tax-payers, wronged and suffering communities, bankrupt municipalities . . . have poured out their wealth, mortgaged their estates . . . that their benefactors may have gilded coaches and palatial residences. They have been developed to death.[15]

Ten other specific proposals calling for fairly drastic railroad regulation were made to the convention by the committee on

[12] Selma *Southern Argus*, December 29, 1876, January 19, September 7, 1877.

[13] *Grange Proceedings* (1874), pp. 16, 26.

[14] *Constitution of 1875*, Art. IV, secs. 54-55.

[15] Selma *Southern Argus*, January 23, 1874. See also Mobile *Register*, May 19, 21, 25, 1875.

corporations. The delegates, however, rejected them all and
adopted a substitute declaring:

> The General Assembly shall pass laws to correct abuses
> and prevent unjust discrimination and extortion in the
> rates of freight and passenger tariffs on railroads, canals,
> and rivers in this state.

The constitution as finally approved contained two other per-
tinent sections. One declared all railroads common carriers,
guaranteed the right of connection between lines, and provided
for the prompt interchange of freight and passengers; the other
prohibited railroads from granting free passes to any legislator
or governmental official.[16]

Thus the new constitution recognized the need for regulatory
legislation but left to the legislature itself the task of formulating
specific laws. The first session under the new constitution,
1876-1877, often called the Granger legislature, heard numerous
proposals to regulate freight rates. Although one such bill passed
the Senate, it failed in the House. The legislature did pass one
restrictive measure making common carriers entirely liable for
all livestock injured along their lines.[17] Popular resentment
against a number of railroad practices continued. Petitions to
the legislature and letters in newspapers demonstrated dissatisfaction with the existing situation; the legislature found it necessary to curtail the prevalent malicious damaging of railroad
property by imposing severe penalties.[18]

By 1880 another factor, the fear of consolidation of Alabama
railroads under out-of-state control, increased the demands for
a railroad commission. As a result of the bankruptcies following
the 1873 panic, practically no new railroad lines were built in
Alabama during the next eight years. Instead, such out-of-state
interests as the Louisville and Nashville, East Tennessee, Virginia, and Georgia, and Central Railroad of Georgia rapidly
bought up Alabama lines for integration into their systems.[19]

[16] *Constitution of 1875*, Art. XIV, secs. 21-23; *Convention Journal* (1875),
pp. 134-135.

[17] *House Journal* (1876-77), pp. 579, 738; *Senate Journal* (1876-77), pp.
247-250; *Acts* (1876-77), p. 54.

[18] See petition from citizens of Butler County in *Senate Journal* (1878-79),
p. 559; Selma *Southern Argus,* October 17, 1879; Montgomery *Advertiser,*
March 26, 1879; *Acts* (1878-79), p. 175.

[19] Doster, *op. cit.,* pp. 24-36; Allen J. Going, "The Establishment of the

These consolidations then placed the transportation lines to some towns, hitherto competitive points, completely under the control of one railroad company. Thus, urban merchants and lawyers now joined the aggrieved farmers in demanding some protection from the threat of unlimited power by single railroad systems. Newspapers in the larger towns began to demand remedial legislation. In February, 1880, the Montgomery *Advertiser* declared that some railroad legislation must be considered, and in November the Mobile *Register* said that from every side came "the cry of an oppressed people against the arbitrary rule of the great railroad corporations."[20] Even the State Bar Association in recommending a railroad commission composed of "discreet citizens," declared:

> These corporations [railroads] do not appear to be amenable to the law of competition . . . . If at any time dangerous competition is established between rival lines, the struggle is settled by direct consolidation of the rival corporation . . . . All this is the more striking and dangerous in States like Alabama, of limited capital, when capitalists come from other states and countries and obtain the control of its railroads.[21]

Walter Lawrence Bragg, one of Alabama's outstanding leaders in the post-war period and first president of the state railroad commission, expressed similar views when he said:

> The greatest difficulty I have found with the railroads of Alabama is the singular want of competition . . . . I am speaking of the pernicious effect of running a system like the Louisville & Nashville in this State . . . which drains but does not develop and build up business in this State along [its] lines.[22]

This consolidation of lines caused more concern in Montgomery than in any of the other large Alabama towns, because of the virtual stranglehold on the railroad lines into that city acquired by the Louisville and Nashville. The columns of the Montgomery *Advertiser* abounded in letters from correspondents

---

Alabama Railroad Commission," *Journal of Southern History*, XII (1946), 373-374. See map p. 128.

[20] Montgomery *Advertiser*, February 22, 1880; Mobile *Register*, November 2, 1880.

[21] *Proceedings of the Second Annual Meeting of the Alabama State Bar Association* (1880), pp. 126-127.

[22] Bragg, *Speech . . . Before the Senate Judiciary Committee*, pp. 2, 5.

and editorials expressing concern and fear over this development.[23] It is not surprising, then, to find shippers of Montgomery
and its environs leading the movement for railroad legislation.
Daniel Shipman Troy, an influential political and business figure
of Montgomery devoted himself to a study of railroad commissions and regulatory legislation in other states. Just before the
legislature met in November, 1880, he outlined an elaborate plan
for an Alabama railroad commission.[24] Although the railroad
commission act was not the work of any one individual,
Troy undoubtedly influenced the legislation more than anyone else.

RAILROAD COMMISSION

Thus by the fall of 1880 anti-railroad sentiment throughout
Alabama had reached a fairly high pitch, and it was clear that
the question would be the most controversial one before the
legislature. Governor Rufus W. Cobb, in his message of November 9, 1880, said that the demand for action on the railroad
question was so general and pressing that the legislators had to
give it their earnest and serious consideration.[25] Within two
weeks regulatory measures had been introduced into both
houses.

Colonel Troy sponsored a series of Senate bills embodying
his ideas of a regulatory body, but none was adopted.[26] Mean-
while Charles Carter Langdon of Mobile introduced into the
House a bill providing for a commission to fix all railroad rates
in the state, a stronger type than that contemplated by Troy.
After lengthy debate during February, 1881, the House altered
somewhat and passed the Langdon bill by a vote of sixty to
twenty-one.[27] The Senate, however, considered the House measure too severe and passed a substitute bill based largely on the
ideas suggested by Troy. Since the session had almost reached

[23] Montgomery *Advertiser*, February 22, 1880. Numerous other excerpts
quoted in Doster, *op. cit.*, pp. 29-34.
[24] Troy, *Proposed Railroad Legislation* (reprinted from Montgomery
Advertiser, October 2-3, 1880).
[25] *House Journal* (1880-81), p. 30.
[26] *Senate Journal* (1880-81), p. 167.
[27] *House Journal* (1880-81) pp. 548-549; Mobile *Register*, November 26,
1880; Montgomery *Advertiser*, January 15, 1881.

its constitutional time limit of fifty days, the House reluctantly, and after much protest, agreed to the Senate substitute.[28]

Practically no opposition to the idea of a railroad commission existed in Alabama in 1881; the controversy centered instead around the question of how strong the powers of the commission should be. Railroad interests recognized as inevitable some type of regulation and confined their efforts to making it as innocuous as possible. W. G. Raoul, vice-president of the Georgia Central, published numerous communications advocating a commission with advisory powers only, such as the commission in Massachusetts.[29] The influential Montgomery *Advertiser* reported both sides of the dispute but favored a commission with mild powers.[30] Governor Cobb believed that the act as finally passed provided too mild a form of regulation, and a number of state newspapers agreed.[31] Colonel Troy and the *Advertiser* felt it necessary to publish a lengthy defense of the legislation.[32]

The railroad commission act can be divided into three parts. The first dealt with the heart of the problem by making any railroad charging more than just compensation guilty of extortion. Questions as to whether or not specific rates exceeded just compensation were to be decided by the courts when actions were brought by aggrieved shippers. If, however, rates had been approved by the railroad commission, they could not be considered "willfully extortionate." The second part of the act prohibited any rebates or reductions from a set tariff and made such practices misdemeanors. The concluding twenty four sections provided for the working machinery of the commission itself.[33]

The commission consisted of a president and two associates serving terms of two years and chosen by the Senate from a list of nine submitted by the governor. Salaries were to be $3,500 for the president and $3,000 each for the two associates. It is

[28] *House Journal* (1880-81), pp. 685, 732, 739, 775; *Senate Journal* (1880-81), p. 488; Montgomery *Advertiser*, February 24, 26, 1881.

[29] Quoted in Montgomery *Advertiser*, November 28, 1880, February 22, 1881.

[30] January-February, 1881, *passim*.

[31] Governor's Message, *House Journal* (1880-81), p. 784; Doster, *op. cit.*, p. 43.

[32] Montgomery *Advertiser*, March 8, 1881.

[33] *Acts* (1880-81), p. 85.

interesting to note that these figures were higher than the average for other state commissioners except those of California, New
York and Massachusetts.[34] It was the duty of the commission to
review all tariffs submitted to it by the railroads and to advise of
any changes necessary. The commissioners also heard all complaints against such approved rates; decisions would not, however, be binding and the complainant's only recourse was to the
courts. The commission had general supervision over all railroads in the state, was required to examine them thoroughly, and
was authorized to demand in writing all needed information.
The commission should also recommend legislation necessary
for the better control of railroads and should confer with similar
bodies in other states. All expenses of the commission, including
salaries, would be met by the proceeds of a special license tax
levied on each railroad according to the amount of its gross income earned within Alabama.

Most observers agreed that the railroad commission act represented a much less mandatory type of control than that originally
contemplated by its backers. Rather than making binding the
commission's rate decisions, the law in a sense bribed railroads
to accept such rates voluntarily, because such an acceptance
guaranteed less judicial controversy. It certainly differed from
the Georgia law, which established a commission with power to
prescribe rates upon its own initiative.[35]

The first commission consisted of Walter L. Bragg as president
and James Crook and Charles P. Ball as associate commissioners.
Bragg, a law partner of Senator John Tyler Morgan, had distinguished himself in politics and had often been mentioned as
a possible gubernatorial candidate. Crook represented the agricultural interests, and Ball represented the railroads, having been
connected with the Western Railroad and the Alabama Great
Southern.[36] Some sections of the state expressed dissatisfaction
over the fact that two members of the commission and the clerk

[34] Report of the Cullom Committee, January 18, 1886, *Senate Reports*,
49 Cong., 1 Sess., no. 46, I, 65-66.
[35] Maxwell Ferguson, *State Regulation of Railroads in the South*, pp.
129-131.
[36] Owen, *History of Alabama*, III, 203-204, 428; Montgomery *Advertiser*,
March 1, 1881.

were all from Montgomery.[37] During the ensuing two years the commissioners vigorously executed their duties. Bragg proved himself to be an executive of considerable ability and tireless energy. Although their terms of office under the law ran for only two years, the Senate in 1883 did not hesitate to reappoint all three for second terms.

In addition to hearing numerous complaints and making a careful inspection of railroads in the state, the commission undertook the troublesome problem of rate revision. All of the railroads submitted their tariff schedules to the commission soon after its creation. Although the rates submitted by each road were considered separately, the general result was a drastic reduction in passenger fares from four or five cents to three cents per mile, but only a moderate revision of freight tariffs. The commissioners themselves said, "The commission was influenced by the idea that the public would be much more benefited by cheap travel than by a corresponding reduction in freight."[38] Since the commission had no direct power to enforce its rates, it hesitated to make drastic reductions in freight rates.

The general effect of the commission upon the state during the first three and one-half years of its existence was reflected to some extent in the reactions of the press and public. The railroads themselves seem to have accepted the commission and its recommendations with fairly good grace. The commission regularly reported co-operation from the roads in furnishing statistics and carrying out recommendations. Although the railroads naturally opposed any reductions in fares or rates, they finally accepted all revised tariffs.[39] Commissioner Bragg said:

> I know that the railroad companies hate a Railroad Commission like the devil hates holy water, and while I say that, my personal relations and those of the other Commissioners have been and are friendly with all the railroad managers and agents of the State.[40]

[37] Mobile *Register,* March 4, 1881; Huntsville *Advocate,* March 2, 1881; Florence *News* quoted in Huntsville *Advocate,* March 23, 1881.

[38] *First Annual Report of the Railroad Commissioners of Alabama* [hereinafter cited as *Railroad Commissioners' Report*] (1881), pp. 150-151. For a detailed account of the work of the commission, see Doster, *op. cit.,* pp. 49-101.

[39] *Railroad Commissioners' Report* (1882), pp. 8, 24, 91; (1885), p. 13.

[40] Bragg, *op. cit.,* p. 38.

The railroads perhaps realized that the regulatory act might have been much more severe, and that a commission with stronger powers would have been much less considerate of their interests. Thus, failure to co-operate might have provoked more stringent regulatory laws. By co-operating with the commission, the railroads also noticeably improved their relations with the public. Both Commissioner Bragg and Colonel Troy noticed this and admitted that by 1884 it was possible for a railroad to receive a fair trial before a jury.[41]

The attitude of the press and public toward the first commission seems to have been rather neutral. Its work aroused neither general condemnation nor enthusiastic praise. The average person probably would have agreed with the newspaper that said, "Alabama's advisory R. R. Commission has worked as well as any."[42] From papers in north Alabama there came some criticism accusing the commissioners of holding sinecures and of accomplishing practically nothing toward curbing railroad power.[43] The legislature of 1882-83 appeared to be friendly to the commission and passed some of the bills suggested by the commissioners. Many more, however, died in a last minute legislative "log jam."[44] It was the legislative session of 1884-1885, however, that witnessed the crucial test to determine whether the new commission should continue as a half-mandatory, half-advisory body or should be given more extensive control.

The controversy over the commission's powers was precipitated by the question of freight rates on through shipments from out-of-state points in the West to Opelika. Commissioners Bragg and Crook rendered a decision specifying that the Opelika rates should be the same as those to Columbus, Georgia. When the Western Railroad objected on the basis that Opelika was not a competitive point, Bragg requested from the legislature additional power to force compliance with the commission's ruling.[45]

[41] *Ibid.*, pp. 35, 38.

[42] Montgomery *Advertiser*, January 16, 1883.

[43] Huntsville *Advocate*, June 29, 1881; Jasper *Mountain Eagle* quoted in Huntsville *Advocate*, August 17, 1881; Florence *News* quoted in Huntsville *Advocate*, March 23, 1881.

[44] Doster, *op. cit.*, p. 83.

[45] *Railroad Commissioners' Report* (1884), pp. 23-28, 45-88; Montgomery *Advertiser*, June 21, December 7, 9, 1884.

There ensued in the legislature a violent debate over the Bragg proposals with the railroads employing every possible device of propaganda and lobbying to defeat them. Practically all newspapers opposed the plans to strengthen the commission.[46] The few papers that did support the proposed changes accused other journals of being paid by the railroads to copy "sentiment of the state press previously subsidized."[47] In contrast to their attitude in 1881, merchants and business men also quite generally opposed Bragg, and Colonel Troy spoke vigorously in the Senate against increasing the commission's powers.[48] Returning prosperity, revival of railroad building, and relaxation of the fear of monopoly all combined to effect this change of heart on the part of urban interests. After lengthy debate the legislature defeated the proposed changes.[49] Commissioner Bragg's efforts to put some "teeth" into the railroad commission law resulted in naught save a great deal of agitation, reverberations from which lasted for some time thereafter.

For a while there existed the possibility that the fight for stronger regulation would be carried into state politics. At the close of the legislative session, eleven senators and nineteen representatives, meeting in Bragg's office, signed an open address to the people of the state, accusing the railroads of having forced a decision on the legislature and urging the people to campaign for the election of "right men" to the next legislature. Of the thirty signatories, twenty resided in eastern and southeastern agricultural counties.[50] Bragg, however, did not pursue the political possibilities of an anti-railroad campaign in the 1886 election; in 1887 he became a member of the first Interstate Commerce Commission and held the position until his death in 1891.

From this time until the first decade of the twentieth century,

[46] Montgomery *Advertiser*, January 10, 1885; Mobile *Register*, December 12, 1884; Birmingham *Chronicle*, January 5, 8, 19, 1885; Birmingham *Age*, November 20, 1885. See other papers quoted in Montgomery *Advertiser*, January 4, 1885.

[47] Opelika *Times* quoted in Montgomery *Advertiser*, January 11, 1885; Selma *Times* quoted in *ibid.*, January 6, 1885.

[48] Quoted in Montgomery *Advertiser*, January 27, 1885.

[49] *Senate Journal* (1884-85), pp. 404, 422, 436; *House Journal* (1884-85), pp. 890, 1020.

[50] Mobile *Register*, February 21, 24, 1885; Grove Hill *Clark County Democrat*, March 5, 1885.

little railroad agitation stirred the people of Alabama. The railroad commission itself assumed the role of a mere fact-finding group leniently supervising the roads, rather than an active agency anxious to increase its own power or to curb that of the railroads. The commissioners did not find favor with many elements in the state except the railroads themselves and those interested in railroad development. It is not surprising, therefore, to find many suggestions for abolition of the commission during the 1880's and 1890's, with Reuben F. Kolb and the Farmers Alliance assuming the leadership in vigorously attacking this "tool of the railroads."[51]

ENCOURAGEMENT AND SUPPORT OF RAILROADS

In spite of suspicion and distrust directed toward railroads from some quarters and attempts to regulate them, railroad building in Alabama flourished during the decade of the 1880's. Between 1880 and 1890 railroad mileage in the state grew from 1,843 to 3,145, a larger increase than during any previous decade. The assessed valuation increased from $10,528,000 in 1877 to $47,883,749 in 1891.[52] Almost all of the new roads that began operation during the 1880's were financed by out-of-state capital and soon became integral parts of larger systems operating in the South.

This rapid building of railroads both resulted from and contributed to the industrial and real estate boom in north Alabama during this period. There appeared in newspapers and pamphlets the same enthusiasm for railroad building that had prevailed during Reconstruction. Some papers went so far as to advocate amending the constitution to eliminate the prohibition against state aid for internal improvements; they argued that the policy itself had never been erroneous but that the Radicals had misused it by permitting corruption and irregularities.[53] A Black Belt paper, however, ridiculed any idea of changing the constitution in this respect by saying: "O, give us back the Steal Age!

[51] J. B. Clark, *op. cit.*, p. 43; Moore, *op. cit.*, pp. 599-600.

[52] *Statistical Abstract of the United States*, (1891), p. 263; Berney, *op. cit.*, p. 115; *ibid.* (1892 ed.), p. 378.

[53] Birmingham *Chronicle*, July 5, October 4, 1885; Tuscaloosa *Times* quoted in Huntsville *Democrat*, July 1, 1885.

We wish to develop the hidden wealth, you know; the hidden wealth of Wall Street."[54]

The constitutional prohibition against railroad aid remained unchanged, but the Democratic administration's attitude toward new or existing railroads could hardly be called hostile. In some instances it actually approved or advocated measures to benefit and assist the common carriers. The adjustment of the state debt did not repudiate all the bonds endorsed for or lent to railroads. Although the debt commission considered the state-aid policy as of "doubtful propriety" and "inopportunely inaugurated," it recommended, and the legislature approved, compromising with the Alabama and Chattanooga bondholders and those who had exchanged endorsed bonds of other roads for Alabama state bonds. The commission explained its recommendation in regard to the Alabama and Chattanooga road by citing the benefits brought to the state by a "first-class railway . . . furnishing traveling and transportation facilities to an intelligent and enterprising population . . . and which would contribute largely to the development of immense mineral wealth."[55]

The state government also followed a lenient policy in relation to the lands granted by the Federal government to the state in aid of railroad construction. In the 1850's Congress had passed a number of bills making generous land grants to Western and Southern states to assist the building of proposed railroad lines. By 1886 Alabama had received a total of approximately 3,000,000 acres of such lands, more than any other Southern state, and 901 miles of land-grant railroad, also more than in any other Southern state, had been built.[56] Most of this land was patented to railroads constructed before or during the Civil War, but large areas were supposed to go to the South and North Alabama and the Alabama and Chattanooga roads, both of which became involved in Reconstruction politics. Since these two roads crossed at Birmingham, some of their land claims overlapped, and the situation became further complicated when the Alabama and Chattanooga was seized by the state government. The first leg-

[54] Hayneville *Examiner* quoted in Huntsville *Democrat,* July 8, 1885.
[55] *Debt Commissioners' Report,* pp. 19, 22.
[56] Lewis Henry Haney, *A Congressional History of Railways in the United States, 1850-1887,* pp. 13-14.

islature after 1874 heatedly discussed a bill to grant these disputed lands to the South and North company. Strong opposition, however, argued that the lands, worth about a million dollars, should be retained as security against further loss on account of the Alabama and Chattanooga. The bill succeeded in passing only one house at that legislative session.[57] At the next session Governor Houston strongly recommended transferring these lands to the South and North road, and the legislature complied.

As part of the debt settlement, the state handed over all of the lands held for the Alabama and Chattanooga Railroad to the English bondholders who had purchased the $2,000,000 worth of state bonds granted to this railroad during Reconstruction. In surrendering their bonds these English capitalists received title to lands their own agent described as the "finest mineral lands, coal and iron, on the face of the globe."[58] These lands were to be exempt from taxation for eight years, but the debt adjustment stipulated that the state was to receive ten per cent of the proceeds from the sale of the lands until it had been reimbursed for the $240,000 paid out in interest on the surrendered bonds. Alabama, however, received nothing from the land sales until 1883 when the legislature agreed to settle for the flat sum of $40,000.[59]

The Democratic legislatures did not object to requesting assistance for railroads from the Federal government. During the 1880's the Alabama legislature passed a number of other memorials requesting aid in the form of Federal lands for railroads running from Florence to Tuscaloosa, Tuscaloosa to Montgomery, and Birmingham to Aberdeen, Mississippi.[60] Senator Morgan introduced the bills to support the two roads terminating in Tuscaloosa, both of which were to be links in major interstate systems. In order to meet expected opposition, he proposed that the lands be sold to the railroads at a nominal price and the proceeds given to public education. None of these bills received

[57] Mobile *Register*, February 23, March 3, 9, 1875; Governor's Message, *Senate Journal* (1875-76), p. 23; Montgomery *Advertiser*, January 2, 1876; *Acts* (1875-76), p. 154.

[58] Report of David A. Wells to Council of Foreign Bondholders, London *Times*, February 18, 1874.

[59] *Acts* (1875-76), p. 130; *ibid.* (1882-83), p. 62.

[60] *Ibid.*, (1880-81), pp. 508, 509; *ibid.* (1882-83), pp. 661, 665.

serious consideration in Congress.[61] One Alabama Bourbon in criticizing Morgan for his proposals said, "Any railroad that cannot now be built without government aid isn't needed."[62]

The legislature also readily appropriated the two and three per cent funds to assist new or proposed railroad lines. During the Civil War and for many years thereafter the United States government refused to turn over to Alabama its allotted shares of these funds, claiming that the state had never paid its share of the 1861 war tax. After the United States Supreme Court ruled against the Federal government in 1887, Alabama received the approximately $44,000 that had accumulated since 1860.[63] In 1889 the legislature appropriated the money received from these funds as follows: Alabama Midland Railroad, $24,000; a railroad from Mobile to Florence via Tuscaloosa, $19,000; and one from Decatur to Meridian, Mississippi, $9,200. The act also designated the railroads to receive future funds derived from this same source.[64]

As in the case of other corporations, the railroad companies in Alabama did not bear an unduly heavy burden of taxation, and occasional complaints were heard that the companies were not paying their just share. In 1877 the legislature created a special board of assessment of railroad property consisting of the governor, secretary of state, auditor, and treasurer. This board assessed the total value of each railroad in Alabama and designated the portion due each county through which the road passed.[65] A comparison of the 1886 assessed valuation of some Alabama railroads with the cost of these same roads as estimated by the railroad commission shows a difference hardly to be accounted for by ordinary depreciation.[66]

[61] Report of Committee on Public Lands, February 6, 1882, *Senate Reports,* 47 Cong., 1 Sess., no. 117; *Congressional Record,* 47 Cong., 1 Sess., pp. 496, 744, 2276; Montgomery *Advertiser,* February 8, 1882.

[62] Robert McKee to John Tyler Morgan, April 7, 1882, McKee Papers.

[63] *United States* v. *State of Alabama* (1887), 123 U. S. 39; Report of Special Agent John H. Caldwell, *House Journal* (1888-89), p. 989.

[64] *Acts* (1888-89), p. 721. See report of special committee on this matter, *House Journal* (1888-89), p. 607.

[65] *Acts* (1876-77), p. 6.

[66] *Auditor's Report* (1886), pp. xxvii-xxviii; *Railroad Commissioners' Report* (1885), p. 60.

	Assessed Valuation	Railroad Commission's Estimated Cost
Alabama Great Southern	$3,108,936	$10,409,854
Georgia Pacific	2,050,897	8,824,943
South and North	2,797,737	10,616,825
Memphis and Charleston	2,085,500	5,467,246

In discussing this situation the railroad commissioners pointed out that there was a "general tacit understanding on the part of corporations and individuals that property, as the subject of taxation, is not listed at its real value."[67]

WATER TRANSPORTATION

During the last half of the nineteenth century in Alabama, as in the entire nation, the railroads rapidly replaced canals and rivers as the chief transportation arteries. Thus, as rail lines penetrated and connected almost every section of the state, Alabama's magnificent system of rivers fell gradually into disuse. Large steamboat companies no longer found it profitable to maintain service or to keep the streams clear of obstructions. Nevertheless, a number of boats continued to operate on the Alabama, Tombigbee, and Tennessee river systems, and in the 1880's fairly strong sentiment backed the revival of water transportation as a means of competing with the rates fixed by railroad combinations and pools. Some Alabamians felt that river transportation would be ideal for conveying heavy mineral products such as coal and iron to the state's own port of Mobile.[68]

In November, 1885, a much publicized rivers and harbors improvement convention met at Tuscaloosa with some two hundred representatives from Alabama and adjoining states. The meeting was addressed by Senator James L. Pugh and heard letters from Senator John Tyler Morgan, Representative Hilary Herbert, and other congressmen. Colonel James B. Eads attempted to win the gathering's approval of his Tehauntepec ship-railway scheme, but the delegates tabled any action on that proposal. The convention passed resolutions petitioning Con-

---

[67] *Railroad Commissioners' Report* (1885), p. 55.

[68] Mobile *Register*, October 19, 1884; Montgomery *Advertiser*, September 28, October 18, 1887; Gadsden *Times* quoted in Montgomery *Advertiser*, October 28, 1887.

gress for additional funds to improve Alabama rivers and Mobile harbor. It stressed the benefical effects such action would have on the volume of transportation and the reduction of railroad rates.[69] In 1887 a similar convention met in Montgomery to urge the opening of the Coosa River. This river was navigable below Rome, Georgia, for about 160 miles, but a 180-mile stretch of the lower river from Wetumpka northward was impassible because of shoals. Although the Montgomery convention urged work on all Alabama rivers, it emphasized especially the necessity of building locks on the Coosa.[70] Similar conventions urging improvements on the Tennessee River were held at Huntsville and Chattanooga in 1880 and 1884 respectively.[71]

During the Reconstruction period the Alabama government spent over $5,000 on a survey of the Coosa River.[72] After 1875, however, the constitutional prohibition against aid to internal improvements prevented the state from becoming involved in any projects to improve Alabama's waterways. Individuals and groups interested in such action pinned their hopes on the Federal government and worked for sizeable portions of the river and harbor improvements appropriations. Between 1870 and 1890 the Alabama legislature directed innumerable petitions and memorials to Congress requesting considerable sums for various projects already under way or contemplated.[73] As a result of these petitions and the work of Alabama's representatives and senators, the appropriations for river and harbor improvements in the state increased considerably during the 1880's. When the Republicans had control of Alabama in the 1870's, the appropriations had been fairly large, but they fell off immediately after 1874. Beginning in 1879, however, they began to grow

[69] *Memorial and Proceedings of the River and Harbor Improvement Convention Assembled at Tuscaloosa, Ala., November 17, 1885,* pp. 12, 25, 32 54, and *passim;* Birmingham *Chronicle,* November 22, 1885; Birmingham *Age,* November 6, 18, 1885; Montgomery *Advertiser,* November 17, 20, 1885.

[70] Montgomery *Advertiser,* March 15, 16, 1887; Mobile *Register,* January 8, 1887.

[71] Montgomery *Advertiser,* January 17, 1880; Huntsville *Advocate,* February 1, 1884.

[72] *Auditor's Report* (1869), pp. iv, xxxii, xl, 41.

[73] As typical examples see *Acts* (1884-85), pp. 823, 824, 831; *ibid.,* (1886-87), p. 1037.

steadily. Before the Civil War the Federal government appropriated a total of $255,751 for the improvement of Alabama rivers and harbors; between 1870 and 1886 the appropriations totaled $1,503,000.[74] Most of the money was used in dredging channels and clearing out obstructions. The government also built two canals at Muscle Shoals and completed the first in a series of locks on the Coosa River. Both of these, as well as a small canal on the Black Warrior, were in operation in 1889.[75]

Alabama Democrats realized that improved transportation facilities were vital to the state's economic progress, but constitutional limitations prevented the government from granting any direct aid. The legislatures constantly petitioned Congress for aid to both railroad and waterways. In its taxing program and debt adjustment, moreover, the Democrats made a number of concessions to the common carriers. Although a wave of anti-railroad sentiment caused the creation of a state railroad commission in 1881, within three years the office of commissioner amounted to little more than a sinecure financed by the railroads and controlled in their interest. There remained among some agrarian groups an underlying distrust of railroads and of other corporate enterprise, but by 1890 the Democratic party in its campaigns and in its actions reflected none of this sentiment.

[74] Laws of the United States Relating to the Improvement of Rivers and Harbors, September 17, 1887, *Senate Miscellaneous Documents,* 49 Cong., 2 Sess., no. 91, p. 481; William Elejius Martin, *Internal Improvements in Alabama,* pp. 42-62.

[75] Analytical and Topical Index to the Reports of the Chief of Engineers, June 18, 1902, *House Documents,* 57 Cong., 2 Sess., no. 439, I, 17, 278 and *passim* I and II.

CHAPTER TEN

Public Education

E F F O R T S to expand educational facilities and to find adequate school revenue created one of the most perplexing problems for the Alabama government during this period. The state's public school system had been established in 1854 but existed little more than on paper prior to the Reconstruction period. Throughout the nation as a whole the last quarter of the nineteenth century witnessed a vast expansion of public school facilities. Alabama felt the impact of this education movement, and practically all newspapers, politicians, and civic leaders accepted the theory of tax-supported schools. The Reconstruction governments organized Alabama's first effective state school system and firmly established the idea of popular education for both Negro and white children. Financial difficulties, however, prevented efficient operation of the schools, and Republicans themselves admitted that educational accomplishments had not measured up to their expectations.[1] Democratic leaders accepted the theory of public education, but because of limited revenue did not always implement the widespread educational program in which they professed to believe.

In the 1874 campaign Democrats denounced the Radical man-

[1] Montgomery *Journal* (weekly), March 25, 1870; Governor's Message, *House Journal* (1873), p. 14.

agement of school affairs, and the Radicals in turn declared that
their opponents intended to wreck the entire educational set-up.[2]
After their victory, the Democrats found the schools in a deplorable condition. During 1873 the state had disbursed no
money to schools, and only those supported by local funds had
been taught. By the end of the fiscal year 1874, the unpaid
sums due to the public schools from the state amounted to
$1,260,511.[3] The Democrats tackled the school problem with two
general reforms in mind. In the first place they proposed a
complete reorganization of the school system. Secondly, they
advocated reducing the financial commitments of the state to a
figure adaptable to the state's revised financial structure.

ORGANIZATION OF THE PUBLIC SCHOOLS

The Constitution of 1868 and subsequent Reconstruction legislation had established on paper an elaborate and centralized
school organization headed by a state board of education. The
constitutional convention in 1875 eliminated the state board, an
agency considered unnecessary by practically everyone. Some
sentiment also existed for eliminating state and county superintendents; the final draft of the constitution provided for a popu-
larly elected state superintendent but made no mention of county
superintendents. It further stated that not more than four per
cent of the total school revenue could be used for expenses other
than the payment of teachers' salaries.[4]

John M. McKleroy, Democratic superintendent of education
1874-1876, did not approve the action of the convention. He
attributed the fine showing of the schools during his first year
in office to the sound organization and financial support made
possible by the 1868 constitution, then in effect. During his
second year Superintendent McKleroy found it impossible to
open any schools until February, 1876, because the legislature
delayed so long in making an appropriation.[5] Contrary to pre-

[2] Mobile *Register* (weekly), July 25, August 29; Montgomery *Journal*,
August-October, 1874, *passim*.
[3] Willis G. Clark, *History of Education in Alabama*, p. 245; Stephen B.
Weeks, *History of Public School Education in Alabama*, pp. 101-105.
[4] *Convention Journal* (1875), pp. 152-158; *Constitution of 1875*, Art.
XIII, secs. 6-7.
[5] *Report of . . . Superintendent of Public Instruction of the State of*

cedent, McKleroy refused to run a second time for the super-
intendency but instead won a seat in the legislature.

The legislature meeting in the fall of 1876 proceeded to work
out a reorganization of the public schools under the new constitution. McKleroy had stated that any radical change in the
school laws would do more harm than good, and he reported
from a House committee a bill embodying his ideas. A minority
of the committee, however, led by S. J. Doster of Dale County
reported a substitute, which the legislature adopted instead of
the majority report.[6] Doster's plan provided for a decentralized
system with little power vested in either the state or county
superintendents. The adopted bill also omitted the word *free*
and thus allowed state funds to go to schools charging tuition.
Doster stated: "It is the object of the law . . . to re-establish the
grand old schools of primary, academic and collegiate; to restore
local self-management of schools to parents, to teachers and to
trustees."[7]

This new school law, which went into effect October 1, 1877,
in reality restored the state system that had existed before the
time of Reconstruction. A state superintendent, elected for two
years with an annual salary of $2,250, presided over the system.
County superintendents were appointed by the state superintendent and received an annual salary of $75 plus one per cent
of all funds distributed in the county. The county superintendents proved to be little more than disbursement agents for the
school fund apportioned to each county by the state superintendent. The law continued the practice, begun in 1873, of having
the school fund for each county turned over by the tax col-
lector directly to the county superintendent; thus the major
portion never went through the state treasury. The responsibility
for establishing schools, contracting with teachers, and paying
teachers fell to the township trustees, elected to serve for four-
year periods. Although the school laws during Reconstruction
had specifically prohibited supplementary contributions from

Alabama [hereinafter cited as *Superintendent of Education's Report*]
(1875), pp. 10-11, 47; *ibid.* (1876), pp. 6, 11; Mobile *Register* (weekly),
January 8, 1876.
  [6] *House Journal* (1876-77), pp. 59, 346, 435, 478, 670.
  [7] Letter quoted in Montgomery *Advertiser*, September 2, 1877.

patrons, these were welcomed and expected under the new law. This new school code did not apply to the increasing number of towns and cities having their own special school laws.[8]

The new law incurred criticism from a number of sources. In a public protest McKleroy and three other Democrats critically analyzed the measure and denounced it as a retrogressive act that would place Alabama's educational system far behind that of other states.[9] One newspaper correspondent asserted that it should not be called an "Act to Establish Public Schools" but rather an "Act to Abolish Public Schools, and to Subsidize Private Schools." The Republicans claimed that the law excluded the poor from all the benefits of public schools.[10] The legislature in 1879 made a number of changes in the school law, one of which increased the authority of the superintendents. The only other alteration of significance in the public school organization during the period under consideration came in 1889 when the legislature, following the recommendation of the state superintendent, provided for popular election of county superintendents in all but twenty-one counties.[11]

The state superintendents after McKleroy seem to have been capable administrators rather than brilliant or crusading leaders in the cause of education. In 1878 a strong movement arose for the selection of Henry Tutwiler of the Green Springs Academy as superintendent. Although Tutwiler enjoyed a reputation as Alabama's most distinguished educator, the Democratic convention failed to nominate him.[12]

Alabama's public school system consisted only of elementary schools, but there was some discussion of establishing high schools. Except, however, for schools supported by certain cities and the district agricultural schools established in 1889, no public high schools were founded under the state system. Another widely discussed but unadopted reform was a compulsory attendance law. General opinion would probably have agreed

[8] *Acts* (1876-77), p. 199; Weeks, *op. cit.*, pp. 116-117.

[9] *House Journal* (1876-77), pp. 632-635.

[10] Montgomery *Advertiser*, February 9, 1877; Elections in Alabama, *loc. cit.*, p. vii.

[11] *Acts* (1878-79), p. 117; *ibid.* (1888-89), p. 396; *Superintendent of Education's Report* (1888), p. 23.

[12] Montgomery *Advertiser*, April 16, 24, June 9, 1878.

with the Democratic newspaper that said: "If the parents of children, when they have the opportunity of sending them to school, will not do so, no free government will attempt to compel attendance."[13]

FINANCIAL SUPPORT OF THE PUBLIC SCHOOLS

The effort to improve and expand Alabama's schools resolved itself basically into a struggle for more revenue. In revising the state's financial structure, the Democrats after 1874 reduced the school fund along with other expenditures and were reluctant to increase it by imposing any new taxes. The Constitution of 1875 considerably reduced the minimum appropriation that the previous constitution had guaranteed for educational purposes. It did continue to guarantee the schools the income, at a reduced rate of interest, from the sixteenth-section fund, the surplus revenue fund, and escheats, plus a poll tax limited to $1.50 per person levied and collected by the county. But where the former constitution had guaranteed one fifth of the state's aggregate revenue, the constitution guaranteed only the flat sum of $100,000. As a result of these reductions the school revenue for 1875-1876 amounted to $348,891, as compared with $484,000 for the previous fiscal year.[14]

Some criticism of the convention's action on education was heard from both within and without the party. One newspaper termed it "a breach of good faith . . . a great wrong . . . done the taxpayers in the interest of the bondholders."[15] The Democrats defended the constitutional provisions by pointing out that it set only a minimum guarantee. Governor Houston admitted the inadequacy of school support but hoped that it might be increased when prosperity returned to the state.[16]

After 1875, increased appropriations to schools were constantly urged by educational meetings, newspaper editorials, official reports, and interested groups. One superintendent declared:

[13] Montgomery *Advertiser,* January 29, 1888, June 1, 1889; *House Journal* (1875-76), p. 108.
[14] *Convention Journal* (1875), pp. 152-158; *Constitution of 1875,* Art. XIII, secs. 3-5. See table below, p. 154.
[15] Mobile *Register,* December 31, 1875. Other criticisms quoted in Weeks, *op. cit.,* pp. 111, 115-116.
[16] Governor's Message, *Senate Journal* (1875-76), p. 19.

"Each year it is made more apparent that the great need of our school system is more money." Another answered critics of the state system by saying: "The trouble is not so much in the system as in a lack of revenue to run it successfully."[17] Both the Grange and the Farmers Alliance expressed the hope that the state might some day appropriate enough money to give every child in Alabama free schools nine months in the year.[18] The few political groups that dared to oppose the Democrats invariably advocated a more liberal appropriation of funds for the education of the masses.[19]

The Democratic adherence to economy and low taxes, however, prevented any increases before the decade of the 1880's. Up until 1883 the annual appropriation to schools did not exceed the $150,000 set in 1876. Combined with other sources of income, this figure put the total school revenue at about $400,000. Beginning in 1883 the legislature appropriated $250,000 for each of the next five years, and for the year 1889-90 another $100,000 was added. Thus, by 1890 the legislature was appropriating $350,000, bringing the total school revenue to nearly $700,000.[20] These increased appropriations were possible because of increasing tax values in the state and resulted in part from the efforts of the superintendent of education ably assisted by the Montgomery *Advertiser*.

These measures constituted significant increases in the public school fund, but it must be remembered that Alabama's growing population brought an ever-increasing school enrollment. The accompanying table shows that the available public funds per capita of school population decreased from $1.47 in 1868-1869 to $ .85 in 1875-1876, and then gradually rose to $1.34 in 1889-1890. Because of the condition of the treasury during the Bourbon period, this was about all the traffic would bear, and

[17] *Superintendent of Education's Report* (1888), pp. 9-10; *ibid.* (1885), p. 31. See also *ibid.* (1884), p. 9.

[18] *Grange Proceedings* (1876), p. 28; *Farmers State Alliance of Alabama Minutes . . .* (1889), p. 11.

[19] As typical, see platform of Greenback-Independent-Labor party in Montgomery *Advertiser,* June 27, 1880.

[20] *Acts* (1875-76), pp. 91-98; *ibid.* (1878-79), p. 28; *ibid.* (1880-81), p. 17; *ibid.* (1882-83), p. 66; *ibid.* (1884-85), p. 77; *ibid.* (1886-87), p. 38; *ibid.* (1888-89), p. 25. See table, p. 154.

Democratic leaders boasted that over one third of the total state expenditures went for school purposes. They also proudly pointed out that practically all of the school fund went directly for the salaries of teachers, with only about three per cent being spent for administrative costs.[21]

Various special methods of increasing the school fund were advocated and some attempted. Superintendents often pointed out that certain improvements in the collection and handling of funds would increase revenues. The poll tax, not then a prerequisite to voting, often went uncollected until a concerted effort in the late 1880's brought about considerable improvement. The total poll tax receipts for 1890 stood at $151,222 as compared to $96,414 for 1876.[22] Laxness or dishonesty on the part of county superintendents was exposed in the investigations prompted by the Vincent defalcation. In 1886 the examiner of accounts revealed that James M. Weems, Lauderdale County superintendent, had been removing funds for his own use from 1871 to 1885. This situation led to an alteration of the method of handling school funds, whereby county tax collectors sent all state taxes directly to the treasurer in Montgomery without first turning over school funds to county superintendents.[23]

Since it seemed impossible to increase state taxes, those interested in Alabama's schools recommended more and more some form of local taxation. Some counties and municipalities did appropriate a portion of their revenue to schools, but the consitution limited city and county tax rates to five mills on the dollar. In the 1880's, the legislature created a number of special school districts and conferred upon them the right to levy special taxes, never over five mills, for the exclusive use of education. In 1887, however, the Supreme Court of Alabama held that a school district as such had no right to impose taxes.[24] Following this supreme court decision, the superintendent, governor, and

[21] Governor's Message, *Senate Journal* (1880-81), pp. 30-31; *ibid.* (1886-87), p. 22; Montgomery *Advertiser*, November 12, 1880, November 15, 1882, July 18, 1888.
[22] *Superintendent of Education's Report* (1875), pp. 71-72; *ibid.* (1876), pp. 8-9; Weeks, *op. cit.*, p. 199.
[23] Montgomery *Advertiser*, February 2, 1886; Birmingham *Chronicle*, October 18, 1886; *Acts* (1886-87), p. 117.
[24] Weeks, *op. cit.*, p. 122; *Schultes* v. *Eberly* (1887), 82 Ala. 242.

ALABAMA PUBLIC SCHOOL STATISTICS, 1868-1891*

Year	School population	Schools	Average attendance	Percentage school population in average attendance	Total revenue	Revenue per capita school population
1868-1869	357,181	2,825	—	—	$524,622	$1.47
1869-1870°	387,057	1,845	52,060	13.4	500,409	1.29
1871-	399,153	3,321	107,666	26.9	581,389	1.46
1871-1872	403,375	—	73,927	18.3	604,979	1.50
1872-1873	404,739	—	—	—	522,811	1.29
1873-1874	405,839	—	—	—	474,347	1.17
1874-1875	406,270	3,898	110,253	27.1	484,214	1.19
1875-1876‡	—	3,632	—	—	348,891	.85
1876-1877	369,447	4,175	103,018	27.9	367,243	.99
1877-1878	370,245	4,796	99,125	27.7	377,560	1.02
1878-1879	376,649	4,671	112,374	29.9	388,215	1.04
1879-1880	387,769	4,597	117,978	30.4	398,465	1.03
1880-1881	388,033	4,572	115,316	29.1	397,479	1.03
1881-1882	401,002	4,624	114,527	28.5	392,905	.98
1882-1883	403,901	4,824	127,016	31.4	418,006	1.03
1883-1884	419,764	5,218	134,410	32.1	506,499	1.21
1884-1885	420,413	5,391	144,572	32.9	511,540	1.22
1885-1886	450,968	5,583	152,776	33.9	523,353	1.17
1886-1887	452,937	5,583	157,718	34.8	515,990	1.14
1887-1888	485,551	5,702	165,009	34.0	566,460	1.17
1888-1889	485,025	6,009	165,528	34.2	713,198	1.47
1889-1890	522,691	6,308	175,168	33.5	698,698	1.34
1890-1891	550,522	—	—	—	699,765	1.27

*Weeks, *op cit.,* pp. 197-199. ‡ not all counties reporting

° 15 month period x 9 month period

teachers association all urged the legislature to initiate a constitutional amendment providing for local school taxation. "Alabama," said the superintendent, "can never, under her present constitution, have the school system she needs and should have, for want of the authority to levy and collect a special local tax for schools . . . ."[25] Such a bill was introduced into the legislature in 1888 by Oscar R. Hundley, backed by the leading state newspapers, and passed by the House. The Senate, however, refused to concur.[26] Thus by the end of the period under consideration Alabama's schools still lacked local tax support, a source from which schools in other states derived the major portion of their revenue. As correctly predicted by Governor Seay in 1890, this situation did not improve until Alabama had a new constitution in 1901.[27]

Some support came to Alabama schools from such outside sources as the Peabody Fund and the Slater Fund. As shown on the accompanying table, certain city systems received fairly large sums from the Peabody Fund during the Reconstruction years, but these amounts dropped to less than one third of the total distributed in the years after 1874.

Many people in Alabama, as in other Southern states, believed that the Federal government should grant direct assistance to the impoverished common schools of the South, which had inherited the task of educating the large number of illiterate freedmen. The 1875 constitutional convention and the legislature at periodic intervals petitioned Congress for land grants to assist Alabama's common schools.[28] Another request was that the United States government return to the state the money collected under the Civil War cotton tax, but Congress took no action on any of these pleas.[29]

[25] *Superintendent of Education's Report* (1888), p. 16; Governor's Message, *Senate Journal* (1888-89), p. 25; *Proceedings of the Alabama Education Association* (1889), p. 16.

[26] *House Journal* (1888-89), pp. 177-178, 1168; *Senate Journal* (1888-89), p. 641; Montgomery *Advertiser*, November 17, 18, 1888; Birmingham *News* quoted in Montgomery *Advertiser*, November 22, 1888.

[27] Governor's Message, *Senate Journal* (1890-91), p. 31.

[28] *Convention Journal* (1875), pp. 212-214; *Acts* (1876-77), p. 313; *ibid.* (1878-79), p. 503; *ibid.* (1882-83), p. 661.

[29] *Senate Journal* (1882-83), p. 731; Montgomery *Advertiser*, September 20, December 6, 1882.

The most widely discussed plan for Federal aid to education was incorporated in the Blair Bill, a proposal to grant money to each state on the basis of its illiteracy rate. During the four Congresses between 1881 and 1889, this plan provoked widespread discussion in both houses and throughout the nation. Although it passed the House, it failed each time in the Senate.

ALABAMA'S SHARE IN THE
PEABODY EDUCATION FUND, 1868-1890*

Year	Public schools	Scholarships to normal schools	Normal schools	Teachers institutes	Total
1868	$6,400				$6,400
1869	7,000				7,000
1870	5,350				5,350
1871	7,300				7,300
1872	9,000				9,000
1873	7,000				7,000
1874	10,000				10,000
1875	3,200				3,200
1876	4,300				
1876	4,300				4,300
1877	3,200				3,200
1878	1,100				1,100
1879	3,600				3,600
1880		$1,200x			1,200
1881		1,800			1,800
1882		4,000	$1,000		5,000
1883	1,000	4,000	1,000		6,000
1884		4,000	900	$ 100‡	5,000
1885	300	4,000	1,000		5,300
1886	950	2,000	3,200		6,150
1887	1,950	3,100	2,528	522	8,100
1888	1,500	2,600	3,000	1,000	8,100
1889	1,000	2,600	3,550°	1,250	8,400
1890	200	2,600	4,300°	1,350	8,450

* Statistics compiled from *Superintendent of Education's Reports* and *Proceedings of the Trustees of the Peabody Education Fund.*
    x For the Nashville school only   ‡ Negro only
      ° Includes $500 to the Birmingham Training School.

In Alabama, newspapers, educators, and the legislature discussed the arguments for and against the Blair Bill. The leading Democratic newspapers and each superintendent of education endorsed the measure, as did Republican and independent groups.[30] Alabama's Senator John Tyler Morgan led the oppo-

[30] Montgomery *Advertiser*, February 24, 1886, February 8, 1887; Mobile *Register*, January 26, 1886, January 18, February 14, 1887; Birmingham

sition in Congress, basing his objections primarily on the dangers of Federal control that some feared would accompany financial assistance. His collegue, Senator James L. Pugh, and Governor Thomas Seay, however, both vigorously supported Blair's ideas.[31] In three different sessions the Alabama legislature discussed the Blair Bill at length but only once did the two houses agree on petitioning Congress in its favor.[32]

NEGRO SCHOOLS

Although the Democratic party in the 1874 campaign had made political capital of the danger of mixed schools, it did not generally oppose educating the Negro in the separate schools that had already been established by the Reconstruction governments. "Intelligent whites," said a leading Democratic newspaper, "realize that the best interests of this section demand that the Negro be educated, so that he can better perform his duty to society and the State."[33] Some leaders, notably J. L. M. Curry, strongly and consistently supported Negro education as in the best interests of everyone concerned and as the chief hope of improving the lot of the Negro race. For a number of years after 1874 the Democrats hesitated to interfere in any way with the Negro schools because of possible adverse criticism in the North and their desire to win Negro political support in the Black Belt.

In spite of the official stand of the party and the actions of the Democratic government, a large number of people individually still opposed Negro education in principle. One of their favorite arguments repeated the familar phrase: "Educate a Negro and you spoil a field hand."[34] Some planters and other landowners complained loudly because so much of their tax money went for the education of a race whose members paid relatively few taxes. The county superintendents often reported

---

Chronicle, January 17, 1885; Huntsville *Advocate,* October 27, 1884; Huntsville *Gazette,* April 15, 22, 1882.

[31] *Congressional Record,* 50 Cong., 1 Sess., pp. 868-875; Governor's Message, *Senate Journal* (1888-89), p. 24.

[32] *Acts* (1882-83), p. 667; *Senate Journal* (1884-85), pp. 285-286; *House Journal* (1886-87), pp. 685-686; *Senate Journal* (1886-87), pp. 370, 630.

[33] Mobile *Register,* September 19, 1885.

[34] Athens *Courier* quoted in Montgomery *Advertiser,* December 2, 1888.

local opposition to the Negro children sharing equally in the benefits of the school fund.[35]

The education laws under the Democratic Constitution of 1875 continued the practice established during Reconstruction of apportioning the school fund according to the school population of each race. Although Negroes sometimes asserted that their race did not receive its fair share because of the wide discretionary powers in the hands of local authorities,[36] it is difficult to prove that any actual discrimination took place before the 1890's. In 1888 salaries paid from the school fund to teachers of Negro schools amounted to 38 per cent of the total; during the same year Negro children constituted 42 per cent of the school population.[37] When sentiment increased during the 1880's for additional financial assistance to public schools, an obvious method was to divert some of the Negro school funds to the use of white schools. The increased appropriations in 1889 came as a result of an understanding that the Black Belt counties could use more of their school fund for white education. A new school law in 1891 made this possible by eliminating the necessity of apportioning the school fund on the basis of the number of school children of each race. Instead, the township trustees were given authority to apportion to each school the amount which "they may deem just and equitable."[38] This action undoubtedly resulted in decreased sums granted to Negro schools, especially in black counties. The state superintendents' reports between 1891 and 1908 fail to report the distribution of funds by races. The report of the latter date, however, shows that the Negro school population made up 44 per cent of the total, but teachers of Negro schools received only 12 per cent of total school expenditures as against 87 per cent to teachers of white schools.[39]

NORMAL SCHOOLS

Alabama educators realized that a crying need for more com-

---

[35] Montgomery *Advertiser*, June 2, 1885, February 5, 15, 1887; Horace Mann Bond, *Negro Education in Alabama*, pp. 142-144.

[36] Elections in Alabama, *loc. cit.*, p. vii.

[37] *Superintendent of Education's Report* (1888), pp. 101, 103.

[38] *Acts* (1890-91), p. 554; Bond, *op. cit.*, pp. 151-159.

[39] Weeks, *op. cit.*, pp. 197, 198, 201; Bond, *op. cit.*, pp. 159-163.

petent teachers existed in the state. As J. L. M. Curry expressed it, too many "pretenders, charlatans, and quacks" used the profession as a "make-shift stepping stone."[40] Normal schools for the training of teachers had first been established in Alabama by the Reconstruction governments. The Democrats after 1874 continued to operate three of these, Florence for whites and Huntsville and Marion for Negroes.[41] The legislature increased the annual appropriation to the Florence school from $5,000 to $7,500 in 1879 and established additional schools for whites at Jacksonville and Livingston in 1883 and at Troy in 1887. The annual appropriations for the first two schools was $2,500 each and for the third $3,000. As shown on the table above, Alabama normal schools received additional financial support from the Peabody Fund. The laws establishing these colleges provided that any student within the proper age limits could attend free of tuition by submitting in writing a pledge to teach in the public schools of Alabama for two years after graduation. For Negroes the legislature passed similar laws and established an additional training school at Tuskegee in 1881.[42]

Considerable controversy developed over the state's policy of teacher training in normal schools. In the interests of economy, the legislature established the schools where some kind of college or academy already existed. The schools continued to offer regular college work, and the tuition fees of non-normal pupils supplied the basic financial support. This arrangement meant that state money, which came out of the public school funds, benefited a few colleges and communities. Others not so benefited either criticized the plan or attempted to have a normal school established in their own communities. One newspaper bitterly asked, "What right or what justice is there in using one-half or probably more [of the school fund] to foster large schools in a few favored localities while a three months apology for a

[40] Lecture delivered at Auburn, July, 1874, Curry Papers, 1st Series, Vol. I.

[41] For the history of the Florence school, see Susan Kirkman Vaughn, "The South's Oldest State Teachers College," *Peabody Journal of Education,* XIII (1936), 282-288.

[42] *Acts* (1878-79), p. 146; *ibid.* (1880-81), p. 395; *ibid.* (1882-83), pp. 392, 520, 523; *ibid.* (1886-87), p. 959.

school is barely sustained in nine-tenths of the school districts of the State?"[43]

The state superintendents defended the normal schools, pointing out that they consumed only a small portion of the total school fund. The legislature, nevertheless, heard numerous suggestions either to prevent normals from sharing in the school fund or to abolish them altogether.[44] In spite of all opposition, normal schools increased between 1875 and 1890 from three to seven, the total annual appropriations rose from $10,000 to $30,000, and the schools turned out about one hundred teachers each year.[45]

The three Negro normals offered a somewhat different type of work. Although their principal purpose was the training of teachers, they also broadened their objectives by stressing vocational, industrial, and agricultural education. The emphasis on vocational education resulted in large part from the strong influence exercised on Negro education in Alabama by Booker T. Washington, principal of Tuskegee, and William H. Councill, principal of the Huntsville school.[46]

The school at Marion consistently received the largest share of state appropriations to the Negro normals. Until 1886 it received $4,000 annually, while Huntsville and Tuskegee received $2,000 and $3,000 respectively.[47] After the Marion school had been moved to Montgomery in 1887, an attempt was made to change its name to the Alabama Colored People's University. The Alabama Supreme Court, however, declared this action unconstitutional because it appropriated money from the public school fund for an institution of higher learning.[48] The Montgomery

[43] Monroeville *Monroe Journal* quoted in Montgomery *Advertiser*, March 6, 1888. See similar criticisms in Montgomery *Advertiser*, November 22, 1884; *Proceedings of the Alabama Teachers' Association* (1884-1890), *passim*.

[44] *House Journal* (1888-89), pp. 217, 1013; *Senate Journal* (1882-83), p. 719; *ibid*. (1888-89), p. 225.

[45] *Auditor's Report* (1876), p. 53; *ibid* (1890), p. 104.

[46] Speeches of both in *Minutes of the First Annual Session of the Alabama State Teachers' Association* (1882), pp. 22-25; *ibid* (1888), pp. 29-30; Bond, *op, cit.*, pp. 203-225.

[47] *Auditors' Reports* (1878-1885), *passim*.

[48] Montgomery *Advertiser*, February 5, 1887; *Acts* (1886-87), p. 198; W. E. Elsberry et al. v. *Thomas Seay* et al. (1887), 83 Ala. 614.

normal school, nevertheless, received the largest state appropriation, $7,500,[49] and was developing into its twentieth-century position as Alabama's chief state-supported institution of higher learning for Negroes.

The most famous Negro school in the state is, of course, Tuskegee, and its origin and history as well as Booker T. Washington and his work are well known. After 1885 Tuskegee received less money annually from the state than the other two schools. In the school year 1890-1891 its receipts totaled $36,290, but only $3,000 of this came from the state treasury.[50] In 1885 the legislature changed the name of the Huntsville school to the State Colored Normal and Industrial School and increased its appropriation from $2,000 to $4,000 per year.[51] This school received some contributions from the North but not nearly so much as Tuskegee. President Councill in 1890 succeeded in obtaining for his school the money that came to Alabama under the second Morrill grant from the Federal government and was designated for the colored agricultural school. This fund amounted at first to about $7,000 per year bringing to $25,713 the school's total revenue for the two-year period ending in 1891.[52]

UNIVERSITY OF ALABAMA

The University of Alabama, the only state-supported institution of higher learning in ante-bellum Alabama, had suffered severely as a result of the Civil War and Reconstruction. Burned to the ground by Federal troops in 1865, the institution was just ready to occupy a new building and open its doors when the bitter factional strife accompanying Radical Reconstruction again delayed its opening until 1871. After that date the school remained free from politics, but did not develop rapidly. When the Democrats assumed control in 1874, the University was suffering from the effects of the depression and a rapid turnover of both faculty and administration.[53]

[49] *Acts* (1888-89), p. 509.
[50] *Superintendent of Education's Report* (1891), p. 142.
[51] *Acts* (1884-85), p. 162.
[52] *Superintendent of Education's Report* (1891), pp. 131-133.
[53] Although there is no history of the University in print, the best treatment for this period can be found in W. G. Clark, *op. cit.*, pp. 89-102.

The Constitution of 1875 abolished the board of regents, which had been instituted during Reconstruction, and restored the University to the control of a board of trustees. This board consisted of one trustee each from seven congressional districts and two from the district containing Tuscaloosa, all appointed by the governor with the advice and consent of the Senate. An act of the legislature further elaborated upon the constitution by providing for financial support, filling of vacancies, organization of the faculty, and other matters.[54]

The new board of trustees, after issuing an appeal to the people of Alabama to support the University, took steps to increase the school's enrollment. They immediately reduced the charges for board and tuition, so that the total cost to each student (or cadet, since the University operated as a military school) was reduced about thirty per cent.[55] Consequently, enrollment increased from one hundred eleven in 1875-1876 to one hundred seventy-nine in 1877-1878. During the next five sessions the enrollment figures declined gradually to a low of one hundred fifty-four.[56] Obviously the University was failing to keep pace with the expanding size and interests of the state. Its enrollment was somewhat smaller than that of the Agricultural and Mechanical College at Auburn and not much larger than that of some private institutions. The presidents during the period unfortunately enjoyed very short tenure of office: Carlos G. Smith, 1874-1878; Josiah Gorgas, 1878-1879; Burwell Boykin Lewis, 1880-1885; Henry D. Clayton, 1886-1889. In 1882 the trustees put squarely before the legislature and the people the sad plight and dire need of their institution.[57]

During this same period criticism and sometimes outright opposition faced the University. One source of these attacks was the private colleges, especially Southern University at Greensboro, whose supporters resented the use of public funds in com-

[54] Constitution of 1875, Art. XIII, sec. 9; Acts (1875-76), p. 268.
[55] Report of the Trustees of the University of Alabama [hereinafter cited as University Trustees' Report] (1876), pp. 12-16; ibid. (1876-78), p. 4.
[56] For enrollment figures year by year from 1831 through 1896, see Report of the Joint Committee to Investigate the University (1896), pp. 35-36.
[57] University Trustees' Report (1880-1882), pp. 7-10.

petition with their own institutions.[58] Some critics considered the University too deeply involved in politics, while others accused the school authorities of laxity in handling problems of student discipline.[59] A more justifiable complaint arose from those who were financially unable to pay tuition costs. One newspaper complained that the two state-supported colleges were "as inaccessible as Leipsic, or Heidleburg, to the mass of poor young men."[60]

The leading state newspapers, however, supported the University and pointed out that improvement and progress depended primarily upon increased financial support. The University fund, originally derived from lands donated by Congress, had been set arbitrarily at $300,000 following the mismanagement and loss of the lands during the ante-bellum period. Since 1861, the state had paid eight per cent interest on this sum, totaling $24,000 per year.[61] This amount supplemented by tuition fees, which averaged annually about $2,000, constituted the entire income of the school. Such a sum sufficed only for operating expenses and could not meet the pressing need for an expanded building program.

Immediately after the war, the state had loaned the University $30,000 for the construction of Woods Hall, a building to serve all housing, academic, and administrative needs. In 1878 the legislature canceled this obligation.[62] The University trustees continued to press for more building money, stating that the institution's "growth, progress—yea, usefulness, depend upon the obtaining of more room." Over the strong protests of economy-minded members, the legislature in 1883 appropriated $60,000 to the University for building purposes.[63] Shortly thereafter, as a result of Senator John Tyler Morgan's efforts, Congress granted

[58] Montgomery *Advertiser,* January 11, 14, July 16, 1880; Mobile *Register,* April 2, 1885.

[59] Selma *Southern Argus,* August 2, 1878; Tuskegee *News* quoted in Monroeville *Monroe Journal,* November 6, December 17, 1885; Birmingham *Chronicle,* November 8, 1885.

[60] Huntsville *Advocate,* February 7, 1883.

[61] *Code of 1876,* Sec. 1298.

[62] *Acts* (1878-79), p. 145.

[63] *University Trustees' Report* (1878-80), pp. 4, 12; *Acts* (1882-83), p. 164.

Alabama 46,080 acres of public lands in compensation for the
burning of the University by Federal troops. Sale of these lands
ultimately brought in $90,000, which the legislature specified
should be used for University buildings and equipment.[64] Utilizing both state and Federal grants, the trustees directed the construction of four new buildings, including Clark and Manly
Halls, and such improvements in the others as circulating water,
drainage, and electric lights.[65]

Increased building and larger endowment brought both increased confidence and enrollment to the University. The number of students rose from one hundred sixty-six in 1882-1883 to
two hundred twenty in 1890-91. The trustees found it possible
to eliminate tuition charges for residents of Alabama and substituted instead a contingent fee of $5.00 per year.[66] The Uni-
versity's troubles, however, were far from over. Its presidents
lacked leadership, and the faculty did not come up to ante-bellum
standards. In the decade of the 1890's increased public attention
focused on the difficulties encountered by the institution in obtaining adequate funds. It was pointed out that in its permanent
endowment the University of Alabama stood next to the bottom
on the list of state universities.[67]

Alabama's only two professional schools were connected with
the University. A law school had been established on the Tuscaloosa campus in 1873, but its enrollment remained small, aver-
aging about twenty.[68] Most law students still obtained their legal
education by reading in a lawyer's office. Although the Medical
College of Alabama at Mobile was in theory a part of the University, to all intents and purposes it operated as a private institution. When established in 1859 the school received from the
state an appropriation for building and equipment. The legislature thereafter granted no regular annual appropriation but
only small sums from time to time for upkeep and maintenance.[69]

[64] Owen, *History of Alabama*, II, 1364; *Acts* (1884-85), p. 109.
[65] W. G. Clark, *op. cit.*, pp. 117-123; *University Trustees' Report* (1886-88), pp. 5-17, 29, 32.
[66] *University Trustees' Report* (1886-88), p. 5.
[67] *Appeal from the Alumni of the University of Alabama* (1896), pp. 3-4.
[68] *A Register of the Officers and Students of the University of Alabama* (1901), p. 504.
[69] William H. Brantley, "An Alabama Medical Review," *Alabama Lawyer*,

The school was controlled by a board of trustees separate from that of the University, and graduated a total of 660 students between 1860 and 1892.[70]

AGRICULTURAL AND MECHANICAL COLLEGE

The other state-supported institution of higher learning, the Agricultural and Mechanical College, attracted more attention from the press and the public than did the University. Perhaps this was due to its recent origin or, more probably, to the growing general interest in technical and practical education as opposed to the liberal and classical offerings of the University. The public press, speeches, and writings of the time alluded often to the pressing need for vocational education. One newspaper, after examining the results of higher education in the state, concluded that "the woods are full" of doctors, lawyers, and teachers who could scarcely make a living, but an educated farmer or mechanic was difficult to find.[71]

Alabama in 1868 formally accepted the 240,000 acres of public lands granted by the Federal government under the terms of the Morrill Act to establish agricultural and mechanical colleges. The legislature then accepted from the Methodist Church the East Alabama College building at Auburn, and there in 1872 the Agricultural and Mechanical College opened its doors. The sale of lands ultimately brought in the sum of $253,500, on which the state treasury paid to the college eight per cent annual interest.[72] A board of directors appointed by the governor controlled the institution until the Constitution of 1875 put it under a board of trustees constituted exactly like that of the University.[73]

The history of the Agricultural and Mechanical College before 1890 can be divided rather easily into two distinct periods. The

---

VI (1945), 260-265; *Acts* (1869-70), p. 10; *ibid.* (1882-83), p. 61; *ibid.* (1890-91), p. 758.

[70] W. G. Clark, *op. cit.*, pp. 147-152.

[71] Montgomery *Advertiser*, May 27, 1883. See also Montgomery *Advertiser*, September 5, 1878; Selma *Times-Argus*, July 3, 1885.

[72] *Report of the Board of Trustees of the State Agricultural and Mechanical College* [hereinafter cited as A. *and M. Trustees' Report*] (1880-82), p. 7; Berney, *op. cit.* (1892), pp. 193-195.

[73] *Acts* (1871-72), p. 85; *ibid.* (1878-79), p. 194; *Constitution of 1875*, Art. XIII, sec. 9.

first decade, under the presidency of Isaac Taylor Tichenor, 1872-1882, was an era of uncertainty and experimentation, with quite limited financial support. Interest on the land fund at $20,280 per year constituted the only source of income, and until 1879 this was paid in depreciated state certificates. Until 1876 tuition had to be charged, but in that year the college authorities substituted a $10.00 per year incidental fee for all students. Between the years 1874 and 1882 the enrollment increased from 88 to 122.[74]

The Agricultural and Mechanical College began by offering, in addition to its agricultural courses, a regular classical and liberal curriculum. Such unwelcome competition naturally incurred criticism from the University and from private colleges. Further objection to the curriculum at Auburn came from individuals and groups in the state who felt that the college was failing to carry out its original purpose by not emphasizing technical and practical education. One newspaper condemned the lack of attention given more practical studies when it said: "What we want first are men who understand how to farm on scientific principles or how to open mines, [and] build railroads . . . Technical education is technical education and halfway measures will accomplish little."[75] Discussions in the state agricultural society meetings also illustrated the prevalent dissatisfaction with the school's curriculum.[76]

In 1882 a new period of prosperity for the college began with the presidency of William LeRoy Broun. Less emphasis was placed on classical studies, and only one degree, bachelor of science, was offered. The year 1883 brought an increase in revenue with passage of the fertilizer tag tax, proceeds from which the school shared with the state agricultural department. This additional revenue made possible the establishment of an experiment station at Auburn, and before the end of the decade branch stations had been established at Uniontown, Athens, and Abbeville. Under the Hatch Act of 1888 Alabama received from

[74] A. and M. Trustees' Report (1875-76), p. 3; ibid. (1877-78), pp. 6, 8; ibid. (1880-82), p. 11.

[75] Montgomery Advertiser, May 29, 1885.

[76] Proceedings of the Alabama State Agricultural Society (1885), pp. 98, 102-105, 107, 128.

the Federal government $15,000 annually for the support and improvement of these agricultural experiment stations.[77]

Although the agricultural interests of the state seemed satisfied with the increased revenue for experimentation and instruction in practical farming, other interests began to demand that the college live up to the "Mechanical" part of its name. There was strong sentiment from the industrial regions of northern Alabama for a new school of technology located "where the greatest inducements are offered for practical tests in mining, manufacturing, and industrial products."[78] Upon the recommendation of President Broun, the trustees of the Agricultural and Mechanical College in 1885 established a department of mechanic arts, and this action was hailed by the industrially minded press of the state as a step in the right direction.[79] The legislature signified its approval by appropriating an additional $12,500 to be used specifically for buildings and equipment for the study of sciences "related to agriculture and mechanic arts."[80]

By 1890 the condition of the Agricultural and Mechanical College had noticeably improved since its founding nearly twenty years earlier. Enrollment had increased to a new high of two hundred eighty-four by 1890-1891. Expansion of facilities had been possible with the annual revenue from state and Federal sources, which had increased from about $20,000 in 1874-1875 to about $65,000 in 1890-1891. The legislature also made special appropriations for buildings, and the Second Morrill Act in 1890 increased the income from the Federal government.[81] The influence of the college was making itself felt increasingly in the agricultural and industrial life of the state.

[77] *Acts* (1884-85), p. 144; *ibid.,* (1888-89), p. 1036; *A. and M. Trustees' Report* (1888-90), pp. 55-58; Montgomery *Advertiser,* February 25, 26, 1888.

[78] Robert H. Sterrett [state senator from Jefferson County] to John T. Morgan, February 5, 1887, Morgan Papers. Similar sentiments in Birmingham *Chronicle,* August 16, 1885.

[79] Report of President Broun to Trustees, December 19, 1884, Broun Papers; Montgomery *Advertiser,* June 21, 25, 1885, September 7, 1886; Selma *Times-Argus,* May 29, 1885; *A. and M. Trustees' Report* (1884-86), pp. 23, 35-40.

[80] *Acts* (1886-87), p. 67.

[81] *A. and M. Trustees' Report* (1888-90), pp. 59-62; *ibid.* (1890-92), pp. 9, 17-23.

EVALUATION

The record of the Alabama Democratic government in the field of public education between 1874 and 1890 was progressive only in the sense that the school system expanded from very limited beginnings during the Reconstruction period. Total expenditures for common schools increased from $275,000 in 1870 to $500,000 in 1880 and to $890,000 in 1890. It is true that Alabama's population also increased during this same period, but the state's expenditures for schools per capita of population rose from $ .28 in 1870 to $ .40 in 1880 and to $ .59 in 1890. Between 1870 and 1890 the number of pupils enrolled grew from 68,000 to 201,615 and the average number of school days per year increased from 49 to 73.[82]

The condition of Alabama schools, however, in comparison with those in other parts of the country was poor indeed. In 1890 the state ranked fourth from the bottom in a listing of various school statistics for all states by the Federal commissioner of education. For the United States as a whole in 1890 school expenditures per capita of population were $2.24 and the average number of school days per year was 134.[83] Alabama made but slight improvement in its deplorable illiteracy rate. In 1880 persons over ten years of age who could not read or write constituted 50.9 per cent of Alabama's population. By 1890 this figure had decreased to 41 per cent. The figure for the country as a whole stood at 13.3 per cent in the latter year.[84]

Alabama's poor showing can be attributed to a number of factors. The theory of free public education still did not go unquestioned, and too often were the schools regarded as charitable institutions or "objects of public contempt."[85] Although Democratic leaders supported the cause of public education, their emphasis on strict economy prevented any large expenditures or additional revenue from new forms of taxation. The maintenance of separate schools for Negroes and whites imposed an additional burden on the educational system; by 1890 the

[82] *Report of the Commissioner of Education* (1890), I, 8, 14, 27. For further evidence of improvements in the Alabama schools, see table, p. 154.
[83] *Ibid.*, I, 14, 27.
[84] *Abstract of the Eleventh Census* (1890), pp. 46-49.
[85] Moore, *op. cit.*, p. 547.

government had definitely begun to divert financial support from the Negro to the white schools.

In the state-supported educational institutions beyond the level of the common schools, Alabama's progress was also relative. Between 1875 and 1890 the number of normal schools had increased from four to seven and the annual appropriations, from $9,000 to $25,700. Although the number of Alabama normal schools in 1890 was double the national average per state, the annual appropriation was considerably below the national average of $35,000.[86] The University and the Agricultural and Mechanical College increased both their size and their revenue, but not sufficiently to enable them to equal the standards of similar institutions in other states.

[86] *Report of the Commissioner of Education* (1875), p. 587; *ibid.* (1890), II, 1030-1031.

Penal System

D u r i n g the post-Civil War period Alabama like other Southern states faced new and difficult problems in its penal system. Demands on the system grew with disrupted post-war conditions and an increasing number of petty offenses committed by freed Negroes. Similar offenses formerly had been handled to a large extent by the plantation owners.

The Alabama penitentiary had been opened in 1841 at Wetumpka and had been operated by various lessees until 1862; thereafter the state administered it directly for a four-year period.[1] Since the penitentiary after the War could not accommodate the growing number of convicts, the legislature authorized the leasing of the prisoners beyond the walls. From 1866 until 1872 the penitentiary and all its inmates were leased to Smith and McMillan, a firm that used the convicts largely in railroad building, principally on the South and North line. Between 1872 and 1875 considerable confusion in the penal system existed. About two-thirds of the convicts were leased out and the remainder worked on a state farm adjacent to the penitentiary.[2]

[1] For general surveys of the history of the Alabama penitentiary system, see Malcolm C. Moos, *State Penal Administration*, pp. 1-23; Gladys King, "History of the Alabama Convict Department" (unpublished M. A. thesis, Alabama Polytechnic Institute, 1937).

[2] Governor's Message, *Senate Journal* (1882-83), pp. 112-115; Berney, *op. cit.* (1892 ed.), pp. 254-266.

After their election in 1874, the Democrats continued the lease system but determined to make it a financial asset rather than the liability it had been ever since the war. The new warden and a legislative investigating committee in 1875 reported financial irregularities and almost complete destitution at the penitentiary.[3] During the next fifteen years the system of handling the convicts changed considerably, resulting in growing financial returns to the state and some improvements in the condition of the prisoners themselves.

ORGANIZATION AND ADMINISTRATION

The Democrats did not immediately alter the system of managing penitentiary affairs but left them in the hands of the warden under lax and infrequent supervision by three penitentiary inspectors. The Code of 1876 contained some regulatory provisions based on the outmoded system of leasing the penitentiary as a unit.[4] The legislature in 1875 provided funds for the destitute institution and reduced the annual salary of the warden from $3,000 to $2,000.[5] Governor Houston in March, 1875, appointed J. G. Bass warden. During the next six years the new appointee steadily increased the revenue derived from convict labor and thereby won the high praise of legislative investigating committees.[6] The committees, however, failed to inspect any of the places where leased convicts worked, and the legislature eliminated the requirement of stationing a penitentiary officer at such places.[7] In spite of reports from the inspectors that prisoners were "well cared for and humanely treated," criticism of Warden Bass's administration began to grow.

A serious disagreement between Governor Cobb and the warden over terms of some convict leases focused attention on the penal problem and led the governor in 1881 to appoint a new warden, John Hollis Bankhead. A law approved in 1879 had

[3] *Annual Report of the Inspectors of the Alabama Penitentiary* [hereinafter cited as *Inspectors' Report*] (1875), p. 3; Penitentiary Committee Report, *Senate Journal* (1874-75), pp. 220-229.
[4] *Code of 1876*, Secs. 4513-4557.
[5] *Acts* (1874-75), p. 162; *ibid.* (1875-76), p. 285.
[6] *House Journal* (1876-77), pp. 323-328; *ibid.* (1878-79), pp. 498-500; *Senate Journal* (1875-76), pp. 301-304.
[7] *Acts* (1875-76), p. 179.

transferred the power of appointing inspectors from the legislature to the governor.[8] A legislative investigating committee in 1881 recommended sweeping changes in the penal system, including the reduction of the "almost supreme and exclusive control" exercised by the warden; one committee member stated, "The present convict system is a blot upon the civilization of this century and a shame upon the State of Alabama."[9]

By 1882 it was clear that an over-all revision of the penal system was necessary. Governor Cobb, just before leaving office in that year, summarized for the legislature the history of the penitentiary, the criticisms leveled at existing practices, and the urgent need for remedial legislation. "From the beginning," he said, "it [penitentiary] has been an utter failure as a reformatory institution; and contrary to the intention of its founders, it has been made a means of punishment more terrible than that it was intended to modify."[10] The leading newspapers likewise emphasized the importance of the question and the necessity of the legislature's taking some steps to correct the flagrant abuses.[11]

Warden Bankhead had worked out a lengthy and detailed plan eliminating the worst abuses of the lease system, many of which resulted from the fact that the warden and inspectors had no power to enforce regulations outside the penitentiary walls. He suggested abandoning completely the penitentiary at Wetumpka and concentrating all convicts in a new prison at some coal mine where they could be supervised directly by the warden and physician.[12] Neither the inspector nor Governor Cobb, however, supported Bankhead's proposal. Cobb argued that such a plan would exclude all competition for the hire of convict labor and would vest so much power in the hands of the

[8] *Ibid.* (1878-79), p. 42.

[9] *Report of the Joint Committee to Enquire into the Treatment of Convicts* [hereinafter cited as *Convict Committee Report*] (1881), pp. 5-8; Jacksonville *Republican* quoted in the Huntsville *Gazette*, September 3, 1881.

[10] Governor's Message, *Senate Journal* (1882-83), p. 126.

[11] Montgomery *Advertiser*, November 14, 1882; Mobile *Register*, December 2, 1882.

[12] *Inspectors' Report* (1882), pp. 3-5, 22; Montgomery *Advertiser*, September 24, 1882.

warden and the sole contractor that they could dictate terms of hire.[13]

The legislature of 1882-83 considered Bankhead's proposal but failed to adopt all of his ideas. It enacted a comprehensive convict law which stipulated that the warden should reside wherever the largest number of convicts were employed, but did not call for the complete abandonment of the Wetumpka establishment. Following Governor Cobb's recommendations, the act provided more stringent regulatory laws and better means of enforcing them, thus for the first time revising the penal code in the light of the existing lease system. The governor was given authority to appoint the warden, three inspectors, and the physician, and could suspend them at will. The warden and inspectors were to adopt rules guaranteeing humane treatment of convicts, and every place of confinement had to be visited by one inspector at least once every week. The salary of each inspector was increased from $200 to $1,000 per year plus expenses, and that of the physician was set at $1,500 per year. The real "teeth" for enforcing these new regulations was the requirement that all contracts must contain a provision whereby the governor might terminate the agreement for any cause at any time. The warden also had the power to dismiss any guard whom he considered negligent or cruel.[14]

In the next legislature Warden Bankhead repeated his recommendation that all convicts along with the entire penitentiary should be transferred to Pratt Mines. The inspectors, Reginald Heber Dawson, William D. Lee, and Albert J. Henly, urged a number of changes, most of which would increase their power and limit that of the warden, especially over financial and contractual matters. They implied that there was little need for a state-paid warden when practically all convicts were worked by one lessee.[15] The legislature adopted most of the inspector's suggestions. The convict law of 1885, in addition to elaborating on lease procedures, abolished the office of warden and transferred

[13] Governor's Message, *Senate Journal* (1882-83), pp. 128-129; *Inspectors' Report* (1882), p. 6.

[14] *Acts* (1882-83), p. 134.

[15] *Inspectors' Report* (1884), pp. 33-35, 67-69; Governor's Message, *Senate Journal* (1884-85), pp. 17-18.

his duties to the penitentiary inspectors, renamed the Board of Inspectors of Convicts. Salaries of inspectors were increased to $1,800 for the president and $1,500 for associates, and a clerk was provided at a salary of $1,000.[16]

The acts of 1883 and 1885 extended the authority of the convict inspectors over convicts leased out by the counties. Immediately after the Civil War, in an effort to relieve the pressure on the penitentiary, the legislature had established a system of hard labor for the county. Only convicts with sentences of two years or more had to be sent to the penitentiary; when the sentence was less than two years, the convict was usually leased out by the county in which convicted.[17] Since revenue from such leases went directly to the county treasury, judges and county commissioners employed every device to prevent as many of the able-bodied prisoners as possible from going to the penitentiary. In 1886 there were 904 convicts at labor for counties as compared with 659 state convicts.[18] A large percentage of the county convicts were leased to individulas or firms far removed from the county of conviction; consequently, it was practically impossible for the county commissioners to supervise their treatment adequately. County officials and contractors kept such poor records, sometimes none at all, that prisoners were known to have been worked for months or even years after the expiration of their sentences.[19]

Governors, investigating committees, and prison inspectors had consistently advocated sending all felons to the state penitentiary, irrespective of the length of sentence. Although the legislature failed to adopt this regulation, revelations of horrible conditions among leased county convicts forced the members to take some action. The 1883 penal law greatly improved the system of keeping records on leased county convicts and provided for quarterly inspection by the state inspectors. For the first time the inspectors' report in 1884 carried lists of county con-

[16] *Acts* (1884-85), p. 187.

[17] *Penal Code of 1866*, Secs. 217-234; *Acts* (1875-76), p. 287.

[18] *Inspectors' Report* (1882), p. 23; *ibid.* (1884), pp. 48-49; *ibid.* (1886), p. 227.

[19] *Ibid.* (1884), pp. 51-53; *ibid.* (1886), p. 23; W. H. Bankhead to Robert McKee, April 16, 1882, McKee Papers.

victs and their location. At the same time, the inspectors pointed out that they still had no means of enforcing their recommendations concerning county convicts.[20] The 1885 law remedied this defect only partially by providing for more frequent inspections; the inspectors in 1886 reported once again that they were held accountable for bad conditions but were given no power to correct them.[21]

The Code of 1886 inaugurated the most significant changes in the county convict system. It gave the inspectors some real authority by providing that the governor could order a probate judge to remove convicts from a lessee when the inspectors reported conditions unsatisfactory. It also applied all state laws and inspectors' rules to county as well as state convicts "except as otherwise provided by law." Finally, it forbade working for any county a prisoner whose combined sentences aggregated more than two years. Three years later the legislature authorized the inspectors to classify and task county convicts just as they did state prisoners.[22] By the end of the decade of the 1880's, county convicts were far better off than they had been ten years earlier, but they still were not so strictly supervised as those from the penitentiary. The total number of county convicts decreased from 904 in 1886 to 654 in 1890.[23]

By 1886 the organization of the Alabama penal system had been stabilized. Although numerous alterations were made later, the general plan remained the same until the end of the lease system in 1928. The almost constant presence of inspectors at places where large numbers of leased convicts worked gave Alabama convicts somewhat better supervision than those in other convict-leasing states.

CONVICT LEASING

The system of hiring out convicts to be worked by lessees came naturally to the post-war Southern states, which were unable to handle in the penitentiary the growing number of offenders and at the same time were anxious to obtain increased

[20] *Inspectors' Report* (1884), p. 54.
[21] *Ibid.* (1886), pp. 24-25.
[22] *Code of 1886*, Secs. 4585, 4588, 4591, 4658; *Acts* (1888-89), p. 47.
[23] *Inspectors' Report* (1886), p. 227; *ibid.* (1890), p. 223.

revenue.[24] Until the 1880's leasing arrangements in Alabama were made by the penitentiary warden subject to the approval of the governor. Warden J. G. Bass, who took office in 1875, leased about one third of the convicts to three coal and iron companies; the remainder were leased to six or eight planters or worked on a branch railroad being built to the Wetumpka penitentiary. The monthly price paid by the lessees was $5 for the better workers and $2.50 for the poorer.[25]

During the last half of the 1870's the revenue from convict labor climbed steadily. At the end of the fiscal year, 1877, the warden turned over $14,000 to the state treasury. In 1880 the penitentiary earned $27,000 and required only $7,790 for expenses.[26] For his work in transforming the penitentiary from a liability into a profitable state agency, Warden Bass received the unqualified approbation of Governor Houston and a large part of the Democratic press.[27]

Some criticism, however, arose over the warden's methods of keeping prison records and financial accounts. In 1879 Governor Cobb began to doubt whether the leases arranged by Bass were the most profitable that the state could obtain. Cobb pointed out that the increased penitentiary income had resulted not from more favorable contracts but from improved accounting procedures and the rapid rise in the number of prisoners sent to the penitentiary.[28] Between 1874 and 1877 the penitentiary population almost trebled; this increase consisted almost entirely of Negroes, who made up 78 per cent of the total in 1871, 88 per cent in 1874, and 91 per cent in 1877.[29]

Since the warden and lessees seemed unwilling to negotiate new contracts, Governor Cobb threatened to advertise for bids

[24] George W. Cable, "The Convict Lease System in the Southern States," *Century Magazine*, XXVII (1884), 582-599.
[25] *Inspectors' Report* (1875), pp. 3-6; *ibid.* (1876), pp. 3-5; *ibid.* (1877), pp. 3-4; *ibid.* (1880), pp. 6-17.
[26] Governor's Message, *Senate Journal* (1882-83), pp. 121-126. See table, p. 180.
[27] Governor's Message, *Senate Journal* (1878-79), pp. 27 28; Montgomery *Advertiser*, July 18, 1876, November 9, 1880.
[28] Governor's Message, *Senate Journal* (1882-83), pp. 123-124; J. W. DuBose, *op. cit.*, p. 1366.
[29] John T. Milner, *A Review of the Convict Situation in Alabama* p. 7. See table, p. 180.

on leasing the entire penitentiary, as he was permitted to do under the law. The Governor withdrew his threat only after most of the contractors agreed to accept new terms calling for an increase of one dollar per month per convict and the maintenance of "dead-heads," who had formerly remained at the penitentiary. Although no contracts were made under this agreement, Warden Bass did negotiate new contracts effective February 1, 1881, providing for $8 per month for first-class hands.[30]

Warden Bankhead, after his appointment in 1881, successfully pushed through the courts action to nullify the contracts made by his predecessor. Under new contracts, lessees paid $12 per month for first-class hands in the mines and $10 for those on farms, thereby increasing considerably the state's revenue from leasing. After the enactment of the revised penal legislation in 1883, another new set of lease contracts were negotiated. These sent four hundred of the approximately five hundred fifty convicts to the mines, with the remainder divided between J. F. B. Jackson's rock quarry in Blount County and Thomas Williams' plantation near Wetumpka.[31] The 1883 act prohibited the hiring of more than two hundred convicts to any one contractor. Thus, only two hundred were leased directly to the Pratt Coal Company and the other two hundred went to Comer and McCurdy, operators for some of the Pratt mines. Critics considered this arrangement an ill-concealed attempt to circumvent the law; in effect it concentrated practically all convicts in one place just as Warden Bankhead desired.[32]

After March 1, 1885, R. H. Dawson, president of the convict inspectors, replaced Warden Bankhead as the chief leasing authority. He agreed with Bankhead that living and working conditions of the convicts could best be supervised with as many of the leased prisoners as possible concentrated in one place.[33]

---

[30] Governor's Message, *Senate Journal* (1882-83), p. 124. The controversy provoked some accusations that Cobb himself had a personal interest in convict leasing. Selma *Southern Argus*, September 26, 1879; Montgomery *Advertiser*, June 5, September 6, 1879.

[31] *Inspectors' Report* (1882), pp. 12-13; *ibid.* (1884), p. 6.

[32] *Acts* (1882-83), p. 134; Montgomery *Advertiser*, May 27, 1883; *Testimony Before the Joint Committee . . . to Examine Into the Convict System* [hereinafter cited as *Convict Committee Testimony*] (1889), p. 75.

[33] Open letter by Dawson in Montgomery *Advertiser*, February 16, 1887.

The Code of 1886 facilitated this concentration by eliminating the maximum of two hundred and substituting a minimum of one hundred state or county convicts that could be leased to any one contractor.[34]

The five-year lease with the Pratt Mines ran until the end of 1887. In 1885 contracts with two planters near Wetumpka were renewed, also to run until the end of 1887. After July, 1887, when J. F. B. Jackson gave up his contract to work convicts at the stone quarry in Blount County, all state convicts were located either at the Pratt Mines or on the two plantations. In January, 1888, after receiving ten bids, primarily from mining companies, the inspectors awarded an exclusive ten-year contract to the Tennessee Coal Iron and Railroad Company, which had taken over the Pratt Mines. Under the lease terms the company was to take all male convicts able to work and was to pay the state for each between $9.00 and $18.50 per month, depending on the convict's classification.[35]

Loud protests from other bidders stirred up so much feeling that the legislature appointed a joint committee to investigate the whole matter. John T. Milner and other mine owners accused the Tennessee Company of reaching a prior understanding with the inspectors as to how the bids should be made. After hearing lengthly testimony, the legislative committee decided that the bid of the Tennessee Company had not been the highest, that the company had not accepted all of the convicts for whom it had contracted, and that the governor should exercise his power to nullify the contract.[36] Governor Seay did not follow this recommendation, however, because the Tennessee Company promised to make the required changes in the contract. Although all of these changes were never made, the contract remained in effect. In September, 1890, the Tennessee Company worked at the Pratt Mines 801 of the 1123 state convicts. The remainder of the convicts, who were unfit for hard work, were kept at the penitentiary in Wetumpka and sometimes leased to

[34] *Code of 1886*, Secs. 4641-4649.
[35] *Inspectors' Report* (1888), pp. 1-3, 251; Montgomery *Advertiser*, January 4, 1888.
[36] Convict Committee Report, *House Journal* (1888-89), pp. 463-470; *Convict Committee Testimony* (1889), pp. 38-39, 45, *passim*.

nearby planters for day labor or worked on a share basis on Thomas Williams' plantation.[37]

Leasing arrangements for county convicts became more standardized during the 1880's with a growing tendency for a few concerns to monopolize most of them. In 1882 John Milner and Comer and McCurdy were the only mine operators using county convicts, and they divided between themselves the counties willing to lease prisoners for mining. After Milner sold his Coalburg property to Sloss Iron and Steel Company, that concern was added to the pooling arrangement.[38] Of all county convicts leased in 1888 and 1890, about seventy-eight per cent went to the mining companies. When Milner gave up his leasing contract in November, 1889, the Tennessee Company and the Sloss Company divided the county convicts. Of the forty-one counties leasing convicts, only eight worked them exclusively within the county; these included Jefferson County, which after 1887 worked all of its convicts on the public roads.[39] Monthly returns from county convicts averaged $8.09 per convict, considerably less than the returns from state convicts because the short terms of the former prevented them from becoming skilled workers.[40]

By 1890 the State of Alabama's business of leasing convicts had grown to sizeable proportions although not nearly so large or remunerative as it was to become in later years. Between 1875 and 1890 the total number of state convicts increased from 368 to 1,123, and the revenue from leasing grew even more. As indicated on the accompanying table, the average amount per convict derived from leasing during the two-year period, 1875-1877, was $30.53; between 1888 and 1890 the average was $164.26. For the fiscal year ending in 1890 the returns to the state from the penitentiary system amounted to $111,133, or about six per cent of Alabama's total revenue. The expense of

[37] *Inspectors' Report* (1890), pp. 1-2, 160-197; *ibid.* (1888), pp. 12-14, 21; *Convict Committee Testimony* (1889), pp. 5-7.

[38] Convict Committee Report, *House Journal* (1888-89), pp. 459-461; *Convict Committee Testimony* (1889), pp. 11, 35; *Inspectors' Report* (1884), p. 131.

[39] *Convict Committee Testimony* (1889), pp. 130-132; *Inspectors' Report* (1890), pp. 198-223; *Acts* (1886-87), p. 818.

[40] *Inspectors' Report* (1888), p. 258.

STATE CONVICTS *

Year	Total number	Statistics as of September 30 Leased to:			Statistics for period ending September 30		
		Farming	Mining	Others	Deaths	Annual percentages of deaths°	Revenue deposited in state treasury
1868	294				93x	18.0	
1869	263				43‡	17.0	
1870	180	25			92‡	41.0	
1871	182			131z	26‡	14.0	
1872			(Figures not available)				
1873	172	50	50		20†	—	
1874	238	131	48		13‡	6.0	
1875	368	200	83		23‡	7.5	
1878	654	393	(not given)		20‡	4.4	$ 6,000‡
1877	655		155	60	45‡	7.5	14,000‡
1876	520		(not given)		18‡	3.0	16,000‡
1880	540	317	139	40	60x	5.0	45,000x
1882	522	239	151	84	61x	6.0	50,029x
1884	527	86	349	63	63x	6.0	54,238x
1886	659	116	358	66	48x	4.5	88,901x
1888	740		596		68x	5.4	103,332x
1890	1123		801		99x	5.2	184,471x

* Information from *Convict Inspectors' Reports*.
z Used primarily in railroad construction.
° Based on average number of state convicts.
x Two years   ‡ One year   † Seven months.

operating the system, including payment of court costs, came to $74,656, thereby leaving a net profit of $36,477.[41] A financial survey of penitentiary systems in the United States in 1886 showed that Alabama's net earnings were far larger than those of any other state reporting.[42]

CONVICT CONDITIONS

Since the principal motive behind the lease system was that of profit, it was almost inevitable that the welfare of the convict would be overlooked in the drive to exploit him. Indeed, many people, believing in retributive justice rather than penological reform, felt that the convicts were treated no worse than they deserved.[43] Nevertheless from time to time the working and living conditions of Alabama convicts came in for the usual exposes that led to some more or less temporary improvements. Although the leased state convicts probably suffered less after 1874 than they had in railroad building under the Smith and McMillan lease, conditions were still terrible.

Warden Bass, in his determination to make the penal system profitable, seems either to have permitted or ignored many abuses. Robert McKee, who investigated closely the convict situation for Governor Cobb, stated that Bass seemed never to have heard of the "gross and flagrant abuses of convicts during his six years' service," and that the inspectors either did not think at all or were too innocent to suspect anything that they did not actually see.[44] Another observer reported that in 1878 the penal system was in a chaotic condition, and that the laws for the protection of leased convicts were poorly executed.[45]

The legislative committee in 1881 made an unusually thorough inspection of the leased convicts and revealed conditions in the coal mines that bore out some of the accusations made by critics of leasing practices. The committee members pointed to inci-

[41] *Auditor's Report* (1890), pp. 21, 44-56.
[42] *Inspectors' Report* (1886), pp. 88-89.
[43] Hilda Jane Zimmerman, "Penal Systems and Penal Reforms in the South Since the Civil War" (unpublished Ph.D. thesis, University of North Carolina, 1947), p. 171.
[44] Article under pen name, "Guian," in Montgomery *Advertiser*, March 2, 1882.
[45] J. W. DuBose, *op. cit.*, p. 1224.

dents of brutal treatment and neglect without specifically nam-
ing the contractors involved. At one mine three convicts had
been subjected to the "water punishment," which the committee
denounced as cruel, dangerous, and contrary to law. In another
instance a contractor was charged with beating to death a convict who had attempted to escape. In some prisons the committee found no water closets or privies for night use; the
convicts were all chained together during the entire night. Testimony before the committee revealed other instances of cruelty
and neglect such as allowing blood hounds to bite an escapee.
The usual punishment seemed to be whipping with from five
to forty lashes.[46]

Warden Bankhead, after his appointment on March 1, 1881,
determined to expose conditions among the leased miners in
order to strengthen his arguments for negotiating new leases. He
requested Dr. John Brown Gaston, president of the Alabama
Medical Association, and Dr. Jerome Cochran, state health officer, to conduct an inspection of convicts working in coal mines.
They strongly condemned the unsanitary conditions at Coketon
and New Castle, repeatedly referring to the convict miners'
bedding and clothing as "filthy and disgusting." Bathing
facilities were far from adequate. They also condemned the
excessive use of shackles. Dr. Gaston contrasted Alabama's penitentiary death rate over the preceding nine years, 8.3 per cent,
with the average in Northern states of a little over 1 per cent.
He condemned the leasing system for its "neglect . . . bad
sanitary conditions in clothing, quarters and food, excessive tasks
and the punishment necessary to enforce them, unnecessary
restraint of body, chaining and packing hard-worked men to
bed like sardines in a box."[47]

A violent controversy between Dr. Gaston and John T. Milner, owner of New Castle Mines, grew out of this report. Milner
published a lengthly reply entitled *A Review of the Convict
Situation in Alabama;* it vehemently denied all of Dr. Gaston's

---

[46] *Convict Committee Report* (1881), pp. 3-5; *Testimony Taken by the
Joint Special Committee to Inquire into the Condition and Treatment of
Convicts* (1881), pp. 5-6, 9 and *passim.*

[47] *Transactions of the Medical Association of the State of Alabama* (1882),
pp. 19-21, 196-204.

accusations. Dr. Gaston in turn published a rejoinder defending himself from the charge of disloyalty to Alabama and reiterating his charges of "injustice, cruelty and misery endured by the convicts."[48] Both the inspectors and the warden now joined in and roundly condemned the lack of sanitation and the cruel treatment of convicts in mines and on railroads. Bankhead described the prisons as completely inadequate in size and ventilation. "They were," he said, "as filthy . . . as dirt could make them, and both prisons and prisoners were infested with vermin. . . . . I found that convicts were excessively, and in some instances, cruelly punished; that they were poorly clothed and fed."[49]

The new leases in 1883, which did not include any of Milner's mines but concentrated the convicts at Pratt mines, were supposed to bring about improved conditions by making supervision easier. For a while, however, conditions failed to improve. The inspectors described the prisons as inadequate, food as insufficient and of poor quality, and cited a number of instances of cruel treatment. A mortality rate of seven per cent at the mines during 1883 led Governor O'Neal to request the state health officer to make a personal inspection. This official attributed the high death rate to unsanitary conditions and lack of hospital facilities.[50] In December, 1883, Governor O'Neal wrote Warden Bankhead that he still did not consider conditions at Pratt Mines satisfactory and requested the Warden to enforce all regulations more strictly.[51]

By 1884 the condition of all state convicts had noticeably improved. The contractors at Pratt Mines and at the quarry in Blount County built new prisons or remodeled old ones under the direction of the warden and inspectors. The reports of state officials, as well as the press, acknowledged these as changes for the better.[52] The state health officer, Dr. Cochran, stated that they constituted virtually a revolution. He added:

[48] Montgomery *Advertiser*, January 28, February 4, 1883.
[49] *Inspectors' Report* (1882),pp. 3-5, 13-15; Mobile *Register*, November 23, 1882; New York *Tribune*, February 3, 1883.
[50] *Inspectors' Report* (1884), pp. 21-28, 247-253; Montgomery *Advertiser*, August 5, 8, 9, 1883.
[51] E. A. O'Neal to John H. Bankhead, December 17, 1883, McKee Papers.
[52] Montgomery *Advertiser*, March 16, October 18, 1884; *Inspectors' Report* (1884), pp. 24, 29, 72-75.

> I do not desire to be understood as holding that our con-
> vict prisons and our methods of prison management are
> all what they ought to be. Far from it. Two years ago they
> were deplorable indeed. Now, with all the improvements
> that have been made, they are barely tolerable, and addi-
> tional ameliorations are still urgently needed.[53]

Under the close supervision of President R. H. Dawson and
his associate convict inspectors, the living conditions of the state
convicts at Pratt Mines continued to improve during the latter
part of the 1880's. By 1890 the Tennesseee Company had built
two completely new prisons, ordered and planned by the inspectors to accommodate adequately the large number of convicts concentrated at these mines. These new prisons were
described as "the best ever built by any contractor in the
South."[54] After an examination of the Pratt Mines in 1890, State
Health Officer Cochran wrote:

> I am not writing a panagyric of these prisons, but am sim-
> ply stating the facts as they have come to my knowledge
> . . . . I want to say as plainly and as emphatically as I can
> that Alabama convicts are not badly treated. . . . When I
> say that the changes for the better have been immense I
> am not using too strong a word. . . . [55]

One of the most troublesome problems connected with convict
mining was the amount of work for which each should be held
responsible. Under the task system each convict was classified
according to his ability and then held responsible for performing
the daily labor specified for his particular class. Regulations
adopted in 1883 required state officials to classify the convicts
according to their skill and ability as miners, not according to
their general physical condition. In the 1888 contracts President
Dawson succeeded in reducing the task of first-class men from
five tons to four tons of coal per day, second-class from four to
three tons, third-class from three tons to two tons, and fourth-
class ("dead heads") from two tons to one ton.[56] If a convict
failed to perform his assigned task, he could be punished by a
flogging administered according to the rules laid down by the

---

[53] *Inspectors' Report* (1884), p. 277.
[54] *Ibid.* (1890), p. 10.
[55] *Ibid.*, pp. 235-237.
[56] Convict Committee Report, *House Journal* (1888-89), p. 468.

inspectors. If he finished his task ahead of time, he could work on his own and would be paid at the same rate as free miners.[57]

Conditions among leased county convicts were much worse than those among state prisoners. Previous to 1883, however, few of the facts came to light because county prisoners were not under the jurisdiction of the inspectors. The 1881 investigating committee exposed appalling conditions among county convicts and urged supervision by the penitentiary inspectors.[58] After 1886 county convicts leased outside the county of conviction were supposed to be under the same regulations and to receive the same treatment as state convicts. The inspectors, nevertheless, found it quite difficult to check on the widely scattered contractors. Public attention was focused on this problem in 1886 when a contractor in Hillsboro whipped a Negro county convict so severely that he died. The Negro had complained of being sick, would not work, and was punished with about one hundred lashes on the bare skin, all in the course of one afternoon.[59]

In 1886 President Dawson published a new set of rules for the treatment of all leased convicts. These covered such subjects as living accommodations, food and clothing to be furnished by the contractors, appointment and conduct of guards, and the imposition of punishments. The rules strictly limited to fifteen lashes a whipping for any offense except attempt to escape, and provided that no convict could be whipped on the bare skin nor more than once on the same day. Alabama and Texas were the only Southern states to limit by law the imposition of punishment.[60] Another evil that Dawson sought to abolish was the immorality resulting from the leasing of women convicts. Although penitentiary officials and contractors denied any knowledge of the situation, testimony taken in 1888 indicated that considerable immorality and cohabitation existed between men and women convicts working on the farms. Consequently the governor and warden agreed that women should not be included

[57] *Inspectors' Report* (1890), pp. 238-239.
[58] *Convict Committee Report* (1881), pp. 6-7.
[59] *Inspectors' Report* (1886), pp. 328-347; Montgomery *Advertiser*, August 7, 1886.
[60] *Rules and Regulations for the Government of the Convict System of Alabama* (1886), *passim;* Blake McKelvey, *American Prisons*, p. 183.

in the lease contracts for 1888. Instead they were kept at the penitentiary, which held seventy-two women convicts in 1890.[61]

In spite of the efforts and accomplishments of inspectors, the fundamental principle of working convicts in the mines still left much to be desired. In 1890 the annual death rate of convict miners stood as follows: 16 per cent at Coalburg, 11 per cent at New Castle, and 6.5 per cent at Pratt.[62] This showed an excessive mortality at the first two mines, worked by county convicts, and was attributed by the penitentiary physician to the fact that most counties sent all leased prisoners to the mines regardless of their physical condition. The deaths at Pratt, worked largely by state convicts, were well above normal. Since the sanitary precautions at Pratt were supposed to be the very best, the physicians and inspectors were at a loss to explain these figures except on the basis of the unhealthfulness and hazards of mining under any condition and the generally unhealthy condition of Negroes when received.[63]

CRITICISM AND REFORM

Criticisms of the lease system and efforts to remove convicts from the mines recurred from time to time during the 1880's. Opposition political parties or independents consistently made political capital out of the convict question by attacking the Democrats for continuing the lease system. Both the Republican and Greenback platforms contained plans denouncing it.[64] and a Negro Republican newspaper asked: "Why should convicts be hired to rich corporations . . .? Are not the great coal mines, which keep coal up at high and extortionate prices able to hire and pay full prices to laborers?"[65] The most consistent anti-Democratic newspaper dedicated itself to the abrogation of the "inhuman, barbarous and vicious convict labor system which now disgraces our State."[66]

[61] *Convict Committee Testimony* (1889), pp. 62-63, 123-127; *Inspectors' Report* (1890), p. 24.
[62] *Inspectors' Report* (1890), pp. 261-262.
[63] *Ibid.*, pp. 262-265, 362-363.
[64] Montgomery *Advertiser*, July 7, August 25, 1878, June 7, 1880, July 7, 1882, July 17, 1886.
[65] Huntsville *Gazette*, February 25, March 11, 1882.
[66] Huntsville *Advocate*, February 1, 1884.

Some Democrats strongly opposed the lease idea, especially where it involved working convicts in the mines. Typical was Frank A. Hall, representative from Montgomery, who bitterly denounced the system in the legislature.[67] In 1884 A. A. Coleman was elected to the legislature from Hale County on a platform calling for penal reform. He unsuccessfully sponsored a bill to prohibit the working of convicts in mines or on railroads.[68] Some denounced the control exercised over penal affairs by a group of lessees usually referred to as the "penitentiary ring." Robert McKee, secretary to the governor, said of the 1883 legislation aimed at concentrating the convicts in one mining establishment, "The ring have shaped, moulded, framed the legislation of the session just closed. . . . "[69]

The Democratic press varied in its attitude, never openly approving the lease system, and sometimes strongly denouncing it. The Montgomery *Dispatch* called it "a shame, a disgrace to the civilization of the age in which we live."[70] Up until about 1886 the Montgomery *Advertiser* mildly opposed working convicts in the mines, but by 1889 seemed convinced that Alabama's penal system was about as good as could be devised.[71] One newspaper reflected general Democratic feeling when it opposed leasing but countenanced it as a necessary evil.[72]

By far the strongest opposition, newspaper or otherwise, came from the Birmingham district. Organized opposition began about 1885 with the establishment of the Anti-convict League, a group dedicated to publicizing the evils of the leasing system. The League pointed out that convict labor gave the mine owners decided advantages in keeping free wages at a minimum and breaking strike threats. It also argued that the very presence of convicts (mostly Negroes) in the mines seriously handicapped any efforts to encourage white immigration.[73] "The State," said

[67] Montgomery *Advertiser*, February 20, 24, 1883.
[68] J. W. DuBose, *op. cit.*, p. 1382; *House Journal* (1884-85), p. 957; Tuskegee *News* quoted in Mobile *Register*, March 28, 1885.
[69] McKee to Thomas R. Roulhac, February 25, 1883, McKee Papers.
[70] February 27, 1886.
[71] September 9, October 18, 1883, February 4, 1885, February 15, July 6, 1889.
[72] Huntsville *Democrat*, January 13, 1886.
[73] Montgomery *Advertiser*, August 4, 1885; Selma *Times*, July 21, 1885; Birmingham *Chronicle*, July 19, August 2, 23, September 6, 1885.

one Birmingham newspaper, "has made Birmingham the dump-
ing ground for crime . . . the Botany Bay of the Common-
wealth." Representatives from Jefferson County repeatedly but
unsuccessfully sponsored in the legislature measures either to
abolish the lease system or to modify its operation.[74]

In spite of considerable criticism and opposition, the lease
system remained. One reason for its continuation lay in the
difficulty of agreeing on any other plan that would cause as
little trouble or produce as large a profit for the government.
The alternative most frequently suggested involved some method
of working convicts on the public roads. It was said, however,
that such a plan would be impracticable and that the conditions
in the road camps would be far worse than in the mines. Indeed, the two counties, Jefferson and Madison, trying this plan
had not achieved particularly good results.[75] Another proposal,
frequently suggested, would have established some sort of manufacturing plant where all convicts would have been worked on
the state's account. Inspector W. D. Lee recommended such a
step, and Governor Thomas G. Jones actually began the movement that resulted some years later in the establishment of a
cotton mill at Speigner. This plan, however, called forth protests from both labor and the small business men.[76]

By the late 1880's the press, public, and most governmental
officials believed that fundamentally the lease system was bad
and that events were moving toward its elimination. "Sooner or
later," said the penitentiary inspectors, "public opinion and
the real interest of the State will force us to abandon the Lease
System."[77] In the meantime those interested in the penal problem concentrated their efforts on reforms within the lease system
as it existed. In 1885 a storm of protest greeted a proposal to
renew the use of convict labor in railway building. Inspector

[74] Birmingham *News* quoted in Montgomery *Advertiser*, January 25, 1889;
House Journal (1874-75), pp. 342, 389-390; *ibid.* (1884-85), p. 866; Montgomery *Advertiser*, November 20, 25, 1886.

[75] Montgomery *Advertiser*, August 17, 1889; Mobile *Register*, November
3, 1886; Birmingham *Chronicle*, August 9, 1885; Huntsville *Advocate*,
July 24, 1878; *Inspectors' Report* (1886), p. 29; *ibid.* (1888), pp. 26-34.

[76] *Inspectors' Report* (1890), p. 69; Montgomery *Advertiser*, March 13,
1886.

[77] *Inspectors' Report* (1888), p. 20; *ibid.* (1890), pp. 35-36.

Dawson declared that no state convict would ever work in a "railroad camp death hole," and the Code of 1886 specifically prohibited the working of any convicts on railroads.[78]

One of the reforms most often advocated was the separation of long-term, hardened criminals from first offenders and young, short-term prisoners. Inspectors and governors continued to urge that all felons be sent to the penitentiary and that misdemeanants be kept in the county of conviction.[79] The legislature in 1885 prohibited working in mines any misdemeanants convicted of offences not involving moral turpitude, but the Code of 1886 altered this law to prohibit merely the working together of felons and misdemeanants convicted of crimes not involving moral turpitude.[80] The legislature discussed but failed to adopt proposals to keep misdemeanants out of the mines. It did require all contractors to return released convicts to the county of conviction.[81]

Julia Tutwiler, Alabama's famous crusader, took an active interest in improving the conditions of leased convicts. "The entire abolition of hiring the convicts to contractors," she said, "is the most needed reform; but it seems hopeless to attempt this in the present state of public opinion."[82] In concentrating on reforms within the system, she advocated a separate prison for women and a reformatory for young boys, who she felt should not be associated with the hardened criminals in the mines. She also pushed the idea of furnishing schooling for the convicts while in prison. "Punishment for crime," she said, "is one great end to be accomplished by the execution of law, but the prevention of future crime, by the reformation of the criminal, is another and no less important."[83] Thanks to her efforts, the legislature in 1887 provided for the instruction of convicts at

---

[78] Mobile *Register*, March 14, 1885; Selma *Times-Argus*, March 13, 1885; Birmingham *Chronicle*, January 27, February 1, 1885; *Code of 1886*, Sec. 4657.

[79] Governor's Message, *Senate Journal* (1888-89), p. 21; *ibid.* (1890-91), pp. 28, 273; *Inspectors' Report* (1886), p. 28; *ibid.* (1888)), p. 41.

[80] *Acts* (1884-85), p. 187; *Code of 1886*, Sec. 4648.

[81] *Acts* (1886-87), p. 90.

[82] Quoted in Clara L. Pitts, "Julia Strudwich Tutwiler" (unpublished Ed. D. thesis, George Washington University, 1942), p. 197.

[83] Open letter in Montgomery *Advertiser*, February 27, 1887.

least two hours each day by teachers paid from the convict fund. Because of lack of space and of means for constructing school rooms, only the convicts at Pratt Mines were able to take advantage of the law.[84] Miss Tutwiler continued her efforts for a reformatory and was supported actively by both white and Negro teacher associations; the legislature, however, failed to adopt this idea until 1899.[85]

Alabama's convict system in the late nineteenth century failed to measure up to the advanced ideas on penology recommended by reformers and inaugurated in progressive institutions in other sections of the country. Instead, the state continued to lease its convicts to private contractors, a policy that appealed to the economy-minded Democrats and to mine owners desirous of a cheap and docile labor supply. In spite of reform efforts, the condition of the leased prisoners was far from commendable on the basis of present-day standards, and the mortality rate of convict miners was exceptionally high. When compared with other lease systems in the South, however, that of Alabama in 1890 did provide stricter supervision, more reasonable treatment, and better accommodations, because the majority of convicts were leased to one concern.[86] As long as the system supplied money to depleted state and county treasuries and as long as conditions were not notoriously bad, there was little chance of abolishing convict leasing.

[84] *Acts* (1886-87), p. 84; Montgomery *Advertiser*, November 30, 1886, February 5, 26, March 1, 1887;*Inspectors' Report* (1888), pp. 10-11.

[85] Owen, *History of Alabama*, I, 20.

[86] Blake McKelvey, "Penal Slavery and Southern Reconstruction," *Journal of Negro History*, XX (1935), 161; Zimmerman, *op. cit.*, p. 146.

CHAPTER TWELVE

The State
and Social Welfare

ALABAMA, like most state governments before the twentieth century, devoted little attention or financial assistance to care of the poor, aged, orphaned, indigent, sick, or other unfortunates. The emphasis on economical government with a minimum of agencies precluded any possibility of the state's undertaking widespread social welfare work. Opinion generally agreed that such matters should be left in the hands of private charities or local governmental authorities. The Reconstruction Constitution of 1868 contained for the first time a clause requiring the General Assembly "to make adequate provisions in each county for the maintenance of the poor."[1] The Constitution of 1875 altered this clause so as to make it the duty of the General Assembly "to require the several counties of this State to make adequate provision for the maintenance of the poor."[2] Under neither constitution, however, did the legislature do much more than re-enact the traditional laws providing for county poor houses to take care of all unfortunates and outcasts.[3]

Just before the Civil War Alabama established two new state welfare institutions, the Alabama Institution for the Deaf and

[1] Art. IV. sec. 34.
[2] Art. IV, sec. 49
[3] *Code of 1876*, Secs. 1729-1747; *Code of 1886*, Secs. 1645-1685.

Dumb and the Alabama Insane Hospital. In 1868 the state took over from the Freedmen's Bureau the Freedmen's Hospital, which had been established to care for indigent and feeble minded Negroes. This institution, located at Talladega, was placed under the superintendent of the deaf and dumb asylum. It housed an average of forty aged, crippled, and otherwise indigent Negroes, and its annual expenditures from the state funds ranged from a high of $6,000 in 1869 to a low of $2,800 in 1874.[4]

After 1874 the Democrats continued to operate the insane hospital and the deaf, dumb, and blind school, but they immediately abolished the Freedmen's Hospital.[5] The Democrats did not establish any new welfare institutions or agencies. One proposal for the better care of paupers was presented in the legislature of 1884-85 but failed to come to a vote. A study of Alabama's welfare problems in 1918 listed eight state-supported institutions, and none of these was established between 1865 and 1900.[6]

INSANE HOSPITAL

The Alabama Insane Hospital opened in Tuscaloosa, April 5, 1861, on the very eve of the Civil War. The superintendent was Dr. Peter Bryce, a young man who had been recommended for the position by Miss Dorothea Lynde Dix, the nationally famous social worker who interested herself in the establishment of the Alabama hospital. The new superintendent had studied and worked in Europe as well as in mental hospitals in South Carolina and New Jersey.[7] During the years of war and the Reconstruction period, the hospital grew in size and in its financial requirements. In 1874 it contained 345 patients and received from the state $52,363 for the maintenance of indigent patients.[8]

By the time the Democrats assumed control of the Alabama government, the hospital was already winning a national reputa-

---

[4] *Acts* (1868), p. 422; *ibid.* (1869-70), p. 146; *Report of the Trustees of the Freedmen's Hospital* (1870), p. 3; *ibid.* (1871) and (1873), *passim.*

[5] *Acts* (1874-75), p. 155; Montgomery *Advertiser*, January 25, 1876.

[6] *Senate Journal* (1884-85), p. 722; Montgomery *Advertiser*, November 23, 1884; Hastings H. Hart, *Social Problems of Alabama*, pp. 21-22.

[7] For a good sketch of Bryce's life see *Biennial Report of the Alabama Insane Hospital* [hereinafter cited as *Insane Hospital Report*] (1892), pp. 91-104.

[8] *Ibid.* (1874), pp. 5, 11.

tion for efficient, economical management and for considerate, humane treatment of the patients. A New York newspaper correspondent wrote from Tuscaloosa in 1884: "It may interest New York people to know that the Alabama Insane Asylum in this city is believed by many persons competent to judge to be the best conducted insane asylum in the country."[9] Legislative committees and government officials likewise consistently praised the institution. "Too much praise," said one committee, "cannot be bestowed upon Dr. Bryce."[10] Governor Seay described the hospital as "absolutely stainless in its entire history," and most Alabamians would probably have agreed with the newspaper that called the Tuscaloosa establishment "a model institution in every department."[11]

One of the most distinctive features of the Alabama hospital was the emphasis placed on cures or relief through kind and considerate treatment. Dr. Bryce was careful to avoid in the hospital any appearance of a jail or house of correction. By 1881 he had eliminated completely all coercive or restraining devices such as strait jackets, restraining beds, or leather cuffs and collars. Dr. Bryce believed, as did other adherents of the nonrestraint school, that coercive measures brought on more violent forms of insanity rather than effected any relief.[12] The superintendent also emphasized occupational therapy as one of the best treatments for most forms of insanity. In accordance with this theory, practically all patients worked at some task and thereby lowered the expenses of maintenance and upkeep of the hospital property. Many assisted in the intense cultivation of the hospital land, which furnished a large share of the food supply.[13]

The efficiency and good reputation of the Alabama hospital are doubly praiseworthy when considered in connection with the limited financial assistance received from the state. The total annual amount from the state treasury did increase from $63,875 in 1878 to $120,773 in 1891, but the revenue per indigent patient

[9] New York *Sun* quoted in Huntsville *Democrat*, May 7, 1884; Montgomery *Advertiser*, May 4, 1884.
[10] Joint Committee Report, *House Journal* (1878-79), p. 430.
[11] Governor's Message, *Senate Journal* (1888-89), p. 13; Montgomery *Advertiser*, November 19, 1888.
[12] *Insane Hospital Report* (1892), pp. 28-29; *ibid.* (1882-1890), *passim.*
[13] *Ibid.* (1892), p. 31.

declined sharply. Although the Code of 1876 had continued the previous appropriation of $4.00 per patient per week, by 1878 the state was paying only $3.50. Superintendent Bryce, after surveying expenditures of other state hospitals, pointed out that the Alabama rate of appropriation was forty per cent below the national average. Nevertheless, by 1891 the appropriation was based on. $2.15 per patient per week.[14]

The hospital's most pressing need during the period was additional space to accommodate the ever increasing requests for admission. As early as 1872 the number of patients had reached capacity, and each year thereafter admissions were always fewer than applications.[15] In granting admission, the superintendent followed the procedure laid down by law, giving precedence to the indigent insane and to the recent cases that had a chance of recovery.[16] A large number of the insane, however, were still unable to gain admission. A legislative committee in 1879 described these unfortunates as "either locked up in the county jails, or chained in outhouses, naked, neglected, ill-fed and often abused, or roaming at large through the country, a terror to their families and the communities into which they straggle."[17]

By 1880 the situation had become critical; the hospital itself was crowded with 402 patients, and 142 applicants had to be turned away.[18] Governor Cobb told the legislature that some action must be taken even though the state treasury could not finance all the improvements and additions requested by the superintendent. The state press joined in this demand for action, and the legislature finally appropriated $100,000 for building purposes, the amount Dr. Bryce had requested.[19] This amount made possible the completion in 1884 of two new wings, which more than doubled the hospital's capacity. In subsequent years

[14] Ibid. (1878), pp. 45, 51; ibid. (1892), p. 38; Code of 1876, Sec. 1499; Montgomery Advertiser, July 1, 1877.

[15] Insane Hospital Report (1872), p. 15; ibid. (1875-1880), passim.

[16] Code of 1876, Sec. 1478.

[17] Joint Committee Report, House Journal (1878-79), p. 433; letter from Dr. Bryce in Montgomery Advertiser, September 26, 1880.

[18] Insane Hospital Report (1880), pp. 10, 13.

[19] Governor's Message, Senate Journal (1880-81), p. 32; Montgomery Advertiser, November 18, 1880; Mobile Register, February 18, 1881; Insane Hospital Report (1880), p. 31; Acts (1880-81), p. 27.

some other additions and improvements were made by utilizing the money left over from the maintenance fund, but no special appropriation for buildings was made by the state again until 1901. In 1891 the legislature did appropriate $12,500 for the purchase of additional farm land adjacent to the hospital property. A general description of the hospital in 1893 estimated the total value of buildings and equipment at $500,000 and the land owned at 450 acres.[20]

The need for expansion, however, was not relieved; the larger the accommodations, the more applications for admission came in. With 1,148 patients in 1892, the superintendent reported the hospital in a "very crowded condition." Reports from county probate judges showed that some 300 insane throughout the state still remained in jails, alms houses, and private homes.[21] Dr. Bryce repeatedly pointed out that one cause of the trouble was the reluctance of the counties to take back their incurable and harmless insane, as required by law. He advocated special county or district asylums to care for feeble-minded, idiots, and harmless insane, but the legislature failed to take action.[22] Another project that Dr. Bryce often recommended but the legislature failed to adopt was some kind of asylum or reformatory for inebriates.[23]

In 1869 the insane hospital records for the first time mentioned the presence of Negro patients. Throughout the period under consideration Negroes in the institution averaged about thirteen per cent of the entire number of patients. They occupied separate wards, and lack of space generally prevented larger numbers from being accepted. By 1878 two frame buildings had been constructed to accommodate about eighty Negroes.[24] Superintendent Bryce in 1886 reported that the most pressing

[20] *Memorial Record of Alabama*, I, 179-180; *Acts* (1890-91), p. 196.

[21] *Insane Hospital Report* (1892), pp. 6, 10, 14-16.

[22] *Ibid.* (1880), p. 17; *House Journal* (1880-81), p. 879; *Senate Journal* (1884-85), p. 722; Montgomery *Advertiser*, November 21, 23, 1880, November 23, 1884.

[23] *Insane Hospital Report* (1870), pp. 14-26; *ibid.* (1878), pp. 39-44; *House Journal* (1880-81), p. 865, Wetumpka *Central Alabamian*, February 24, 1880.

[24] *Insane Hospital Report* (1869), p. 8; *ibid.* (1878), pp. 6, 45-46; *ibid.* (1880), p. 18.

need of the institution was additional room for Negroes, and the legislature in the following year appropriated $20,000 for that purpose. A new building enabled the hospital in 1892 to care for 288 Negro patients, but it was not until the turn of the century that the present separate institution at Mt. Vernon became available for insane Negroes.[25]

DEAF AND BLIND INSTITUTE

Alabama's other pre-war eleemosynary institution, a school for the deaf, was established in Talladega in 1860. It received a number of increases in financial support from the Reconstruction governments, and in 1867 the legislature established a school for the blind in connection with the institution. Dr. Joseph Henry Johnson, a native of Georgia who taught for a number of years in the deaf and dumb institute of that state, served efficiently as superintendent of the Alabama school from 1860 until his death in 1893. He was succeeded by his son.[26]

Unlike the insane hospital, the deaf and blind institute operated with less than capacity enrollment during the 1870's. The number of students dropped from sixty-eight in 1874 to forty-nine in 1876 and to fifty-four in 1878. Since the Democrats after 1874 had not changed the annual appropriation of $18,000, the superintendent found it possible, through the practice of rigid economy, to use some of the maintenance fund for buildings and improvements.[27] In 1877 a dormitory building was completed, in 1880 a three-story building containing class rooms and a chapel, and in 1881 a laundry building. By 1882 the school consisted of nine buildings, five brick structures and four wooden ones, affording accommodations for one hundred children.[28] In spite of the fact that the Alabama school required much less

[25] Ibid. (1886), pp. 21-22; ibid. (1892), p. 10; Acts (1886-87), p. 59.

[26] For brief accounts of the early history of the school, see W. G. Clark, op. cit., pp. 152-153; J. H. Johnson, "The Alabama Institute for the Deaf," Histories of American Schools for the Deaf, pp. 3-5; Bi-ennial Report . . . of the Alabama Institute of the Deaf [hereinafter cited as Deaf Institute Report] (1892), pp. 47-55.

[27] Deaf Institute Report (1876), pp. 11-12; ibid. (1878), p 21; Report of the Joint Committee to Visit the . . . Institute, House Journal (1878-79), pp. 470-472.

[28] Deaf Institute Report (1878), p. 10; ibid. (1880), pp. 7-10; ibid. (1882), p. 12.

financial support per pupil than similar schools in other states, the legislature in 1879 reduced the annual appropriation to $15,000.[29]

Time and again the superintendent and trustees urged the people of Alabama to support the institution by seeing that the handicapped children attended. One explanation for the small attendance was the fact that the law failed to provide clothing or transportation for those unable to furnish themselves. The law did stipulate that clothing expenses for the poor could be collected from the treasurer of the county from which the student came, but the process of collection proved too complicated to be effective.[30]

During the 1880's the deaf and blind institution benefited, along with other state agencies as a result of more liberal grants from the state treasury. In 1885 the legislature restored the annual appropriation to $18,000 and added $2,000 for repair of the buildings.[31] The school began to grow in size with one hundred seven registered during the two-year period ending in 1884 and two hundred twelve registered during a similar period ending in 1892.[32]

Because of overcrowded conditions, Superintendent Johnson recommended the establishment of a separate school for the blind. In 1887 the legislature complied with this recommendation and created two separate schools, the Alabama Institute for the Deaf and the Alabama Academy for the Blind, both at Talladega and under the same board of trustees. Appropriations were placed on a per pupil basis, $230 annually for the blind and $217.50 for the deaf. An additional $20,000 was voted to the blind school for building purposes, and was increased two years later.[33] By 1892 the blind school consisted of three new brick buildings located about a half mile from the deaf school. Eighty-nine students were enrolled during the latter year. These im-

[29] *Acts* (1878-79), p. 34; Montgomery *Advertiser,* February 6, 1879.
[30] *Deaf Institute Report* (1875), p. 15; *ibid.* (1876), p. 11; *Code of 1876,* Secs. 1311-1323.
[31] *Acts* (1884-85), pp. 124, 158.
[32] Montgomery *Advertiser,* December 14, 1884; *Deaf Institute Report* (1892), pp. 15, 19.
[33] *Deaf Institute Report* (1886), p. 18; *Acts* (1886-87), pp. 56, 70; *ibid.* (1888-89), p. 22.

provements prompted one newspaper to proclaim that no state in the union was doing more for its deaf and blind children than Alabama.[34]

Throughout the 1880's Superintendent Johnson and the trustees had consistently emphasized the need for a Negro deaf and blind school, and Governor Seay in 1890 urged the legislature to take action on this appeal which for some time had been awaiting "with patience the pleasure and ability of the State."[35] In 1891 the legislature established a school for the Negro deaf and blind at Talladega operated under the management of the trustees for the two white institutions. For the construction of this school the state provided $12,000 plus $6,000 annually for maintenance. On six acres located about a half mile from the Academy for the Blind, a three-story brick building was constructed for the Negro school. It opened in January, 1892, and had a total of thirty-four pupils by the end of that year.[36]

PUBLIC HEALTH

One of the first actions of the Alabama Democratic government after 1874 was the establishment of a state board of health to regulate and integrate the administration of public health laws. In the years before 1870, Alabama, like other states, had passed only a few public health laws, the administration of which was left in the hands of local officials or local boards of health.[37] During the 1870's the movement for the establishment of state health boards gained momentum throughout the country, and Alabama in 1875 was the sixth state to adopt such a system. Southern states in particular felt the need for such boards because of the ever present danger of yellow fever epidemics.

Most states modeled their public health systems on that established by Massachusetts in 1867, but there was a tendency in the South for physicians and medical associations to dominate

[34] *Deaf Institute Report* (1892), p. 19; Berney, *op. cit.* (1892), pp. 201-210; Montgomery *Advertiser*, August 17, 1886.

[35] *Deaf Institute Report* (1882), pp. 7, 12; *ibid.* (1884), p. 11; Governor's Message, *Senate Journal*, (1890-91), p. 19.

[36] *Acts* (1890-91), p. 458; *Deaf Institute Report* (1892), pp. 21-22.

[37] Jerome Cochran, "The Medical Profession," *Memorial Record of Alabama*, II, 114-117; William H. Brantley, "An Alabama Medical Review," *Alabama Lawyer*, VI (1945), 248-257, 279-285.

the boards.[38] Alabama went to the extreme in this matter and, unlike any other state, vested complete control over the public health system in its medical association. The dynamic leader in this development was Dr. Jerome Cochran of Mobile. He engineered the reorganization of the Alabama Medical Association under a new constitution in 1873 that provided for a highly centralized, oligarchical control vested in a board of ten censors elected indirectly by the association members. Dr. Cochran hoped that the association under such a constitution would prove efficient enough to operate a public health system.[39] He presented his plan for a state health board to three legislative sessions before it was finally approved in 1875.[40]

The 1875 act constituted the state medical association a state board of health required to "take cognizance of the interests of health and life among the people of the State . . . and . . . be in all ways the medical advisers of the State." The law also designated as county boards of health all county medical societies affiliated with the state association; the duties and powers of county boards were to be worked out with county and municipal officials. Details of organization and duties were left up to the association itself. That group vested complete control over public health matters in its boards of censors, which assumed the additional title, committee of public health. This committee elected for a five-year term a public health officer, a position held by Dr. Cochran until his death in 1896.[41] The legislature at first appropriated no money for public health activities, and the lack of funds prevented any significant work. In 1879, however, the legislature set up a small annual appropriation of $3,000 to

[38] Francis R. Allen, "Development of the Public Health Movement in the Southeast," *Social Forces*, XXII (1943), 70-73.

[39] Carey V. Stabler, "The History of the Alabama Public Health System" (Unpublished Ph.D. thesis, Duke University, 1944), pp. 45-65; William H. Sanders, "The History, Philosophy and Fruits of Medical Organization in Alabama," *Transactions of the Medical Association of the State of Alabama* [hereinafter cited as *Medical Association Transactions*] (1914), pp. 510-579.

[40] *Medical Association Transactions* (1873), pp. 10, 23; *ibid.* (1874), pp. 19, 22-23; *ibid.* (1875), pp. 28-33.

[41] *Acts* (1874-75), p. 130; *Book of Rules of the Medical Association of the State of Alabama* [hereinafter cited as *Book of Rules*] (1883), pp. 114-115.

be expended by the board of health as it saw fit. Of this sum, $1,800 went as annual salary to the state health officer.[42]

Alabama's unique arrangement for a public health system met with general approval among physicians; they considered their own organization best qualified to give advice on and to administer public health laws. The plan also received considerable attention in medical circles throughout the nation because of its unusual features.[43]

The primary function of the state health board was to prevent and combat the dreaded yellow fever epidemics. Dr. Cochran and other physicians of the time, unaware of the true cause of the disease, believed that the best approach was a strict quarantine against any locality where the fever had been definitely proven to exist. "The golden rule for the prevention of the spread of yellow fever," said Dr. Cochran, "is non-intercourse — isolation — the keeping of the well away from the sick, away from infected things, and very specially away from infected localities."[44] Control over both maritime and land quarantines in Alabama was vested in local authorities with some financial assistance from the state to counties bordering on Florida and the Gulf of Mexico. Complaints against unduly strict quarantines were numerous, and both Governor Seay and Dr. Cochran recommended placing a greater degree of control over quarantines in the hands of the state board of health.[45] The legislature, however, would not confer complete power upon the board. In 1887 it passed an act giving the governor power, upon the recommendation of the board of health, to proclaim a quarantine anywhere in the state; to carry out the intent of this act, $5,000 was appropriated. The law specifically stated, however, that such action should not prevent the establishment of local quarantines by towns and counties.[46]

---

[42] Acts (1878-79), p. 33; The Report of the Board of Health of the State of Alabama [hereinafter cited as Board of Health Report] (1888), p. 24.

[43] Stabler, op. cit., pp. 70-72; J. N. Baker, "Alabama's Contribution to Public Health," American Journal of Public Health, XXX (1940), 860.

[44] Book of Rules (1889), p. 156.

[45] Code of 1886, Secs. 1260-1277; Governor's Message, Senate Journal (1888-89), p. 13; Jerome Cochran, Problems in Regard to Yellow Fever and the Prevention of Yellow Fever Epidemics, p. 8.

[46] Acts (1886-87), p. 105.

The state health officer served as a specialist in diagnosing suspected cases of yellow fever, and in case of epidemics gave advice and assistance to local health officers and other officials. In 1889 the legislature empowered the state health officer to relax or increase the stringency of the quarantine laws upon consultation with the local officials concerned.[47] In addition to its work with quarantines the state board of health also published numerous rules and suggestions in an attempt to prevent the outbreak or spread of yellow fever. Dr. Cochran and the board took an active interest in interstate quarantine conferences, one of which in March, 1889, met in Montgomery.[48]

The Alabama board of health showed some interest in other problems of public health, but took little concrete action. Some members suggested a compulsory vaccination law as the only sure way of avoiding the danger of smallpox, but Dr. Cochran prevented any such recommendation from going to the legislature.[49] The board attempted to establish a program for the collection of accurate vital statistics, which were essential in acquiring a complete picture of the various public health problems confronting state and local boards. As recommended by the state board, the legislature in 1881 passed an act providing for the collection of vital statistics and more clearly defining the duties of county health boards and officers. This vital statistics law was one of the earliest in the country and attracted considerable attention from physicians and public health officials elsewhere. The machinery for collecting the statistics did not operate efficiently, however, and probably not more than seventy-five per cent of all births and deaths in Alabama were reported to the state health officer during the first fifteen years of the operation of the law.[50]

Although Alabama's public health system did not attract a

[47] *Board of Health Report* (1888), pp. 49-70; Montgomery *Advertiser*, November 16, 28, 1888; *Acts* (1888-89), p. 72.

[48] Montgomery *Advertiser*, August 6, 1879; *Book of Rules* (1889), pp. 154-162; *Proceedings of the Quarantine Conference held in Montgomery, Ala.*

[49] Stabler, *op. cit.*, pp. 94-95. For an account of the smallpox epidemic in 1883, see *Board of Health Report* (1884), pp. 126-135.

[50] *Acts* (1880-81), p. 76; *Medical Association Transactions* (1880), pp. 112-116; Stabler, *op. cit.*, pp. 83-89.

great deal of attention from laymen, the occasional comments were usually favorable. Some criticism, however, led to an attempt to legislate Dr. Cochran out of his position as state health officer. Cochran had incurred considerable opposition because of his virtually absolute control over both the board of health and medical association and because of numerous disagreements over matters of quarantine. The legislature of 1884-85, however, failed to pass a bill that would have cut off all appropriations to the health board.[51] Although Alabama's public health system was carefully worked out, it accomplished little of significance during this period, and fell far short of the aims and promises of its founders.

Closely related to public health problems was the question of regulating and standardizing the practice of doctors, dentists, and pharmacists. Before 1877 licenses to practice were granted to physicians, dentists, and druggists by local medical boards, which set up their own methods of determining a candidate's ability or qualifications. "Regular graduates of medical colleges in the United States" might use their diplomas as licenses, and the licensing system did not apply to those practicing an "irregular" system of medicine.[52]

Early in the 1870's the state medical association strongly recommended that the legislature establish a better regulated method of qualifying physicians. The physicians felt that the "alarming growth in number of incompetent doctors, charlatans and quacks" necessitated such action.[53] In 1877 the legislature passed a bill on this subject that had been recommended to it by the association. The new act designated as boards of medical examiners the boards of censors of state and county medical societies. No person could practice a "regular" system of medicine without being qualified by one of these boards; physicians already practicing and in good standing were entitled automatically to certificates of qualification. Any person desiring to practice an "irregular" system of medicine had to have a diploma

---

[51] *House Journal* (1884-85), p. 650; Montgomery *Advertiser*, January 23, 29, 31, February 5, 1885; Birmingham *Chronicle*, February 8, 1885.

[52] *Code of 1867*, Secs. 1223-1236.

[53] *Book of Rules* (1889), p. 103; *Medical Association Transactions* (1874), pp. 24-26; *ibid.* (1875), p. 21.

or certificate in "anatomy, physiology, chemistry, and the mechanism of labor." The leaders of the medical association pointed with pride to this new law which placed complete control over qualifications in the hands of the association.[54]

The Code of 1886 made some significant changes in the qualification law. It eliminated any mention of "irregular" physicians; homeopathic and other "irregulars" thereafter had to pass the same kind of qualifying examinations as the "regular" allopathic physicians.[55] This action brought forth loud protests from the "irregular" physicians. One newspaper correspondent pleaded for justice to the homeopaths and protested against the complete domination of Alabama's qualifying boards by allopaths. In 1887 the executive committee of the Eclectic and Homeopathic Physicians Association issued a protest against this domination by "the Old School, or Allopathic, Physicians."[56]

Before 1881 those desiring to practice dental surgery had been licensed by the same boards that handled applicants to practice medicine. The Alabama Dental Association had been organized in 1869, lapsed in 1873, and was revived in 1880. This organization worked to obtain a board of dental examiners under their own control rather than under the control of the medical association.[57] The legislature in 1881 established such a board consisting of five dentists, members of, and elected by, the Alabama Dental Association. The board granted licenses without examination to all graduates of incorporated dental colleges and to other applicants "who undergo a satisfactory examination."[58]

For some time pharmacists also were licensed by the medical boards. In 1881 the Alabama Pharmaceutical Association was organized in order "to improve the science and art of Pharmacy, to restrict the dispensing and the sale of medicine to regularly educated Druggists and Apothecaries." The association regularly petitioned the legislature for an effective pharmacy law, but

[54] *Acts* (1876-77), p. 80; Brantley, "Alabama Medical Review," *loc. cit.*, pp. 270-271; *Medical Association Transactions* (1878), pp. 171-172.

[55] *Code of 1886*, Secs. 1296-1307; Thomas D. Parke, *A Study of the Medical Laws from an Ethical Standpoint*, p. 4.

[56] Montgomery *Advertiser*, February 22, 1887, November 23, 1888.

[57] Owen, *History of Alabama*, I, 483-485; Cochran, "Medical Profession," *loc. cit.*, II, 132-133.

[58] *Acts* (1880-91), p. 82.

opposition from the country store keepers, who felt that it would injure their business, prevented its passage in 1883 and 1885.[59] In 1887 a pharmacy law finally passed, but its provisions applied only to towns with a population of one thousand or more, reduced two years later to nine hundred or more. Under this act the governor appointed a three-man pharmacy board that would give to pharmacist applicants either oral or written examinations. The members of the board had to be pharmacists with at least five years experience in Alabama.[60]

CONFEDERATE PENSIONS

An important aspect of Alabama's social welfare work was the financial assistance given to aged and disabled Confederate soldiers and widows. Before 1890, however, the state made only small payments because of the limited revenue of the state government. Most Confederate veterans during the twenty to twenty-five years after the war were comparatively young and still able to support themselves and their families. Principal attention during this early period was directed toward assisting maimed or disabled veterans.

In 1867 an act appropriated $30,000 to be used in the purchase of artificial limbs for ex-soldiers who had lost a leg in action. The governor was to contract for the manufacture of the limbs and then have them distributed to those qualified, the handling of applications and distribution being left in the hands of the probate judge of each county. The legs were expected to cost from $50 to $75, and a direct grant of $100 was made to any veteran in such bad condition that he could not use an artifical limb.[61] No additional appropriations were made during Reconstruction, and in 1875 the Democratic legislature reappropriated the $9,500 balance left from the fund provided by the original 1867 act.[62]

For the first few years after the Democrats regained control of the government, financial stringency allowed only very small

---

[59] *Proceedings of the Alabama Pharmaceutical Association* (1881), p. 9; *ibid.* (1885), pp. 8, 10, 17-21.

[60] *Acts* (1886-87), p. 106; *ibid.* (1888-89), p. 59.

[61] *Acts* (1866-67), p. 695.

[62] *Ibid.* (1874-75), p. 161; Selma *Southern Argus,* January 31, 1879.

appropriations to the veterans. As the state's revenue increased in later years, the total amounts devoted to Confederate pensions steadily increased. The legislature appropriated $5,000 in 1876, the same in 1877, but none in 1878. Benefits were restricted to legless veterans as under the 1867 law, but the $75 for each artifical limb went directly to the beneficiary. Under the 1876 and 1877 acts approximately 160 veterans received benefits.[63] In 1879 the legislature appropriated $10,000 for disabled veterans. Any veteran who had lost a limb could receive the regular $75, provided he had received no previous benefits. The remainder was to be divided pro rata among the other disabled veterans who had benefited under other acts. An additional act provided $1,800 to aid blind soldiers. As actually distributed, the money went to 10 blind soldiers who received $150 each and to about 350 maimed soldiers who received $30.12 each.[64]

During the 1880's Alabama increased somewhat the total payments to veterans and liberalized the requirements for pension eligibility. The 1880-1881 legislature increased pension appropriations to $15,000 and included not only those who had lost limbs but also those "materially disabled by wounds received in . . . service." The same provisions were repeated in 1883 with the added requirement that each recipient must be "physically incapable of making a livelihood by labor." In neither act did the legislature distinguish between blind and maimed soldiers or those benefiting or not benefiting under previous acts. When the pro rata distributions had been worked out, each veteran received $14.77 under the 1881 act and $17.96 under the 1883 act.[65]

During the next three legislative sessions pension appropriations increased rapidly: $25,000 in 1885, $30,000 in 1887, and $50,000 in 1889. The 1887 act for the first time included widows of Confederate soldiers killed in the war or who had died later as a result of diseases or wounds contracted during the war.

[63] *Acts* (1875-76), p. 263; *ibid.* (1876-77), p. 31; *Auditor's Report* (1876), pp. 44-45; *ibid.* (1877), pp. 65-66. For a list of these sums year by year, see Owen, *History of Alabama*, I, 341.
[64] *Acts* (1878-79), pp. 34, 36; Montgomery *Advertiser*, January 22, 1879; *Auditor's Report* (1879), pp. 36-41; *ibid.* (1880), pp. 48-49.
[65] *Acts* (1880-81), p. 20; *ibid.* (1882-83), p. 181; *Auditor's Report* (1882), pp. 63-81; *ibid.* (1884), pp. 59-75.

These three acts also prohibited payments to anyone who owned property up to a specified value: $2,000 in the 1885 act, $1,000 in the 1887 act, and $400 in the 1889 act. In spite of these restrictions, the numbers receiving benefits increased to 1,596 in 1886 and to 4,035 in 1890.[66] By 1890 pension payments had come to be a fixed policy of the state government and required yearly an ever increasing share of appropriations. In 1891 the legislature passed a special half-mill tax to meet these payments. By 1916 Alabama was paying annually to Confederate veterans and widows $1,024,326 in pensions.[67]

In its attitude toward problems of social welfare, the Alabama Democratic government was influenced by the prevalent lack of interest in such matters and by its own emphasis on economy. Although it continued to operate both the insane hospital and the deaf school, appropriations per inmate were far below the national averages. Nevertheless, under efficient and economical management, the two institutions grew, and the hospital under Superintendent Bryce won an excellent national reputation. The inauguration of a state board of health resulted not from the efforts of governmental officials but from those of Dr. Cochran and the state medical association. Its operation cost the state very little, and its accomplishments before 1900 were negligible.

[66] *Acts* (1884-85), p. 157; *ibid.* (1886-87), p. 64; *ibid.* (1888-89), p. 83; *Auditor's Report* (1886), pp. 92-93; *ibid.* (1890), pp. 93-94.
[67] Owen, *History of Alabama*, I, 340-341.

CHAPTER THIRTEEN

Conclusion

IT SEEMS clear that the term *Bourbon* in its literal sense of having learned or forgotten nothing would not accurately describe the Alabama Democratic party and government between 1874 and 1890. It is true that some of the agrarian Democrats espoused an extremely conservative, Bourbon attitude toward such matters as debt adjustment, concessions to business and industry, encouragement of immigration, and further expansion of governmental activities. Other elements within the party, however, believed that a different policy was necessary if Alabama was to keep step with the rest of the nation in its industrial and business progress. This difference of opinion caused the Democratic party at times to follow a dual role with some conservative and some progressive aspects. It also led to numerous intra-party conflicts, some of which resulted in independent movements.

When formally organized after the Civil War, the Alabama Democratic and Conservative party included diverse elements from a number of ante-bellum parties and thus contained from the beginning the seeds of disagreement on policy. The one unifying factor after 1868 was opposition to Radical Reconstruction, but previous to the election of 1874 agreement was lacking on the question of how to attack the opposition. In that election the Democrats centered their campaign on the exclusive issue of white *versus* Negro rule and, with other factors in their favor, won control over all branches of the state government. During the years immediately after the 1874 victory, a conservative, agrarian-minded policy dominated the Democratic party and government. The Constitution of 1875 imposed strict prohibitions against increased taxes and state aid to railroads and industry; it further required the reduction of governmental salaries and expenditures. The first few legislative sessions were dominated largely by Grangers and farmers that had long been skeptical of the Republicans' interest in and encouragement of Alabama's mining, railroad, and industrial resources. By reducing expenditures and eliminating a number of offices and agencies established during Reconstruction, they faithfully carried out the mandate of the new constitution for economy in government. They also imposed a number of regulations and curbs on what they considered the increasingly dangerous practices of corporations and monopolies. Foremost among these measures were the establishment of a railroad commission in 1881 and fertilizer inspection through an agricultural commissioner in 1883. Much of the immediate post-Reconstruction farmer legislation was designed to strengthen the control exercised by landowners over their laborers and tenants.

Even during the 1870's, however, an agrarian, conservative program did not wholly characterize the Alabama Democratic party. Many innovations and changes had been made in the interests of the masses of people, both white and black, during the Reconstruction period, and these the Democrats could not oppose or change openly after 1874. Neither the 1875 constitutional convention nor the legislatures dared to abolish guarantees of exemptions, popular election of judicial officials, or the principle of public school education for all children. Indeed, the Constitution of 1875 in its organization and wording more closely resembled the Republican 1868 document than it did any previous constitution. On the important question of debt adjustment the Bourbon elements also lost out to those interested in preserving Alabama's credit standing so that her chances of business and industrial growth would be better. Instead of repudiating all of the state debts incurred during Radical Reconstruction, as Robert McKee and his conservatives wished, the adjustment reduced only the interest on the debt incurred for state purposes and compromised on some of the railroad indebtedness. This action effectively prevented an immediate reduction in the tax rate, because the adjusted debt required such a large percentage of the state's revenue.

During the 1880's as the remembrance of Reconstruction bitterness became more remote and as economic conditions improved, bringing prosperity and booms to north Alabama towns, the outlook of the Democratic party changed somewhat. More and more leaders and newspapers, largely in the northern part of the state, advocated a forward-looking, New-South policy for Alabama. They urged the legislature to encourage immigration, grant more concessions to new industries, and renew the program of state aid to railroad building; at the same time they criticized some Black Belt Democrats for sacrificing Alabama's progress to the party shibboleth of a strictly economical government. Although the legislature never did return to the Reconstruction program of open aid and encouragement to business enterprises, it did not hesitate to petition Congress for grants in aid of railroads and for relaxation of restrictions on the sale of mineral lands. Total expenditures of the state government, moreover, rose as a result of increasing assessment valuations and new forms of taxation, until by 1890 they exceeded Reconstruction expenditures. Alabama's revenue would have been much larger if the legislature, under pressure from landowners, had not consistently reduced the rate of taxation. Some of the increased governmental activity was designed to benefit the farmers through the encouragement of agricultural organization, establishment of experiment stations, and dissemination of information. Agrarian conditions, however, failed to improve because of falling prices, scarcity of credit, and inefficient labor; the condition of the average Alabama farmer became much worse in the late 1880's.

In any consideration of the activities of the Alabama government during this period, two fundamental conditions must be borne in mind. In the first place, the retarded economic development of the state coupled with constant reductions in the tax rate made available funds quite scarce. Secondly, the last quarter of the nineteenth century was a period in the country's history when *laissez faire* and a minimum of governmental activity characterized the political thinking of almost everyone, North and South, Democratic and Republican. Immediately after their 1874 victory, Alabama Democrats reduced salaries, employees, and activities of the state government to a minimum. During the succeeding sixteen years no important increases in salaries occurred, and the work of governmental divisions increased only in proportion to the general growth of the state. Three new agencies, a board of health, a railroad commission, and an agricultural commissioner, were created, but none carried out extensive or significant work. The Alabama government operated far more economically than efficiently, although some improvements followed the embarrassing defalcation of Treasurer Isaac Vincent in 1883.

After debt payments, the Alabama government spent the next largest share of its income on education. The state-supported schools and colleges, however, were still far below national standards, and Alabama's illiteracy rate remained extremely high. The school fund was at first apportioned evenly between Negroes and whites, but in 1891 a new law made possible the diverting of Negro school funds to improve white schools. The sincere interest of Democratic leaders in the theory of public education pointed to the coming educational renaissance in the early twentieth century. In their operation of the penal system, the Democrats, primarily interested in making a profit, continued to lease practically all prisoners to mining and farming interests. By concentrating most of the leased convicts in the mines of the Tennessee Company, the inspectors could exercise somewhat better supervision than in the average leasing arrangement. The inevitably bad conditions, however, combined with the attacks of free miners to strengthen the growing opposition to the system. The Democrats created no new eleemosynary institutions but continued to operate the insane hospital and the deaf and blind institute, both of which had been established before the Civil War. In spite of its limited income, the insane hospital operated as a model institution, admitting both white and Negro patients.

In their policies and activities, the Alabama Democrats encountered little serious opposition from Republican or other political parties after 1876. They made sure of retaining control and of thwarting any resurgence of a Republican-Negro combination by rewriting election laws and by employing innumerable extra-legal devices to control or nullify Negro and other unwanted votes. More serious threats to Democratic hegemony came from disagreements and threatened bolts within their own party. In an effort to avert these, control over party affairs rested in the hands of comparatively small groups that could dictate the selection of candidates, but this very fact often led to independent movements aimed at destroying "ring control." The most effective method of preserving party harmony was the emphasis in every campaign on white *versus* Negro rule, and the strict avoidance of all such controversial issues as public school support, convict leasing, and election laws. The only serious opposition before 1890 came from the Greenbackers beginning in 1878. Although the movement won a number of victories in the 1880 and 1882 elections, it declined rapidly in Alabama after the death of Congressman William M. Lowe in the latter year.

In conclusion it may be said that the Alabama Democratic and Conservative party after 1874 made a contribution in instituting an economical government managed by native Alabamians in whom the public generally had confidence. The party organization and methods of controlling elections were far from creditable and instituted many practices detrimental to the best interests in a true democracy. On economic questions the party could not be termed literally Bourbon, but rather exemplified aspects of both a progressive and conservative policy. This seeming inconsistency grew out of an effort to satisfy the diverse elements that made up the Democratic party and often led to serious internal friction. These disagreements failed to cause an open breach in party unity until precipitated by agrarian difficulties and the Populist revolt of the early 1890's.

APPENDIX

RETURNS IN GUBERNATORIAL ELECTIONS

	DEMOCRATIC		OPPOSITION	
1870	Lindsay	76,977	Smith (Republican)	75,568
1872	Lindsay	81,371	Lewis (Republican)	89,878
1874	Houston	107,118	Lewis (Republican)	93,928
1876	Houston	99,255	Woodruff (Republican)	55,582
1878	Cobb	89,571	—	
1880	Cobb	134,908	Pickins (Greenback)	42,363
1882	O'Neal	100,591	Sheffield (Greenback)	46,386
1884	O'Neal	139,580	Lane (Independent)*	305
1886	Seay	144,737	Bingham (Republican)	37,116
			Tanner (Prohibitionist)	576
1888	Seay	149,591	Ewing (Republican)	42,805
			Orr (Prohibitionist)	301
1890	Jones	139,912	Long (Republican)	42,390

* Refused to accept nomination

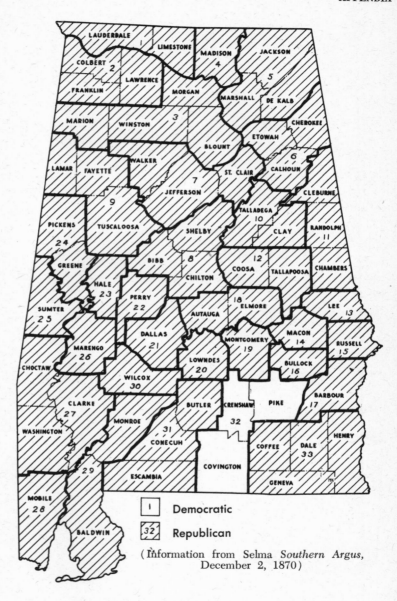

☐ 1   Democratic

☐ 32   Republican

(Information from Selma *Southern Argus,*
December 2, 1870)

Membership of Alabama Senate, 1870-1871 Session

Democratic 67

Republican 33

°No representation for these counties
The figures indicate number of representatives where county had more than one

(Information from Selma *Southern Argus*, December 2, 1870)

Membership of Alabama House of Representatives, 1870-1871 Session

(Information from Montgomery *Advertiser*,
November 17, 1872)

Membership of Alabama Senate, 1872-1873 Session

47 Democratic	°No representation for these counties
5/ Republican	The figures indicate number of represen-
2 Independent	tatives where county had more than one

(Information from Montgomery *Advertiser,*
November 17, 1872)

Membership of Alabama House of Representatives, 1872-1873 Session

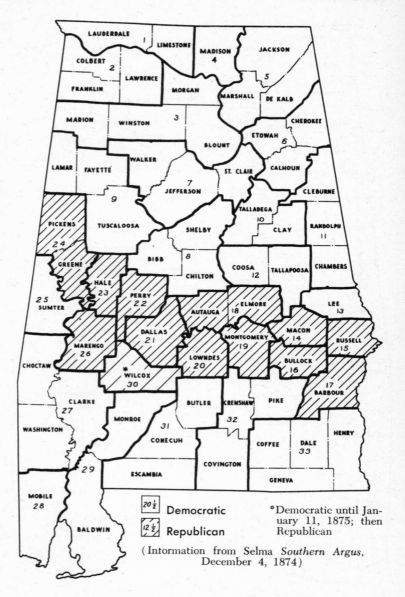

Democratic until January 11, 1875; then Republican

(Intormation from Selma *Southern Argus*, December 4, 1874)

Membership of Alabama Senate, 1874-1875 Session

	Democratic	°No representation for these counties

6 4 Democratic
3 5 Republican
Independent

°No representation for
these counties
The figures indicate
number of represen-
tatives where county
had more than one

(Information from Selma *Southern Argus,*
December 4, 1874)

Membership of Alabama House of Representatives, 1874-1875 Session

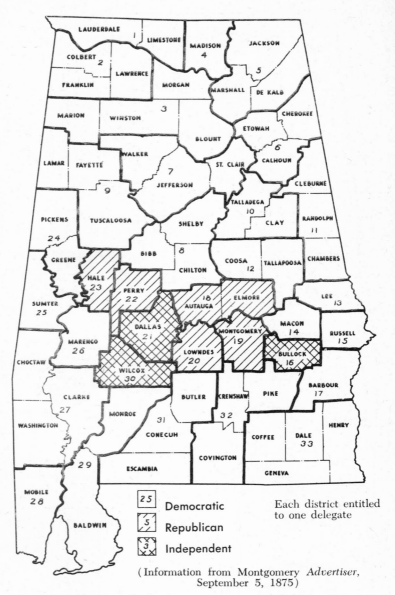

(Information from Montgomery *Advertiser*,
September 5, 1875)

District Delegates in Alabama Constitutional Convention of 1875

56 **Democratic**

6 **Republican**

4 **Independent**

°Each county entitled to one delegate except Mobile which had two

(Information from Montgomery *Advertiser*, September 5, 1875)

County Delegates in Alabama Constitutional Convention of 1875

(Information from Montgomery *Advertiser*,
September 15, 1876)

Membership of Alabama Senate, 1876-1877 Session

79 **Democratic**

18 **Republican**

3 **Independent**

The figures indicate number of representatives where county had more than one

(Information from Montgomery *Advertiser*, September 15, 1876)

Membership of Alabama House of Representatives, 1876-1877 Session

31 Democratic

2 Independent
   and Greenback

(Information from Montgomery *Advertiser*,
August 24, 1878)

Membership of Alabama Senate, 1878-1879 Session

91 Democratic

Republican,
Independent,
and Greenback

°No representation
until 1882
The figures indicate
number of represen-
tatives where county
had more than one

(Information from Montgomery *Advertiser*,
August 24, 1878)

Membership of Alabama House of Representatives, 1878-1879 Session

33 | Democratic

(Information from Montgomery *Advertiser*, November 9, 1880)

Membership of Alabama Senate, 1880-1881 Session

(Information from Montgomery *Advertiser*, November 9, 1880)

Membership of Alabama House of Representatives, 1880-1881 Session

(Information from Montgomery *Advertiser*,
November 14, 1882)

Membership of Alabama Senate, 1882-1883 Session

80 | Democratic
20 | Others

The figures indicate number of representatives where county had more than one

(Information from Montgomery *Advertiser,* November 14, 1882)

Membership of Alabama House of Representatives, 1882-1883 Session

30 Democratic

3 Independent

(Information from Montgomery *Advertiser*,
November 11, 1884)

Membership of Alabama Senate, 1884-1885 Session

LAUDERDALE 2
LIMESTONE 2
MADISON 3
JACKSON 2
COLBERT
LAWRENCE 2
FRANKLIN
MORGAN
MARSHALL
DE KALB
MARION
WINSTON
CULLMAN
CHEROKEE
ETOWAH
BLOUNT
LAMAR
FAYETTE
WALKER
ST. CLAIR
CALHOUN
CLEBURNE
JEFFERSON 2
TALLADEGA 2
PICKENS 2
TUSCALOOSA 2
SHELBY
CLAY
RANDOLPH
GREENE 2
BIBB
COOSA
TALLAPOOSA 2
CHAMBERS 2
HALE 2
CHILTON
PERRY 2
ELMORE
LEE 2
SUMTER 2
AUTAUGA
MACON
DALLAS 4
MONTGOMERY 4
RUSSELL 2
MARENGO 2
LOWNDES 2
BULLOCK 2
CHOCTAW
WILCOX 2
BARBOUR 3
CLARKE
BUTLER
CRENSHAW
PIKE 2
MONROE
WASHINGTON
CONECUH
COFFEE
DALE
HENRY
COVINGTON
ESCAMBIA
GENEVA
MOBILE 4
BALDWIN

93 Democratic
7 Independent

The figures indicate number of representatives where county had more than one

(Information from Montgomery *Advertiser,*
November 11, 1884)

Membership of Alabama House of Representatives, 1884-1885 Session

BIBLIOGRAPHY

I PRIMARY MATERIALS

MANUSCRIPT COLLECTIONS

Frederick G. Bromberg Papers. Southern Historical Collection, University of North Carolina.

Frederick G. Bromberg Papers. Library of Congress.

William LeRoy Broun Papers. Southern Historical Collection, University of North Carolina.

Clement C. Clay Papers. Duke University.

Rufus W. Cobb Papers. Alabama State Department of Archives and History.

Jabez Lamar Monroe Curry Papers. Library of Congress.

Hilary A. Herbert Papers. Private possession.

George Smith Houston Papers. Duke University.

Robert Jemison Papers. University of Alabama.

Robert McKee Papers. Alabama State Department of Archives and History.

John Tyler Morgan Papers. Library of Congress.

Edward A. O'Neal Papers. Southern Historical Collection, University of North Carolina.

Lewis E. Parsons Papers. Alabama State Department of Archives and History.

John W. A. Sanford Papers. Alabama State Department of Archives and History.

OFFICIAL FEDERAL DOCUMENTS

Affairs in Alabama, February 23, 1875, *House Reports,* 43 Cong., 2 Sess., no. 262. Washington: Government Printing Office, 1875.

Congressional Documents, 42 Congress (1871)—58 Congress, (1905).

Congressional Record, 47 Congress (1881)—50 Congress (1889).

Elections in Alabama, March 3, 1877, *Senate Reports,* 44 Cong., 2 Sess., no. 704. Washington: Government Printing Office, 1877.

234 BOURBON DEMOCRACY IN ALABAMA

Memorial of the Republican Members of the Legislature of
Alabama, February 25, 1875, *Senate Miscellaneous Docu-
ments*, 43 Cong., 2 Sess., no. 107. Washington: Government
Printing Office, 1875.

Ku Klux Report, February 19, 1872, *Senate Reports*, 42 Cong.,
2 Sess., no. 22, 13 vols. Washington: Government Printing
Office, 1872.

*Report of the Committee of the Senate upon the Relations
between Labor and Capital, and Testimony Taken by the
Committee*, 5 vols. Washington: Government Printing Office, 1885.

Reports of the Commissioner of Education, 1870-1890.

Rowell, Chester H. (comp.), *A Historical and Legal Digest of
all the Contested Election Cases in the House of Representatives* . . . Washington: Government Printing Office, 1901.

Statistical Abstracts of the United States, 1879-1890.

United States Census Reports, Ninth (1870)-Thirteenth (1910).

United States Statutes at Large, vol. 22 (1881-1883).

United States Supreme Court Reports, vol. 94 (1877)—vol.
123 (1887).

OFFICIAL ALABAMA DOCUMENTS

Acts of the General Assembly, 1865-1901.

An Agreement Entered Into, 17th May, 1869, Between . . .
Commissioners on the Part of Florida . . . , *and* . . .
Commissioners on the Part of Alabama . . . , *Setting Forth
the Terms of Annexation of West Florida to the State of
Alabama*, n.p., n.d.

*Alabama, A Few Remarks Upon Her Resources, and the
Advantages She Possesses as Inducements to Immigration.*
Published by the Commissioner of Industrial Resources.
Montgomery: Jno. G. Stokes & Co., 1869.

*Catalogue of the Officers and Alumni of the Alabama Poly-
technic Institute*, 1872-1906. Montgomery: Brown Printing
Co., 1906.

Circular of Information from Department of Education . . .
As to Alabama's Educational Status from 1855 to 1898.
Montgomery: Brown Printing Co., 1898.

Codes of Alabama, 1852, 1866, 1867, 1887, 1897.

*Compilation of the Laws Relating to the Government and
Management of the Penitentiary and Convicts.* Montgomery: W. D. Brown & Co., 1883.

Constitutions of Alabama, 1865, 1868, 1875, 1901.

A General Description of the State of Alabama . . . *Complied
by the Department of Agriculture. Montgomery:* W. D.
Brown & Co., 1884.

*Journal of the Constitutional Convention of the State of Ala-
bama, Assembled in the City of Montgomery, September
6th 1875.* Montgomery: W. W. Screws, 1875.

*Journals of the Board of Education and Board of Regents,
1871-1873.*

Journals of the House of Representatives, 1865-1891.

Journals of the Senate, 1871-1891.

*Register of the Officers and Students of the University of Ala-
bama* 1831-1901. Tuscaloosa: University of Alabama, 1901.

*Report of Joint Committee to Enquire Into the Treatment
of Convicts.* Montgomery: Alfred & Beers, 1881.

*Report of M. G. Moore, Special Commissioner, To Settle Lease
of Penitentiary.* Montgomery: Arthur Bingham, 1873.

Report of the Commissioner of Swamp and Overflowed Lands.
Montgomery: Barrett & Brown, 1878.

*Report of the Commissioners Appointed in Pursuance of the
Act Approved February 17, 1885, "To Revise and Reduce
into a Code . . . . "* n.p., [1886].

*Report of the Commissioners of the State of Alabama to the
Universal Exhibition, at Vienna, Austria.* Montgomery:
Arthur Bingham, 1873.

*Report of the Commissioners to Adjust and Liquidate the
Indebtedness of the State of Alabama.* Montgomery: Barrett & Brown, 1879.

*Report of the Committee on Contingent Fund and Other Irre-
gularities in the State Government.* Montgomery: W. W.
Screws, 1875.

*Report of the Committee on the Memorial Addressed by the
Republican Members of the General Assembly of Alabama
to the Congress of the United States.* Montgomery: W. W.
Screws, 1875.

*Report of the Joint Committee in Regard to the Amendment
of The Constitution.* Montgomery: W. W. Screws, 1875.

*Report of the Joint Committee of the General Assembly,
Appointed to Investigate the Conduct, Transactions, etc., of
Isaac H. Vincent, Lately State Treasurer.* Montgomery:
W. D. Brown & Co., 1883.

*Report of the Joint Committee of the General Assembly of
Alabama, in Regard to the Alleged Election of Geo. E.
Spencer, as U. S. Senator.* Montgomery: W. W. Screws,
1875.

*Report of the Joint Committee to Visit Tuscaloosa and Inves-
tigate the University.* n.p., [1897].

*Report of the Special House Committee Appointed to Inves-
tigate Railroad Matters.* Montgomery: W. W. Screws, 1872.

Report of the Special Joint Committee Appointed to Visit the State University. Montgomery: Barrett & Brown, 1879.

Report of the Special Joint Committee of the General Assembly of Alabama, to which Was Referred the Report of the Commissioner of S. and O. Lands. Montgomery: Barrett & Brown, 1879.

Report of the State Land Agent. Montgomery: Brown Printing Co., [1915].

Reports of the Adjutant General, 1871-1890.

Reports of the Agricultural and Mechanical College, 1874-1892.

Reports of the Attorney General, 1884-1890.

Reports of the Auditor, 1869-1891.

Reports of the Board of Health, 1884, 1887, 1888.

Reports of the Commissioner of Agriculture, 1886, 1888, 1890.

Reports of the Commissioner of Immigration, 1876, 1878.

Reports of the Commissioner of Industrial Resources, 1869-1874.

Reports of the Freedmen's Hospital, 1870, 1871, 1873.

Reports of the Insane Hospital, 1867-1892.

Reports of the Inspectors of the Penitentiary, 1868-1884.

Reports of the Inspectors of Convicts, 1886-1890.

Reports of the Institution for the Deaf, Dumb, and Blind, 1869-1892.

Reports of the Railroad Commissioners, 1881-1890.

Reports of the State Geologist, 1873-1892.

Reports of the Superintendent of Public Instruction, 1869-1876.

Reports of the Superintendent of Education, 1877-1890.

Reports of the Supreme Court, vol. 58 (1877)—vol. 127 (1899).

Reports of the Treasurer, 1869-1890.

Reports of the Trustees of the University, 1876-1890.

Rules and Regulations for the Government of the Convict System of Alabama. Montgomery: Barrett & Co., 1886.

Skinner, Thomas E., *Alabama Constitution Annotated.* Birmingham: Birmingham Printing Co., 1938.

Testimony Before the Joint Committee of the General Assembly, Appointed to Examine Into the Convict System of Alabama. Montgomery: Brown Printing Co., 1889.

Testimony Taken by the Joint Special Committee of the Session of 1880-81, to Enquire Into the Condition and Treatment of Convicts of the State. Montgomery: Allred & Beers, 1881.

Testimony Taken by the Special Joint Committee of the General Assembly of Alabama to Which Was Referred the

Report of the Commissioner of S. & O. Lands. Montgomery: Barrett & Brown, 1879.

OFFICIAL PUBLICATIONS OF ORGANIZATIONS

The Books of Rules of the Medical Association of the State of Alabama, 1883, 1889.

Farmers State Alliance of Alabama, Minutes of the Fourth Annual Session, August 6-8, 1889. Dadeville: New Era Job Print, [1889].

Memorial and Proceedings of the River and Harbor Improvements Convention: Assembled at Tuscaloosa, Alabama, November 17th, 1885. Cincinnati: Ohio Valley Press, 1886.

Minutes of the Alabama State Teachers' Association [Negro], 1883-1889.

Minutes of the Eleventh Annual Reunion of the United Sons of Confederate Veterans. Nashville: Brandon Printing Co., 1907.

Proceedings of the Alabama Educational Association, 1886-1890.

Proceedings of the Alabama Agricultural Society, 1884-1888.

Proceedings of the Alabama Teachers' Association, 1884-1885.

Proceedings of the Annual Meetings of the Alabama State Bar Association, 1879-1890.

Proceedings of the Annual Sessions of the Alabama Pharmaceutical Association, 1881-1890.

Proceedings of the Quarantine Conference Held in Montgomery, Ala., on the 5th, 6th, and 7th days of March, 1889. Montgomery: Brown Printing Co., [1889]

Proceedings of the State Grange of the Patrons of Husbandry of Alabama, 1873-1876, 1888-1891.

Proceedings of the Trustees of the Peabody Education Fund, vol. 1 (1867-1874)–vol. 4 (1888-1892).

Transactions of the Medical Association of the State of Alabama, 1869-1890.

PERIODICALS

Alabama Law Journal, vol. II (1883). Tuscaloosa.

Alabama University Monthly, vol. I (1873)—vol. XIV (1887). Tuscaloosa.

Appletons' Annual Cyclopaedia and Register of Important Events, vol. X (1870), vol. XVI (1876)—XXVIII (1888). New York.

Commercial and Financial Chronicle, vol. XX (1875)—vol. XXIV (1877), vol. XXXI (1880). New York.

The Farm Journal: A Monthly Magazine for the Field and Fireside, vol. I (1878), vol. III (1880). Montgomery.

The Maxwell Almanac, 1870-1884. Tuscaloosa.

N. W. Ayer & *Son's American Newspaper Annual,* 1887. Philadelphia.
The New South, vol. II (1886), vol. III (1887). Birmingham.
The Rural Alabamian, vol. I (1872))—vol. II (1873). Mobile.
The Southern Plantation, vol. I (1874-1875), vol. III (1876-1877). Montgomery.
The World Almanac, 1892. New York.

NEWSPAPERS

Birmingham *Age-Herald,* 1889-1890.
Birmingham *Alabama Sentinel,* 1887-1889.
Birmingham *Alabama True Issue,* 1880-1881.
Birmingham *Chronicle,* 1885-1886.
Birmingham *Herald,* 1887.
Birmingham *Independent,* 1879-1881.
Birmingham *Iron Age,* 1881-1887.
Birmingham *News,* April 13, 1947.
Birmingham *Observer,* 1880.
Brewton *Escambia Banner,* 1883-1885.
Grove Hill *Clarke County Democrat,* 1869-1885.
Huntsville *Advocate,* 1869-1872, 1878-1884.
Huntsville *Democrat,* 1872-1879, 1882-1888.
Huntsville *Gazette,* 1881-1891.
Huntsville *Independent,* 1880-1883, 1885-1889.
Huntsville *Mercury,* 1880-1882, 1884-1889.
Huntsville *New South,* 1885-1886.
London *Times,* 1874-1876
Mobile *Register,* 1869-1890.
Mobile *Tribune,* 1874-1876.
Monroeville *Monroe Journal,* 1878-1889.
Montgomery *Advertiser,* 1869-1890.
Montgomery *Alabama State Journal,* 1868-1876.
Montgomery *Colored Citizen,* 1884.
Montgomery *Dispatch,* 1885-1888.
Montgomery *Mail,* 1869-1870.
New York *The South,* April 5, 1873.
New York *Tribune,* 1875-1887.
Selma *Mail,* 1882-1884, 1888.
Selma *Southern Argus,* 1872-1879.
Selma *Times,* 1881-1886.
Selma *Times-Argus,* 1884-1886.
Troy *Enquirer,* 1875-1890.
Tuscumbia *North Alabamian,* 1875-1878.
Tuscaloosa *Clarion,* 1879-1882.
Tuscaloosa *Gazette,* April 17, 1895.
Tuskegee *Macon Mail,* 1881-1884.

Warrior *Advance*, 1885.
Warrior *Advance and Guide*, 1885.
Warrior *Enterprise*, 1885.
Wetumpka *Central Alabamian*, 1880.

CONTEMPORARY SPEECHES, BOOKS, ARTICLES, AND PAMPHLETS

Address of the Democratic and Conservative State Executive Committee. n.p., [1875].

Address to the Republicans of Alabama by the Republican State Executive Committee. n.p., [1892].

Anderson, William H[enry], *The City of Mobile: And the Contiguous Country About the Gulf Coast as a Winter Resort.* Mobile: Daily Register Steam Print, 1882.

An Appeal from the Alumni of the University of Alabama to the Legislature of the State. Tuscaloosa: Burton & Weatherford, 1896.

Bragg, W[alter] L[awrence], *Speech . . . Before the Senate Judiciary Committee on Bills Pending in Reference to Railroad Legislation,* n. p. [1884].

Bryce, P[eter], *Moral and Criminal Responsibility.* Tuscaloosa, [1888].

Campbell, John L., *A Physical Survey Extending from Atlanta, Ga., Across Alabama and Mississippi to the Mississippi River, Along the Line of the Georgia Pacific Railway.* New York: E. F. Weeks, 1883.

Cochran, Jerome, *Problems in Regard to Yellow Fever and the Prevention of Yellow Fever Epidemics.* Reprint of paper read before the American Public Health Association. Concord, N. H.: 1888.

Curry, J[abez] L[amar] M[onroe], *Address Delivered . . . in Response to an Invitation Extended in a Joint Resolution of the Senate and House of Representatives of Alabama.* Montgomery: Barrett & Co., 1885.

Facts and Statistics Concerning Northeastern Alabama. Nashville: F. M. Paul, [1890].

Gaston, J[ohn] B[rown], *A Review of "The Convict Situation in Alabama," by John T. Milner.* n.p., [1883].

Haines, Hiram, *L'Etat d'Alabama.* Paris: Imprimerie Simon Racon et compagnie, 1867.

Haines, [Hiram], *Report on the Traffic Resources of the South & North Alabama Railroad.* Montgomery: Barrett & Brown, 1872.

Herbert, Hilary A[bner], "Grandfather's Talks About His Life Under Two Flags." Unpublished manuscript in private possession.

The Hill Country of Alabama: Or the Land of Rest. London and New York: E. & F. N. Spon, 1878.

Hodgson, Joseph (ed.), *Alabama Manual and Statistical Register for 1869.* Montgomery: Mail Building, 1869.

Homes and Investments in the South . . . 600,000 Acres of Land in the Hill Country of Alabama on the Alabama Great Southern Railway for Sale and Settlement. London: Alabama Coal, Iron, Land, and Colonization Co., Ltd. 1882.

Manning, J[oseph] C[olumbus], *Politics of Alabama.* n.p., 1893.

Milner, John T[urner], *Alabama: As It Was, As It Is, and As It Will Be.* Montgomery: Barrett & Brown, 1876.

Milner, John T[urner], *A Review of the Convict Situation in Alabama.* Montgomery: Barrett & Co., [1882].

Milner, John Turner, *White Men of Alabama Stand Together: 1860 & 1890.* Birmingham: McDavid Printing Co., 1890.

Mobile County eine passende Heimath fur dem Deutschem Farmer. St. Louis: 1874.

Mohr, Charles, *The Lands of the Louisville and Nashville R. R. in Alabama as Homesteads for the Settler.* Birmingham: Roberts & Son, 1884.

Morgan, John T[yler], "The Danger of the Farmers' Alliance," *Forum,* XII (1891), 399-409.

Munroe, Kirk, "The Industrial South: Birmingham, Alabama," *Harper's Weekly,* XXXI (1887), 213-216, 223.

Parke, Thomas D[uke], *A Study of the Medical Laws from an Ethical Standpoint.* Reprint of paper read before Jefferson County Medical Society. n.p., [1888].

The Queen City of the South: Huntsville. Birmingham: Caldwell Printing Co., 1888.

Radical Falsehood Exposed: Grant's Attorney General Exposes the Falsehoods of Senator Morton and Spencer's Ku Klux Speeches. n.p., [1870].

Reliable Information as to the City and County of Tuskaloosa, Alabama. Tuskaloosa: Board of Industries, 1876.

"Retrogression in Alabama," *Nation,* XXXVII (1883), 372-373.

Scott, S[utton] S[elwyn], *The Political Situation.* Columbus, Ga.: Thos. Gilbert, 1878.

Screws, Benjamin H[arrison], *The "Loil" Legislature of Alabama: Its Ridiculous Doings and Nonsensical Sayings.* Montgomery: H. W. Offutt & Co., 1868.

Smith, William H[ugh], *Letter from . . . in Defense of His Administration.* Montgomery: Barrett & Brown, 1870.

Troy, D[aniel] S[hipman], *Proposed Railroad Legislation.* n.p. [1880].

Walker, L[eroy] P[ope], *Speech of . . . on State and National Affairs.* n.p., [1878].
Which Was the Lawful Legislature of Alabama? Senator Spencer's Case. Washington, D. C.: Gibson Brothers, 1874.

II SECONDARY MATERIALS

STATE HISTORIES AND GENERAL WORKS

Berney, Saffold, *Hand Book of Alabama: A Complete Index to the State.* Mobile: Register Print, 1878. 2nd edition, Birmingham: Roberts & Son, 1892.

Beverly, John W[illiam], *History of Alabama.* [*Montgomery*]: author, 1901.

Brewer, Willis, *Alabama: Her History, Resources, War Record, and Public Men, from 1540 to 1872.* Montgomery: Barrett and Brown, 1872.

Brown, William Garrett, *A History of Alabama.* New York: University Publishing Co., 1900.

Cable, George W[ashington], *The Silent South.* New York: C. Scribner's Sons, 1885.

DuBose, Joel C[ampbell], *Notable Men of Alabama,* 2 vols. Atlanta: Southern Historical Association, 1904.

DuBose, John Witherspoon, "Forty Years of Alabama, 1861-1901, A History of the Lapse and Recovery of Civil Government." Unpublished manuscript in the Alabama State Department of Archives and History, Montgomery.

Garrett, William, *Reminiscences of Public Men in Alabama.* Atlanta: Plantation Publishing Co., 1872.

Herbert, Hilary A[bner] (ed.), *Why the Solid South? Or Reconstruction and Its Results.* Baltimore: R. N. Woodward & Co., 1890.

Hillyard, M. B., *The New South.* Baltimore: Manufacturers' Record Co., 1887.

Howard, M[ilford] W., *The American Plutocracy.* New York: Holland Publishing Co., 1895.

Johnson, Allen and Dumas Malone (eds.), *Dictionary of American Biography,* 20 vols., index, and supplement. New York: Charles Scribner's Sons, 1928-1944.

Kelley, William D[arrah], *The Old South and The New.* New York: G. P. Putnam's Sons, 1888.

Kendrick, Benjamin Burks and Alex Mathews Arnett, *The South Looks at Its Past.* Chapel Hill: University of North Carolina Press, 1935.

King, Edward, *The Great South.* Hartford, Conn.: American Publishing Co., 1875.

McClure, Alexander K[elly], *The South.* Philadelphia: Lippincott, 1886.

Manning, Joseph Columbus, *The Fadeout of Populism*. New York: T. A. Hebbons, 1928.

Manning, Joseph C[olumbus], *Rise and Reign of the Bourbon Oligarchy*. Birmingham: Roberts & Sons, 1904.

Memorial Record of Alabama, 2 vols. Madison, Wis.: Brant & Fuller, 1893.

Moore, Albert Burton, *History of Alabama*. University, Ala.: University Supply Store, 1934.

Murphy, Edgar Gardner, *Problems of the Present South*. New York: Macmillan Co., 1905.

Nordhoff, Charles, *The Cotton States in the Spring and Summer of 1875*. New York: D. Appleton & Co., 1876.

Northern Alabama: Historical and Biographical. Birmingham: Smith & DeLand, 1888.

Otken, Charles H., *The Ills of the South*. New York: G. P. Putnam's Sons, 1894.

Owen, Thomas McAdory, *A Bibliography of Alabama*. Reprinted from *Annual Report of the American Historical Association*, 1897. Washington: Government Printing Office, 1898.

Owen, Thomas McAdory, *History of Alabama and Dictionary of Alabama Biography*, 4 vols. Chicago: S. J. Clarke Publishing Co., 1921.

Riley, B[enjamin] F[ranklin], *Alabama As It Is: The Immigrant's and Capitalist's Guide Book to Alabama*, 2 edition. Atlanta: Constitution Publishing Co., 1888.

Riley, B[enjamin] F[ranklin], *Makers and Romance of Alabama History*. Birmingham: author, 1914.

Skaggs, William H[enry], *The Southern Oligarchy*. New York: The Devin-Adair Co., 1924.

The South in the Building of the Nation, 13 vols. Richmond: The Southern Historical Publication Society, 1909-1913.

W[alker], R[obert] H[enry], *Alabama Politics from 1890 to 1938: As Viewed by a Country Editor*. n.p., n.d.

MONOGRAPHS, BIOGRAPHIES, AND SPECIAL STUDIES

Alabama Blast Furnaces. Woodward, Ala.: Woodword Iron Co., 1940.

Armes, Ethel M[arie], *The Story of Coal and Iron in Alabama*. Birmingham: Chamber of Commerce, 1910.

Bond, Horace Mann, *Negro Education in Alabama*. Washington: Associated Publishers, Inc., 1939.

Brantley, William H[enderson], *Chief Justice Stone of Alabama*. Birmingham: Birmingham Publishing Co., 1943.

Bright, John Clinton, "Some Economic and Social Aspects of the History of Cullman, Alabama." Unpublished Master's thesis, University of Alabama, 1937.

Bromberg, Frederick G[eorge], *The Reconstruction Period in Alabama.* Papers of the Iberville Historical Society, no. 4, n.p., [1914].

Broun, Thomas L., *Dr. William LeRoy Broun.* New York: Neale Publishing Co., 1912.

Buck, Paul H[erman], *The Road to Reunion, 1865-1900.* Boston: Little Brown, 1937.

Burgin, Maggie, "The Direct Primary Election System in Alabama." Unpublished Master's thesis, University of Alabama, 1931.

Clark, John B[unyan], *Populism in Alabama.* Auburn, Ala.: Auburn Printing Co., 1927.

Clark, Willis G[aylord], *History of Education in Alabama.* Bureau of Education, Circular of Information, whole no. 163. Washington: Government Printing Office, 1889.

Cooke, Leonard Calvert, "The Development of the Road System of Alabama." Unpublished Master's thesis, University of Alabama, 1935.

Crane, Mary [Powell], *The Life of James R. Powell and Early History of Alabama and Birmingham.* Brooklyn: Braunworth & Co., 1930.

Dabney, Charles William, *Universal Education in the South,* 2 vols. Chapel Hill: University of North Carolina Press, 1936.

Davidson, Elizabeth H., *Child Labor Legislation in the Southern Textile States.* Chapel Hill: University of North Carolina Press, 1932.

Doster, James F., *Alabama's First Railroad Commission 1881-1885.* University, Alabama: author, 1949.

Dryer, Edmund H., *Origin of Tuskegee Normal and Industrial Institute.* Birmingham: author, 1938.

DuBois, W[illiam] E[dward] Burghardt, *Black Reconstruction, 1860-1880.* New York: Harcourt Brace and Co., 1935.

DuBose, John Witherspoon and James K. Greer, *Alabama's Tragic Decade: Ten Years of Alabama, 1865-1874.* Birmingham: Webb Book Co., 1940.

Ferguson, Maxwell, *State Regulation of Railroads in the South. Columbia University Studies in History, Economics, and Public Law,* vol. 47, no. 2. New York: Columbia University, 1916.

Fleming, Walter L[ynwood], *Civil War and Reconstruction in Alabama.* New York: Columbia University Press, 1905.

Haney, Lewis Henry, *A Congressional History of Railways in the United States, 1850-1887.* Bulletin of the University of Wisconsin, Economics and Political Science Series, vol. 6, no. 1. Madison: 1910.

Hart, Hasting H[ornell], *Social Problems of Alabama*. Study made by the Russell Sage Foundation. Montgomery: 1918.

Hyatt, Oscar W., *The Development of Secondary Education in Alabama Prior to 1920*. Nashville: George Peabody College, 1933.

Johnson, J. H., "The Alabama Institute for the Deaf, 1858-1893," in *Histories of American Schools for the Deaf*, 3 vols. Washington: Volta Bureau, 1893.

Jones, Walter B[ryan], *History and Work of Geological Surveys and Industrial Development in Alabama*. Geological Survey of Alabama, Bulletin no. 42. University, Ala.: 1935.

King, Gladys, "History of the Alabama Convict Department." Unpublished Master's thesis, Alabama Polytechnic Institute, 1937.

King, Gladys Victoria, "The Blair Education Bill with Special Reference to Southern Attitudes." Unpublished Master's thesis, University of North Carolina, 1943.

Knight, Edgar W[allace], *Public Education in the South*. New York: Ginn & Co., 1922.

Lewinson, Paul, *Race, Class and Party: A History of Negro Suffrage and White Politics in the South*. London: Oxford University Press, 1932.

McGrane, Reginald C[harles]. *Foreign Bondholders and American State Debts*. New York: Macmillan & Co., 1935.

McKelvey, Blake, *American Prisons*. Chicago: University of Chicago Press, 1936.

McMillan, Malcolm Cook, "Constitutional Development in Alabama, 1819-1901." Unpublished doctoral dissertation, University of North Carolina, 1948.

Manning, Joseph Columbus, *From Five to Twenty-Five: His Earlier Life*. New York: T. A. Hebbons, 1929.

Martin, Roscoe C[oleman), *The Growth of State Administration in Alabama*. University, Ala.: Bureau of Public Administration, 1942.

Martin, William Elejius, *Internal Improvements in Alabama. Johns Hopkins University Studies in Historical and Political Science*, series 20, no. 4. Baltimore: Johns Hopkins Press, 1902.

Mitchell, Martha C., "Birmingham: Biography of a City of the New South." Unpublished doctoral dissertation, University of Chicago, 1947.

Moos, Malcolm C[harles], *State Penal Administration in Alabama*. University, Ala.: Bureau of Public Administration, 1942.

Owens, C[larence] J., *Secondary Agricultural Education in Alabama*. U. S. Department of Agriculture, Office of Experiment

Stations, Bulletin no. 220. Washington: Government Printing Office, 1909.

Pitts, Clara L., "Julia Strudwich Tutwiler," Unpublished doctoral dissertation, George Washington University, 1942.

Sapp, Fannie Ella, "The Convict Lease System in Alabama, 1846-1895." Unpublished Master's thesis, George Peabody College, 1931.

Scott, Emmett J. and Lyman Beecher Stowe, *Booker T. Washington: Builder of Civilization.* New York: Doubleday Page & Co., 1916.

Scott, William A[masa]. *The Repudiation of State Debts.* New York: T. Y. Crowell & Co., 1893.

Sellers, James Benson, "A History of Negro Education in Alabama." Unpublished Master's thesis, University of Chicago, 1925.

Sellers, James Benson, *The Prohibition Movement in Alabama. The James Sprunt Studies in History and Political Science,* University of North Carolina, vol. 26, no. 1. Chapel Hill: University of North Carolina Press, 1943.

Stabler, Carey V., "The History of the Alabama Public Health System." Unpublished doctoral dissertation, Duke University, 1944.

Thrasher, Max Bennett, *Tuskegee: Its Story and Its Work.* Boston: Small, Maynard & Co., 1901.

Washington, Booker T[aliaferro], *Up From Slavery: An Autobiography.* New York: A. L. Burt Co., 1901.

Weeks, Stephen B[eauregard], *History of Public School Education in Alabama.* U. S. Bureau of Education Bulletin, 1915, no. 12, whole no. 637. Washington: Government Printing Office, 1915.

Williams, Arthur, "The Participation of Negroes in the Government of Alabama." Unpublished Master's thesis, Atlanta University, 1946.

Worley, Lillian, *Alabama's People.* University, Ala.: Bureau of Public Administration, 1945.

Zimmerman, Hilda Jane, "Penal Systems and Penal Reforms in the South Since the Civil War." Unpublished doctoral dissertation, University of North Carolina, 1947.

PERIODICAL ARTICLES

Allen, Francis R., "Development of the Public Health Movement in the Southeast," *Social Forces,* XXII (1943), 67-75.

Baker, J. N., "Alabama's Contribution to Public Health," *American Journal of Public Health,* XXX (1940), 859-865.

Bond, Horace Mann, "Social and Economic Forces in Alabama

Reconstruction." *Journal of Negro History*, XXIII (1938), 290-348.

Brantley, William H., "An Alabama Medical Review," *Alabama Lawyer*, VI (1945), 243-285.

Cable, George Washington, "The Convict Lease System in the Southern States, " *Century Magazine*, XXVII (1884), 582-599.

Caffey, Francis G., "The Annexation of West Florida to Alabama," *Proceedings of the Alabama State Bar Assocation*, 1901, pp. 108-133.

DuBose, John Witherspoon, "History of the Alabama Railroad Commission," Birmingham *Age-Herald*, June 3, 1906.

Dunning, William A., "The Undoing of Reconstruction," *Atlantic Monthly*, LXXXVIII (1901), 437-449.

Gates, Paul Wallace, "Federal Land Policy in the South, 1866-1888," *Journal of Southern History*, VI (1940), 303-330.

Going, Allen J., "The Establishment of the Alabama Railroad Commission," *Journal of Southern History*, XII (1946), 366-385.

Herbert, Hilary A., "How We Redeemed Alabama," *Century Magazine*, LXXXV (1913), 854-862.

Hesseltine, William B., "Economic Factors in the Abandonment of Reconstruction," *Mississippi Valley Historical Review*, XXII (1935), 191-210.

McKelvey, Blake F., "Penal Slavery and Southern Reconstruction," *Journal of Negro History*, XX (1935), 153-179.

Moore, Albert Burton, "Railroad Building in Alabama During the Reconstruction Period," *Journal of Southern History*, I (1935), 421-441.

Sanders, William H., "The History, Philosophy and Fruits of Medical Organization in Alabama," *Transactions of the Medical Association of the State of Alabama*, 1914, pp. 510-579.

Vaughn, Susan Kirkman, "The South's Oldest State Teachers College," *Peabody Journal of Education*, XIII (1936), 282-288.

INDEX

Date Due

6/10/63			